contact

D0012260

contact

MOUNTAIN CLIMBING AND ENVIRONMENTAL THINKING

EDITED BY Jeffrey Mathes McCarthy

UNIVERSITY OF NEVADA PRESS | RENO & LAS VEGAS

University of Nevada Press, Reno, Nevada 89557 USA
Copyright © 2008 by University of Nevada Press
All rights reserved
Manufactured in the United States of America
Design by Carrie House, HOUSEdesign llc
Library of Congress Cataloging-in-Publication Data
Contact : mountain climbing and environmental thinking /
edited by Jeffrey Mathes McCarthy.
p. cm.
ISBN 978-0-87417-746-6 (pbk. : alk. paper)
1. Mountaineering—Anecdotes. 2. Ecology.
I. McCarthy, Jeffrey Mathes
GV199.82.C66   2008
796.522—dc22   2007040981
The paper used in this book is a recycled stock made from
50 percent post-consumer waste materials and meets
the requirements of American National Standard for
Information Sciences—Permanence of Paper for Printed
Library Materials, ANSI/NISO Z39.48–1992 (R2002). Binding
materials were selected for strength and durability.

EXCERPT CREDITS: "Climbing Into a Life" by John Daniel
from "West," *Winter Creek: One Writer's Natural History*
(Minneapolis: Milkweed Editions, 2002). Copyright
© 2002 by John Daniel. Reprinted with permission from
Milkweed Editions, www.milkweed.org. "Freeing the
Nose" from *Climbing Free: My Life in the Vertical World* by
Lynn Hill, with Greg Child. Copyright © 2002 by Lynn Hill.
Used by permission of W. W. Norton & Company, Inc. "The
Mountain," "Spirit Lake," "The Climb," and "Atomic Dawn,"
copyright © 2004 by Gary Snyder from *Danger on Peaks*.
Reprinted by permission of Shoemaker & Hoard Publishers.
"Denali" by Jonathan Waterman from *In the Shadow of
Denali* (Lyons Press, 1998). Copyright © 1998 by Jonathan
Waterman. Reprinted with permission from Lyons Press.

FIRST PRINTING
17 16 15 14 13 12 11 10 09 08
5 4 3 2 1

Frontispiece: © Tommy Chandler Photography

For Robin McCarthy, who taught me to read

contents

3: connection 166

preface

Contact is a book about climbing. *Contact* is a book about the environment. In the mountain stories collected here, human beings do bold things amid big peaks. The pattern of human relations to the natural world is explicit in some, implicit in others. These climbing stories are arranged and introduced to define North American attitudes to nature. But this is not an insistently didactic arrangement; you can read these stories for their amazing adventures, or you can read them in the context of environmental history.

Either approach works.

These are first-person accounts of serious climbs by the most prominent climbers of the last fifty years, a couple of classic nineteenth-century accounts, and unpublished archival work from earlier decades. You see, climbers rub endlessly against the natural world, and a pearl of environmental awareness grows to differing shapes in each climber and each climb.

Lynn Hill falls on the crux "changing corners" pitch of the Nose, until she sees a heart pattern on the granite, feels connected, and then sends. Steve House teeters atop three thousand feet of forbidding limestone on Mount Alberta's north face and thinks of history. Barry Blanchard squeezes himself like a fist against a "turbine of snow and screaming wind" and understands his tears will melt into the creek that leads, in time, to the river that runs through his childhood. Steph Davis knows fear in Patagonia, but finds these harsh conditions sustain a complex and subtle weave of life. Gary Snyder climbs Mount Saint Helens and returns through wind and smoke to read of nuclear bombs blasting Japan. These stories draw readers for adventure, for famous names, for new voices, and for fine writing. *Contact* delivers all this, and also a readable explanation of the environmental context that suffuses the best climbing writing but has never been recognized. This anthology is for climbers, outdoor lovers, and people involved with environmental issues.

You'll see that this book interprets climbing stories according to three influential discourses of wilderness: conquest, caretaking, and connection. These are reference points, like distinctive hills on an open landscape, and so they shouldn't limit mental journeys, but rather point those journeys in one intriguing direction or another.

Look at the table of contents. Some of the voices in this volume are famous, some less known. They all describe the rock and the ice and the wind-slapped ridges in different ways, and behind them all is the steady backbeat of the tangible, alpine world, in all its glorious forms.

acknowledgments

This project has been a long, satisfying journey; in the nature of journeys, *Contact* has accumulated many friends and influences along the way. I am especially grateful to this book's contributors—for their writing of course, but also for the enthusiasm that made this hopeful plan seem not only possible but necessary. Thanks again to all of you.

There have been so many friends and climbers who have tied in with me along the way that I bow to all of you. A few of the most patient are Oli, Dave, Pratt, Sean, Jenn, Luther, Matt, Doug, Morgan, and Cory.

This book got its start while I was a Fulbright Fellow to Canada; so I want to thank the Fulbright Foundation for sending me, the University of Calgary Humanities Center for hosting me, and the Whyte Museum of the Canadian Rockies for keeping me. Westminster College awarded me two Gore Summer Research Grants and a Merit Leave for research; these professional development opportunities were crucial to the project. A special nod is due to my colleagues in English and Environmental Studies at Westminster. Other academic support has been important to me throughout, and I'm glad to acknowledge Gordon Sayre, Paul Peppis, Rick Davis, Dawn Marano, Paul Armstrong, and Ian Campbell for all they've done.

Finally, there have been a few absolute stars in this process, helping me with the heavy lifting and the breaking of trails. So here's to you Katy Ryan, Mikel Vause, Bob Palais, Derek and Rieko Holtved, Kirk and Jay Huffard, Bronwyn Ben Mac Jed Gus and Nene Huffard, and Robin and Ted McCarthy.

contact

introduction

Have you noticed a change in the weather? A greener Christmas, glaciers cringing into nothingness on your favorite peak, maybe some natural gas derricks bobbing where the antelope played?

Some of this world's alterations we see; others we read about over breakfast. The Alaska Range gets hotter every year, and every year water tables get lower in the Sacramento Valley. There's mercury in the Ottawa River, there are fewer cod off the Grand Banks, fewer salmon in the Yukon, and it seems the air we breathe causes Parkinson's for the old, asthma for the young, and an uncertain fate for those in between. Technological solutions have been promised, attempts at mitigation have been made, but the cars on the highway get fatter and wider. The environment we inhabit is being changed fast, and with glaciers receding, species disappearing, and human beings breeding, the solution isn't a new machine—it's a new way of thinking.

These are generalities. I'm looking for something as specific and hopeful as a fist jam—a clean hold amid the loose rock of environmental degradation—and I think I see it in the interpretive shifts that periodically transform our culture's understanding of the natural world. Yes, I'm saying that our environmental policy and our environmental practice depend on our environmental perception. I might sound crazier than a sport climber in the rain, but climbing narratives reveal how our culture interprets nature. Listen closely to the words mountains speak through climbers, and hear where our culture's attitudes have been and, also, where those attitudes are going.

This introduction asserts something controversial: environmental thinkers can learn from mountain climbers. From our position at the beginning of the new millennium, mountaineers offer a vision of human relations to nature, and a version of how these relations might transcend this historical moment's distinctive attitudes and approaches. Indeed, an academic might study the verb "transcend" and in it find evidence of climbing's visionary associations. "Transcend" derives from the Latin words *scandere,* meaning "to climb"—from which we get the familiar verb "to scale"—and *tran,* meaning "over." So, all the time we use "transcend" about metaphysics or belief, that word is rooted firmly in the physical act of climbing.

I suggest we understand the mountaineering narrative as a symptom of Western civilization, and a measure of civilization's shifting approaches to the environment. To make this idea stick, I'll first classify climbing attitudes, second explore a cultural moment when vested attitudes to nature were abruptly deposed, and in the end argue that the corporeal, bodily fact of climbing points us toward the possibility of a sustainable relation between human beings and the natural world.

|||

Let's get historical. Until a few centuries ago civilized people disdained mountains. There were no alpine holidays, no glacier tours, no crowds in Chamonix . . . all because of an established set of attitudes toward the mountain environment. Before the Renaissance people believed mountains were not only inhospitable, but had been cursed by God into barbarity, and were thus seats of evil. Lucretius called mountains waste places of the earth in the first century BC, and as late as the seventeenth century travelers did little to burnish this reputation—"strange, horrid & firefull crags" John Evelyn sweated into his diary. But, by the time North America's great ranges startled Western consciousness, alpine environments were already undergoing a shift in European perception. Mountaineer and "Eminent Victorian" Leslie Stephen testifies: "before the turning-point of the eighteenth century, a civilized being might . . . regard the Alps with unmitigated horror. After it, even a solid archdeacon, with a firm belief in the British constitution, and Church and State, was *compelled to admire,* under penalty of reprobation. It required as much originality to dislike as it had previously required to admire." Stephen jests, but his point is a serious one for us: a new way of interpreting the alpine environment came quickly and powerfully to reshape British consciousness. Eighteenth-century Romantic poets and travelers contradicted received wisdom to extol each mountain from Chamonix to Skye for its awesome beauty. Their appreciation mixed fear and wonder, awe and desire, and in 1757 the young Irishman Edmund Burke insisted his peers call it "sublime." Thirty years later Jean-Jacques Rousseau testified, "I must have torrents, rocks, pines, dead forest, mountains, rugged paths to go up and down, precipices beside me to frighten me." In short, he wanted the same alpine terrain John Evelyn so lately abhorred. The eighteenth century in its wigs and stockings seems staid and hidebound to us, but it hosted many radical changes, including the shift in attitude toward the alpine world. Climbing matters because it's both symptom and cause of a changed appreciation for nature.

A move to a new way of knowing nature seems especially important today, when a chorus of environmental voices insists that transforming human attitudes toward nature is the only solution to the "environmental crisis." Their fundamental point is that our estrangement from the natural world is shaped by the inherited view of nature as another to be manipulated. Half a century back, Aldo Leopold wrote that our concept of land dooms efforts at conservation: "We abuse land because we regard it as a commodity belonging to us. When we see land as a community to which we belong, we may begin to use it with love and respect." So, an epistemological advance, not a technological or bureaucratic one, is the precondition to sustaining harmony between people and environment. Mountain guide Jack Turner comments, "We realize that our ecological crisis is not, *at the roots,* caused by industrialization, capitalism, and technology, but by a particular form of the human self." Turner echoes

Leopold in asserting that environmental and human well-being depend on reimagining humanity and recognizing a unity in the lives of people and their environment.

Environmentalists, philosophers, activists, and even vice presidents tell us our problem is a deep-rooted structure of knowledge that grows always toward homocentric dominion and expansion, while the solution is a shift in thinking—a unified awareness of civilization's fundamental connection to landscape. The question to ask Turner, Leopold, and our climbing selves is, What evidence exists that any such mental shift is on our horizon?

Three Ways

Let's search for evidence of that mental shift, expedition style; we'll go the long way, and in covering all that ground we'll get a fully supported, fully nourished answer. I propose we measure climbing narratives according to three primary categories—conquest, caretaking, and connection.

Look at the writing.

For certain climbers the story is all about conquest and domination; putting a flag on a peak, a name on a route, or a summit photo on the wall is their fundamental experience. Caretaking narratives emphasize appreciation for the mountain environment. Here climbing appreciates the land and conserves wilderness resources against the pressure of industrial, consumer culture. Still other mountain writing emphasizes an intense connection between the human climber and the alpine environment.

This spectrum of climbing is pertinent to environmental thinking because these are three of the primary modes for experiencing nature in the culture that surrounds us, from suv advertisements to debates in Congress. I see them every day here in Salt Lake City where huge mines tear mountains into dust, where National Wilderness lands insist we "Leave no trace," and where a tribe of climbers and skiers has come to make a life in and for the Wasatch Mountains. Climbing stories are types of our culture's master narratives about nature, and climbing stories that step beyond a consumerist, extractive model of interaction are a hopeful possibility for a later, evolving, master narrative. In sum, climbing engages the whole spectrum of attitudes toward nature, and that's why climbing matters.

| | |

The category of conquest is easy to understand—think flags on summits, national pride, domination of a mountain foe. In the conquest model of climbing, the perceiving, active climber overcomes an inanimate world. Take, for instance, the Reverend George Kinney who, in 1909, set out to be first on Mount Robson. Kinney treats the alpine wilderness in the familiar terms of conquest when he reaches what he thinks is the top: "In the name of Almighty God by whose strength I have climbed her, I capture this peak, Mount Robson, for my own country and for the Alpine Club of Canada." It's rather a letdown from this mighty peroration to find that he was actually on a secondary shoulder of the peak, well below the true summit, but the vocabulary illuminates the familiar conceits of feminizing and capturing nature, getting God's blessing for human domination, and claiming a mountain for some social abstraction.

I don't mean to criticize Kinney, whose courage and hardiness were formidable; it's just that he approaches mountains as a space where human striving gathers meaning by dominating the natural world. Of course, conquest is one approach to mountaineering that didn't end in the early twentieth century. The century closed with a flurry of attention to mountaineering narratives thanks largely to the Mount Everest debacle recorded most famously by Jon Krakauer's *Into Thin Air*. Whatever motivation the guides and Sherpas may have felt, for most of the clients this was the chance to be photographed atop the world's highest hill. The guide Scott Fischer tells Krakauer: "We've got the big E figured out, we've got it totally wired. These days, I'm telling you, we've built a yellow brick road to the summit." That "yellow brick road" demanded gold and nothing but. Many of the Everest clients were (and are) unfamiliar with crampons, unable to lead, and motivated by the desire to "capture this peak." Unlike Kinney, though, the capture is not for God or country, but for self en route to the seven summits, or a picture on the wall. This is the vocabulary of conquest, and here the climber's efforts become significant insofar as they succeed in dominating the natural world.

But conquest is more than overt claims of domination—there's a legacy of conquest in Western thinking about nature expressed in ways as various as route names or fixed anchors, scientific exploration or ascetic trials. You see, conquering can be as much internal as external, and in many climbing experiences the alpine opponent is in fact the hungry, quivering, unruly self. Further, very few climbs are now structured by hostile opposition. Conquest is embodied in certain ascents, and briefly inhabited and then abandoned in others. So, climbing narratives put the torch of commitment to confrontations with the alpine world, and the resulting blaze shows us our interaction in a circle of light broader than simple oppression.

We should pause here—a water break—to say these three approaches overlap like leaves on a forest floor: conquest, caretaking, connection. The goal is not to put people or approaches in simple boxes, but to show that the attitudes we take to climbing are the attitudes our culture brings to the natural world. You know and I know that we can't honestly reduce the variety of mountain experience to cast categories. But it is productive to recognize that approaches to the world slide along a spectrum from domination to spiritual identification, and that some climbs pull more than one attitude from the climbers involved.

The second of my three categories, caretaking, is worth the work to grasp because it's the dominant outlook of today's mountain enthusiasts. In this case, climbers eschew talk of overcoming an enemy, or claiming a peak for some club or nation. Instead, climbing is a physical test that offers lessons about oneself, about others, and about the environment. These narratives show sympathy for a natural world of glaciers and streams and rock faces that merit protection from overuse by industrial culture.

John Muir and Teddy Roosevelt's famous connection occurred, after all, at Yosemite. As early as 1922 the president of the Alpine Club of

Canada argued his club should "devote more attention to the conservation of our great mountain heritage, as undoubtedly the tendency of this very commercial age is to lose a proper sense of proportion, and alienate, and even destroy, areas of natural beauty which can never be replaced." The caretaking vision is about rescuing the sublime so that it may be experienced indefinitely. Ironically, this tension between being saved and being a savior is enacted in a setting that is itself at risk from development and use.

Caretaking's historical incarnations inform contemporary treatments of wilderness. A tension between preservation and exploitation is evident across North American history because our civilization identifies with nature with one hand and destroys nature with the other. You see, the smoke had barely cleared from the American Revolution when development brought us into the uplifting wilderness, and thus threatened that wilderness. If frontier experiences made us Americans better than our prissy European cousins . . . where were we headed with all these saw mills, farms, and saloons? By the mid-nineteenth century, Americans celebrated and then agonized over the factories and railroads sullying that wild nature they had identified as uniquely American. The emergence of Transcendentalism, Walt Whitman, and James Fenimore Cooper are protest and compensation.

Here's where climbing mountains comes in—the mountains are a symbolic freedom from this dilemma because even today the doughty mountaineer continues conquering, but in the name of the sublime. By identifying with the mountains they explore, climb, and name, mountaineers can maintain the now plainly contradictory poses of nature lover and wilderness conqueror. Caretaking in climbing, then, is like conservation because it treats the mountains as a resource. Conservation efforts in alpine North America have achieved great things because climbers believe that the preservation of alpine wilderness is the preservation of something for recreation and for society's well-being. In this sense, mountains are protected as more than an effort to stop development; they become a medicine chest from which climbers may withdraw doses of vigor. See the paradox? Caretaking is the illogical attention of *Outside Magazine*'s regular "Last Great Places" issue, where readers are instructed to renew themselves by going to some "undiscovered" corner of the alpine world, all at once. Caretaking is the constructive ministrations of John Muir and *Freedom of the Hills* in that the more North America's mountain landscape is threatened, the more mountaineering is deployed as a mode for appreciating—for taking care of—a clean and powerful nature.

Okay, one more.

The third category of climbing narrative is connection, and it holds the promise of knowing nature another way. Connection is the most exciting of my three categories because it insists that human beings are fundamentally intertwined with their environment. Ron Kauk's imperative "Make friends with the rock" may sound clichéd, but this attitude continues to appear in peoples' experience and writing. One version is the transcendence climbers report when summiting a peak, or waiting out a storm. They come to know thoroughly and deeply they are not just witnesses to mountain splendor, but part of it. Yvon Chouinard offers a version of connection when he describes extended effort and commitment on the Muir Wall in Yosemite: "with the more receptive senses we now appreciated everything around us. Each individual crystal in the granite stood out in bold relief." Chouinard's prose sounds like the caretaker's category of engaged appreciation, but with his next sentence he points to something new: "This unity with our joyous surroundings, this ultra penetrating perception gave us a feeling of contentment we had not had for years." Here the climbers developed a pronounced sensitivity to the mountain, and with their heightened receptiveness were able to succeed in what became a cooperative venture with the peak instead of a conquest over it.

Similarly, Chouinard's crony, California mountaineer Doug Robinson, interprets connecting experience as the discovery of a new "visionary" self. In the mountains, he writes, "The climbs will provide all the necessary rigor of discipline . . . and as the visionary faculty comes closer to the surface, what is needed is not an effort of discipline, but an effort of relaxation, a submission of self to the wonderful, supportive, and sufficient world." Through physical practice, Robinson says, the climber approaches insight into the oneness of the human and the natural worlds. "Both the laborious and the visionary parts of climbing seemed well suited to liberating the individual from his concept of self, the one by intimidating his aspirations, the other by showing the self to be only a small part of a subtly integrated universe." So, Robinson and Chouinard both point toward climbers transcending ego-centered subjectivity, and gaining a felt knowledge of human integration with the natural world.

Connection isn't New Age, crystal-hugging shamanism; this is a human relation to the environment that has been obscured by the matrix of culture and consumption you and I inhabit every day. Climbing stories strain through the mists of convention and usage to a way of knowing connection. We're looking at an active partnership linking nature to humans. And you don't have to be in California to perceive connection; even the dour Scots offer examples—W. H. Murray wrote of a moonlit winter climb: "in the architecture of hill and sky, as in great art and music, there is an everlasting harmony with which our own being had this night been made one."

Interestingly, contemporary philosophers have theorized a similar intermingling between human and environment, but have struggled to provide examples of it in action. For instance, ecologist Neil Evernden writes, "the establishment of self is impossible without the context of place," because human beings are a mixture of brain, body, and the spot where it all sits. Likewise, philosopher Edward Casey argues that each body is integrated with the environment in which it lives in a genuine give and take between the self and the setting: "place, we might say, has its own operative intentionality that elicits and responds to the corporeal intentionality of the perceiving subject. Thus place integrates with body as much as body with place." So, noted philosophers wonder when we'll recognize that our lives are defined by the places we live them. This point matters because if we are not beings separate and distinct from lakes, pine trees, or sagebrush, then we are, instead, actively formed by our environment.

We asked if there's evidence of a shift in thinking about the environment, and I've answered by categorizing climbing stories. Why? Because while philosophers and ecologists cast about for a changed consciousness to solve environmental problems, climbing narratives offer a lived expression of the very shift they seek.

A Romantic Mirror

Attitudes change.

The Romantic poets may have outraged their contemporaries, partied across Europe, left bastards, suicides, and tears in the wake of short lives, but they sure revolutionized attitudes to alpine scenery. If today's environmentalists want to change minds about the environment, they should look where the Romantics looked—to the hills. Seventeenth- and eighteenth-century aesthetics register the interpretive shift: in critic Marjorie Hope Nicolson's words, "The rough, jagged, monstrous stones that had once seemed the rubbish of the world have become an integral part of a savage or solemn Nature whose majesty is enhanced rather than marred by their presence and who seems to take as much delight in asymmetry and irregularity as she once felt in the limited, the restrained, the patterned." From "monstrous" "rubbish" the mountain environment came eventually to embody the grand and soul-touching beauty we know from William Wordsworth to John Muir to Galen Rowell.

The point for us in our Subarus and Gore-Tex is that perception changes, consciousness changes, and these changes reshape the way people experience nature. This means that the mountain peaks that appear immutable are instead open to the various meanings staged upon them. Therefore, in those moments when one way of interpreting nature solidifies into either orthodoxy or revolt, we can read the peaks both for a society's values and its direction. So, if we are interested in new ways of making sense of the environment, perhaps the same mountains that moved Europe toward Romanticism herald some mode of perception otherwise buried in our culture's constellation of interests, fears, and desires.

Let me give you some particulars to chew on: Romantic prime movers like Byron and Shelley trundled forward a profound change in attitudes toward alpine nature as irrevocably as you would roll a boulder from a great height. They show us what an interpretive shift looks like in practice.

I live not in myself, but I become
Portion of that around me; and to me
High mountains are a feeling, but the hum
Of human cities torture.

So chants Lord Byron's Childe Harold, and

Are not the mountains, waves, and skies, a part
Of me and of my soul, as I of them?

The speaker is "portion of that around me," and exemplifies the new connection between self and nature in a social world that is otherwise insensitive to such an outlook. Maybe in the Romantics we have a distant mirror of our own world, and an image of the individual embracing the environment against cultural odds. Clearly for Byron appreciating nature became a merger that entailed deeper feeling than "human cities" could muster, and in his poetry changing attitudes toward nature are apparent in a vocabulary of connection to the mountains.

Now this isn't an essay on Romantic nature, or I'd talk about Wordsworth and Coleridge, Emerson and Burns. Instead, this is a peek, a snapshot of a generation where received wisdom about the environment was overthrown, and new attitudes led to new practices in the wild.

Another example of nature's power and danger comes from America's Romantic, Henry David Thoreau. His intense experience on Mount Katahdin in 1846 has been variously interpreted, but makes the most sense in terms of what I call connection. In this much-taught narrative, Thoreau describes the wilderness that he expected would inspire him toward the summit, but actually upsets him: "Nature was here something strange and awful, though beautiful." This seems like standard sublime fare for Thoreau's intended audience of New England journal readers, until Thoreau develops his experience in terms that destabilize the separation of self and other. "I stand in awe of my body, this matter to which I am bound becomes so strange to me. . . . What is this Titan that has possession of me? . . . *Contact! Contact! Who* are we? *Where* are *we*?" Thoreau's questions and italics show that he boggles at the redefinition of self that connection inspires. For Thoreau on the mountain, physical life is revealed and reconsidered in terms of "awe" and "possession" and especially a dizzying "Contact!"

Most commentators hold that "Ktaadn" is the record of his fear and trembling before the antihuman wilderness. On the contrary, I maintain that "Ktaadn" is an experience of connection because Thoreau emphasizes that his body's "contact" is an episode of startling consanguinity with this wild place. Thoreau's body "becomes so strange" to him because he recognizes, there atop "Ktaadn," that his self is also the wilderness. Thoreau's vertigo is induced by the breakdown of the human/nature binary that buttressed a unitary version of self the mountain has exploded. Thoreau's talent as a writer allows him to describe the emotional impact of an inkling that his "self" goes beyond his flesh and mind to include and integrate this wild, alpine world.

The Romantics deliver us an attitude that embraces alpine life, and that in a generation transformed received attitudes toward the ridges and rocks and the whole natural world. The fact that an intellectual transformation could reshape attitudes to the alpine world, then, should give environmentalists hope now. If there are new ways for us to know nature, there are new ways for us to live in nature.

The Body in Conclusion

Look at the ground we've covered.

We decided that tipping to a new way of thinking could sustain the environment, we laid out three modes by which climbers make sense of the natural world, and we talked about the distant mirror of Romantic sea change. My concluding idea is that these strands braid in a particular place: the human body. Now stick with me here, because this idea speaks to the way you turn a page or place an ice screw—it's physical first. The physical necessity of bodily movement is how climbing demonstrates people's connection to nature. You see, the progressive continuity between person and place manifests through the body's thick nerves and heavy flesh, not the wavering, lambent mind.

Climbing is a physical activity. The union between human and nature produced by climbing animates both the material world and the experiencing body. French philosopher Merleau-Ponty argues that perception is fundamentally an interplay between perceiver and perceived—"a coition, so to speak, of my body with things"—and thus it is in bodily activity we clarify that interplay, that intermingling. Climbing matters because it can reveal that humans and nature intermingle, overlap, connect, instead of exist side by side as active subject and passive object. Thoreau asks us in *Walden:* "Shall I not have intelligence with the earth? Am I not partly leaves and vegetable mould myself?" This "intelligence" comes through the growing, perspiring, material body, the same body where climbing, above all, insists we adapt.

My reading of climbing narratives suggests that the life of the body pushes people beyond egocentrism. I know, you've run into enough self-adoring crag rats to sink a porta-ledge, but what's a great climber's attitude to the mountain? Messner, Blanchard, House, Hill, or Chouinard? It's modesty, it's awareness, it's respect. Recall that Doug Robinson connects the laborious with the liberating "visionary faculty" through the body in an alpine environment. If during a climb's extended focus the swinger of ice axes begins to intuit the ripples in the ice, to swing naturally into the one best place, to swing always with the correct force . . . that person climbs and on hard ice survives because the ice speaks to the climber and is heard. For philosophers like Casey and Merleau-Ponty, as for Robinson, Chouinard, and Thoreau, the body is the active vehicle of recognition, the means by which the world becomes intertwined with the human. We can all find examples of the body working as an autonomous connector in the mountain writing we know, and even the climbs we do.

Climbing unfolds something. John Elder writes that "Land is not merely soil: it is a fountain of energy flowing through a circuit of soils, plants, and animals," and he describes a circuit that charges humanity through the body. My point is that climbing sensitizes the body, opens it to the land's current, and thereby animates it to awareness of the natural world. Of course, implicit in this fountain of sensitivity is the body's very doom, and it is a trademark of climbing writing that this lurking fear should be recognized but, like some long-gone lover, never introduced. From this perspective you see that the risk is not the point. It is important to have consequences, but the goal is what the fear makes possible in the body's charged openness to the world around it.

We've seen that the challenge for environmentalists is to change attitudes to nature, but unlike the philosophers I say this change can come through the human body. I say that climbing can animate our fleshly, sensory sympathies to show that somewhere in our physical being there is the knowledge—the *Contact!*—that humans are part of nature and nature is part of humans. Therefore, instead of making climbers mystic seekers or cheerless masochists who incidentally rub shoulders with the sublime, mountaineering can be an activity that enforces a connection to nature and eventually overcomes the established mode of perception that treats nature as another. To recognize climbing in this way—and here is the move I ask readers to consider—is to discern the presence of an actual integration between the natural setting and the human subject. If the body is where we actually exist, then activities that mark the body's being-in-nature are crucial to any reconsideration of our culture's idea of nature. A person who, like Byron, feels "portion of that around me" is rather less likely to strip-mine, or clear-cut, or dump mercury into the same waves that float this body.

| | |

This chapter shows that Western society can change, has changed, and will change. The examples from Romantic culture prove that attitudes shift and that—like Earth's climate—a gathering of small forces tips circulation in favor of a whole new atmosphere. That said, I wouldn't insist that climbers are an indicator species, or that a conversion is right around the corner. What I will insist, though, is that climbing narratives deserve our attention first because they embody the spectrum of our culture's attitudes toward nature in all their power and confusion, and second because they demonstrate the possibility of connecting self and setting through the body.

The climbing narrative is one form that suggests a new way of being in the world. Looking back across acres of dusty books, I see that historical responses to the alpine experience have been guided by established forms of storytelling, foremost among which is surely conquest. If latterly the dominant trope has become caretaking, then we can, I believe, say yet another genre is emerging, and this third genre presents the alpine environment as a place for connection between the physical human and the ice-rock-snow of nature's body.

Does everyone need to go climb a rock tomorrow? Not really.

Not every eighteenth-century soul was obliged to tour the Alps or pen a lyric admiring glaciers either—and still the shift in outlook was culture-wide. So, the possibility of change, of a new attitude and way of being is right in front of us. And yes, it is modeled in climbing, and in the precedent of significant, sudden shifts in the way minds consider and bodies live this world we call home.

1: conquest

The first category of climbing narrative is conquest, and we all know why. Conjure your image of an explorer claiming a peak for country and queen, or a parka-puffed figure holding the stars and stripes with glaciers spreading behind. But conquest isn't only a flag on the summit; it's a picture on the wall, a line in the guidebook, a name on a route. Conquest is a state of mind that's close to home, and it can flourish as readily on a local top-rope as on a Himalayan giant. In conquest, the climber objectifies the climb as something separate to confront, dominate, and claim.

Last week a catalog came in the mail, and in it were listed scores of mountain books from the early twentieth century. Look at these titles: *The Assault on Mount Everest, The Conquest of Mount McKinley, The Fight for Everest, Kamet Conquered, Five Miles High: The Story of the Attack on the Second Highest Mountain in the World, Four Against Everest,* and Sir John Hunt's *The Conquest of Everest.* These titles bring to life a philosophy of experiencing the world that shaped both the hard climbers who wrote them and the many readers who read them—a philosophy of confrontation and mastery. This approach no doubt respects the mountains and delights in them, but it seems also to cast each mountain as a separate and defiant entity to overcome.

Now it's the twenty-first century, and conquering has become unfashionable for mountaineers. But we should listen when people say that the impulse to conquer emerges from the human necessity to eat, to create shelter, to stay warm and happy. We enjoy real benefits from the attitude that holds nature at arm's length and asks, "How might I use this?" Long ago, the effort to live in a powerful and intimidating nature pushed human beings to focus first on the tools and the meals and the shelter nature affords. If you've spent a night in the rain or fished out of hunger, you'll know why.

Conquering peaks is one expression of the energetic human impulse to use the environment. The philosopher Theodor Adorno writes that people "have always had to choose between their subjection to nature or the subjection of nature to the self." Perhaps this is one way to feel Warren Harding's three hundred holes that rat-a-tat-tat a finish on El Cap's Wall of Early Morning Light. To live in this world that snows, that rains, that threatens with predators and parches with sun, humans have found some purchase by objectifying it, by making it a separate and inert toolbox from which to build survival. And we have wrought wonders.

The downside of domination is apparent too—in clear-cuts and pollution, in strip mines and the endless appetite for growth and profit and progress in a world not endless. You can stand with some philosophers and call this the subject/object divide or you can call it instrumental rationality, and then you can blame Genesis, or the Enlightenment or capitalism . . . but from any perspective we're a civilization that approaches nature as something to be manipulated, and we're starting to see limits to how much manipulation this world can sustain.

Thus, climbing that objectifies a mountain and marches a route across its hostile bulk is founded in a grand and important philosophical tradition. Conquest is clearly an influential human attitude to nature, and one that recurs in climbing tales across the centuries. By holding it up for examination in these stories, we can, perhaps, get a better understanding of the ways it shapes our culture from George Washington to George Bush, from the Access Fund to the Arctic National Wildlife Refuge.

The first story here is the Reverend George Kinney's wonderful tale of exploration, challenge, transcendence, and illusion. You see, his march through the wilds of British Columbia is a mix of mountaineering and exploration gone to us in these days of helicopter pickups and glacier pilots. We can wonder how high he really got on Mount Robson, along with those who've doubted his claim since 1913, but we can't doubt his resilience in hunting for his supper, cutting a trail through thick forest, and being swept away by a flood.

If Kinney's rhetoric is overtly triumphalist, others in this section deploy a more nuanced vocabulary of conquest. Direct claims to domination are easy to recognize, but there are more subtle encounters with landscape shaped by conquest's inherited patterns and attitudes and structures of feeling. For some of the writers below, conquest is a personal battle pitting fear against discipline. For others, climbing confronts history or gender roles or family expectations as a force to transcend. So conquest comes in many sizes, and in its variety informs the experience climbers have with their alpine world. In sum, there is a legacy of confrontation in human dealings with the natural world, and that legacy is usefully illuminated, complicated, and even changed by the stories climbers tell.

I won't introduce every writing in this section, but I do want to flag three more efforts that exemplify the climber's compulsion to confront a hard, hard world. Steve House's "The Mind of the Observer" takes us back to Canada for some of the scariest alpine climbing in North America. He and Marko Prezelj fight the unrelenting north face of North Twin and wrestle with their precursors in the pantheon of climbing history. House's essay describes life on the knife-sharp line that separates using nature from failing under its weight. Young Chris McNamara describes the unusual effort to make El Cap's first "girdle traverse"—to travel not vertically but horizontally across all that stone and above all that air. In this retelling the reader feels the heat, feels the creaking granite flakes, and also McNamara's desire to fight the battle by fair means. He could surely force a way with endless bolts and long spells of drilling, but that's no contest. As clear as California sun, this game climber's play depends on the challenge between mute rock and determined assailants. The final story in the Conquest section takes us back into the cold—Barry Blanchard's not-very-fictional rendering of solo ice. Here you might say the steep ice wins, and the man retreats. But Sisyphus is to some a hero, and like that ancient character, we feel Blanchard's protagonist could rise to push himself up that hill, to fight the fight against himself in that glittering arena, again and again.

The Capture of Mount Robson | Reverend George Kinney

I left the mountain that fall, believing that I had had my last try at it. But by the time the spring of 1909 had come, Mount Robson had such a hold on me that I could not rest satisfied till I had had another try at it. I then made arrangements with John Yates, our packer of the year before, for another trip to Mount Robson.

In May I received word that foreign parties were about to attempt Mount Robson. Telegraphing Yates that I was starting at once and expected to meet him on the trail, I hurriedly borrowed some money, and the second of June 1909, left Victoria for Edmonton to outfit an expedition of my own.

From that moment things began to happen. I had counted on one of my brothers making the trip with us, but at the last moment he could not get off. A washout on the C.P.R. delayed me in Vancouver a few days. At Calgary, the president being away I could not accept the grant of a hundred dollars that the Alpine Club had made me, because I was alone at the time and could not get anyone to make the trip with me. About an hour's run out of Calgary, the northbound passenger on which I was traveling ran off the track and piled up in a wreck in the ditch, nearly killing the conductor. At Edmonton, money that I had expected to be in the bank for me failed to materialize. And a letter of introduction that would have made matters easy I found I had misplaced.

I was in Edmonton a week before I could get my outfit together. That week's delay nearly cost me the prize, for by it I got caught in the floods of the Athabaska. Another disappointment awaited me in the shape of a letter from Yates, telling me that it would be utter folly to think of starting on a trip to Mount Robson at that time, for the rivers were in a flooded condition and the unusually late snows still buried deeply all the passes. But I had gone too far to turn back then, and snow and floods or not, I would make the attempt.

III

On Friday, June 11, 1909, with three good horses packed with three months' provisions, I started off alone for Mount Robson, hoping to pick up someone on the trail who would share fortune with me. But for hundreds of miles across the prairies and through mountain fastness, I fought alone the fearful difficulties of that trip, threading my way across treacherous bog, or swimming my horses across mountain torrents.

At one place in trying to cross a rude pole bridge across a muskeg, the horses got mired, and one of them, after getting stuck several times, finally rolled off the poles, and lay on top of his packs, with all four feet helplessly pawing the air.

At the Pembina I passed a pack outfit that had left Edmonton nearly a week before I did. Owing to a flood they lost several hundred dollars worth of packs in the river. Several other pack trains were waiting for the flooded river to subside. But I could not wait, so swam my horses across, and succeeded in getting my stuff over without serious difficult.

At the Big Eddy on the McLeod, a young fellow made up his mind to go with me to Mount Robson, but changed his mind, and I left the place to again plunge alone again into that glorious wilderness.

At Medicine Lodge, on the McLeod, I met Mr. S. McBride, an old-time lumberjack, who was spending a few weeks on the McLeod, living on the trout which were abundant. Mac concluded he would like to go with me to see the country around Mount Robson, and possibly spend the winter in those parts hunting and trapping. But he had no horse or outfit. I finally agreed to sell him one of my horses and half of my provisions on condition that he go with me, from the Indians at the Yellowhead Pass.

For nearly a week we had the finest kind of weather. But the warm days were flooding the rivers from the melting snows higher up in the mountains, and things began to happen. Had I got off a week earlier I would have been high up in the mountains and avoided the floods.

On July 5, after resting our horses over Sunday, we started to ford the Rocky River, a big tributary that empties into the Athabaska just below Jasper Lake. The river was muddy and swift, but I had had no trouble in crossing that place the year before, and was so confident that I knew the ford that I did not unpack my saddle horse and try the place as was my custom, but climbed up on top of his two-hundred-pound packs and led the pack train into the river. But the river ice of that spring had ploughed out the channel of the river several feet deeper than it was the year before. When I reached this channel I suddenly found myself and horse in swimming water. Slipping out of the saddle to relieve my now overloaded horse, I swam alongside of him till I had him nicely headed for the other side, and then struck out for myself and after going through some big rapids reached the shore in safety. The other horses had swum back just in time and were safe.

But my saddle horse had not fared so well. The heavy packs had soon become water-soaked and were dragging him down, while that raging torrent rolled him over and over. He stuck on a bar in midstream, with all four legs stuck up helplessly in the air and his head underwater. But he was a fighter and would not give up, and struggled into swimming water again. Several times he got stuck, then he was rolled and tossed again. I called him once and he swam to the edge of the eddy near me, but the current seized him again and bore him across the river help-lessly toward a logjam. He turned again to come to me, but this time I scolded him and with stones drove him from me to the shelter of a big eddy on the other side, just in the nick of time. He was almost all in. He could not get his feet on the bottom, but he gradually drifted down to the quiet water above the jam. I was helpless on the other side of the river. I shouted to Mac to come and save my horse. Three times the horse started to swim out of the eddy to come across the river to me, but I succeeded in keeping him there till Mac could get down and get him out. He had put up the pluckiest fight for life that any horse could have done, and won out. I was chilled to the bone by my bath in those icy waters, but my pack train was on the other side of the river, so there was nothing for me to do but plunge in the river with all my clothes on and swim to the other side.

We got our horses back to the camp spot we had just left and spent the morning in drying my packs. My camera and notebooks, and all my photographic outfit had been rolled half a mile down that river, but by quick work I was able to save my notebooks and most valuable negatives and enough supplies for a splendid set of pictures that I took later on at Mount Robson.

That night a great cloudburst drowned the whole country. Next morning, to our astonishment, our fairly high camp was flooded. We had to wade waist deep and shift our stuff to a third camp spot before the floods began to subside, our horses being stranded on a distant island.

Mac insisted on stopping, but I had to get on, and every mile counted. Among the great sand dunes of Jasper Lake, we found that the water was so deep that we would have to swim our horses across the outlet of Fish Lake. That was too much for Mac. He would go no farther into such a country.

I made a raft, and the next day, swimming my two horses across the river and rafting my stuff, I said goodbye to Mac and continued my journey alone. By Saturday, July 10, 1909, I had reached John Moberley's, the breed who would canoe me across the Athabaska. Here I found a temporary village. Two or three parties of prospectors had found traveling impossible, and even a couple of small parties of Indians were waiting for the river to subside.

That night the Indians held a potlatch and we were the honored guests. For hours the tom-tom banged and the fire in the center of the big teepee lit up a weird scene. As the Indian warriors circled slowly around that little fire, singing their doleful songs, we thought of days when no white man lived in Canada.

When I got back to my little camp that night, I found that the dogs had eaten up all my supply of meat, and it was impossible then to procure more. The Indians even were completely out of Pemica, so I would have to depend on what wild game I could get.

The next day Donald Phillips rode into camp. On the side of his Stetson hat was the silver badge that bore the legend of "The Guide Association of Ontario." At twenty-five years of age, that blue-eyed, curly-headed, clean-lived Canadian entered that little frontier scene perfectly fit for the undertaking I had in hand. We were soon exchanging confidences. He had been out alone in the hills, looking up the country for guiding purposes, for the Grand Trunk would soon be bringing the tourists into those parts; and he was now returning for provisions.

I told him to come along with me and I would show him the chief beauty spot in all our alpine world, and that I was going to try to climb Mount Robson, the highest peak in all the Canadian Rockies. Thus Phillips and I came together. And a more cheerful, handy, and willing camp companion I never met.

We left the Miette, with its meadows and its graphite, and crossing the Yellowhead, swung rapidly past Mount Peelee and the lakes and down the Fraser. Then when Grant Creek and Moose River joined, we left the Fraser and climbed the hills, following the Moose to its sources. Oh, those were days of glorious weather and more glorious scenes, but days of hard toil and exposure. Our camp fire lit the deep shadows of Moose Pass, on the flowering alps near a hanging glacier, and in another day we saw Mount Robson.

The spring had indeed been late. Great snowslides were still heaped up amid the flowers of those upland meadows. Within twenty feet of any one of those slides of snow, were distinctly shown all the stages of progress from midwinter to midsummer. We stepped out of the tall flowers and grasses of midsummer, and as we approached a pile of snow, the vegetation became more backward till we came to the earliest signs of spring, and the crocuses were boldly lifting their purple heads right out of the hard crust of snow itself.

Our trail up the Smokey was a hard one, yet by the middle of the afternoon we rounded the last turn in the valley, and Mount Robson, white and beautiful, swung into view. Exclamations of surprise and wonder burst from our lips. As I saw this monarch for the third season I was more convinced than ever that only by supreme effort could his summit be reached.

On the following day, Saturday, July 24, 1909, the last stage to the mountain was made, and we turned our horses loose to graze for several weeks where they pleased.

Mount Robson certainly cannot be excelled, for grandeur and extreme beauty of surroundings in all the wide world of alpine scenery. Its lofty peak rises eleven thousand feet above its deep-gouged valleys, or over seven thousand feet above tree line. And so abrupt is its rise, that its steep slopes present an average angle of over sixty degrees.

Sunday we rested. Monday afternoon, July 26, 1909, found us struggling up the cliffs of that north shoulder, and at sunset that day we had carried our packs of blankets and provisions to our high-up camp at Island Cliff, a little bluff that stood on a big shale slope at nearly ten thousand feet altitude. We had spent no time looking for a way up the mountain, for we followed the way up the cliffs that I had discovered the year before.

It was glorious weather. Far and wide, to the south and west and north from horizon to horizon, stretched the endless procession of irregular snow-capped peaks. Now fields and glaciers ploughed every upland valley. While thousands of feet below us the "Valley of a Thousand Falls" was musical with the subdued murmurs of countless waters, that slipped over the edge of its walls of rock. While now and then some distant snowslide added its muffled thunders to the orchestry of the hills.

But the little fleecy clouds, that had turned to gold and deepest crimson, put on somber grays and blacks. While the blues of the valleys had darkened to deepest indigoes, and the silver half-moon changed the scene to another world.

We rose with the dawn and drank in afresh those ever-changing views. The high-up shoulder I had climbed alone last year in a blizzard was a mile or more around to the west and south of us. That was one of the landmarks of the route I had planned on following. But the streaks of snow on the steep cliffs above us seemed to offer a shorter route to the peak, so we concluded to try the north face.

All day we climbed those walls of rock, and cut steps up those icy ravines. The climbing was so difficult and those cliffs were so steep that by three o'clock that afternoon we had attained an altitude of not more than eleven thousand feet. It was useless to try to get higher that day, and as we would have to reposition for another climb, we concluded to return to our camp at the foot of the mountain.

Phillips had never climbed mountains before that summer, but I found him to be so coolheaded and surefooted that there are few experienced men who can excel him in the work. We soon scrambled down the cliffs that had been so hard to climb. We left my camera and most of our supplies cached under a rock, at nearly eleven thousand feet altitude, for we expected to return there and try a new way we had found.

All day the avalanches from the mountains nearby boomed and roared. The afternoon sun loosened slides of rock and snow from the cliffs above us. In climbing the steep couloirs, we had to be extremely cautious, for we were directly in the track of the falling debris. Every now and then, rocks came whizzing and screaming by us. We could usually hear them coming clattering down among the cliffs. But they would not always give us warning. Sometimes they would come from so high up that they would bound over the cliffs above us, and the first we would know of their presence would be when they would suddenly hiss by us in the air like winged messengers of destruction. Glissading down a long slope of snow, we worked down the cliffs of the north shoulder to Camp Robson, where the humming birds used to visit us on sunshiney days.

The next afternoon we made our "higher up" camp on a little ledge in the cliffs above the big shale slope at over ten thousand feet. Our little bed was so narrow that we had to lie very close together, and even then had to build a wall of rock to keep us from falling off the mountainside.

We spent an uncomfortable night because of the wind and cold, but the next day dawned clear and gave promise of a fine day. By nine o'clock we had made such good climbing that we were again at the eleven-thousand-foot level. But there a wall of rock too steep to climb rose abruptly above us. The steep ice of the couloir offered us the only possible way up that we could find. We chopped steps in that wall of ice, till we came to a narrow gorge, where for twenty-five feet we had to climb straight up. We managed to reach the top to that cliff but only to find new difficulties. The cliffs we had been climbing had up till then been quite free of snow; now we found every ledge and possible shelter piled high with ice and snow. Places that would have offered fair climbing were now almost impossible. To add to our difficulties, the western sun began to melt the snows so that they not only made us wet and cold, but the loosened masses of rock and ice began to tumble all about us.

On a jutting crag, where we ate our lunch, I built a cairn at about eleven thousand feet. But the ice cutting and the dangers due to the melting snows were too much for us. We had reached an altitude of twelve thousand feet, but it was three o'clock in the afternoon. The north side of the peak seemed to be only a few hundred feet above us, but I knew we could not reach the summit that afternoon and be able to return in safety, it being too risky to get caught out overnight on those cliffs.

For more than a thousand feet down those upper cliffs of rock our every step was fraught with fearful danger. Not only did we have to get down gullies dripping and streaming with water, where falling rock and avalanches were a constant menace, but the now melting masses that covered every ledge threatened to slide from under our weight and drag us over the cliffs. We found the steps we had cut in the ice slope of the couloir below had nearly melted away, and that the whole mass looked as if it would slip down over the cliff if we so much as touched it. Yet we could only get down by way of those dripping ravines and gullies.

When we had got down to about the ten-thousand-five-hundred-foot level, I left Phillips in charge of my pack, while I followed a series of ledges around to the west and south for nearly half a mile. I wanted to see what the western side was like from the top of the knob of cliffs on the summit of the great west shoulder.

I reached the point desired just as the sun was setting. Phillips was a mere dot on the cliffs to the north. The lake that Dr. Coleman named after me, and the "Valley of a Thousand Falls," lay eight thousand feet directly below. These and the valley of the Fraser were being engulfed by the shades of night. But above me swept a long slope of snow clear to Mount Robson's highest pinnacle. A number of cliffs darkly threaded its gleaming white, and it was tipped at a fearful angle, but in contrast to the mighty cliffs we had been climbing for the past four days, the slope looked easy. With hope and expectation strong in my heart once more, I hurried back to tell Phillips.

We had still five hundred feet of cliffs to go down before we would be able to reach camp "higher up." These were so steep and the step cutting in the couloirs took us so long that we had to get down the last few hundred feet in the dark. We had planned to sleep comfortably at Camp Robson that night, but as it was long after dark when we reached our little ledge on the cliffs, "Camp Highest Up," we knew it was necessary to spend that night also at over ten thousand feet.

The wind rose and the storm clouds swept around us and blotted out the stars and the snow-capped peaks. As we snuggled together, on that little ledge, the fury of a mountaintop storm broke loose upon us. I did not know that the wind could blow so hard. It seemed like some furious monster seeking to tear the very cliffs asunder in order to get at us. It was very cold, and we spent a most uncomfortable night. The rocks that had been warmed by the sun still retained enough heat to melt some of the snow that fell, so that by morning the drip from the cliffs had wet our blankets through, making it necessary for us to seek shelter below. It was so cold that we could not eat any breakfast; so rolling up our wet blankets we set off in the storm to seek Camp Robson below.

For eleven days furious storms buried the mountain peaks. Our provisions were now nearly all gone. For eleven days we explored the mountains round about, chasing in vain the big game of the hills, for our crooked rifle would not shoot them. But with our pistols we bagged the marmot, and grouse, and gopher.

We camped under the cedars and birches of the shores of Lake Kinney, and rafted across its emerald waters. We even went without provisions for a day or two.

|||

For seventeen days we fought a losing fight for the peak. Then Thursday, August 12, dawned fine and clear. As we had plenty of time to get to our camp up the mountain, we spent most of the morning mending our boots and clothes. After several hours' hard work, we finally reached our cache of packs stowed away among those fearful cliffs. We had to cut steps up steep icy gullies and traverse narrow snow-covered ledges. But in five hours' time we at last threw down our fifty-pound packs on the top of that great west shoulder, at an altitude of over ten thousand five hundred feet, or equal to that of Stephen at Field. With my axe I chopped away a couple of feet of ice and snow and leveled off a place where Phillips and I feathered our bed with dry slate stones. We slept with all our clothes on, and wrapped up in our robes spent a wretched night in the wind and cold. The scenes about us were wonderful. We watched the clouds nestle to sleep in the sheltered nooks of the peak. We saw the sun gild all the crests of white and paint blood red each dome and pinnacle. The sunset shadows deepened to royal purples and darkest indigo, till the silver moon transformed the scene again to blacks and whites.

Friday, August 13, 1909, began fine. At dawn we made a little fire of dried sticks we had carried up there, and when the stew was hot we stood wrapped in our blankets and shivered around that little fire, eating out of the pot with sticks for spoons. By sunrise we faced the cold wind and stormed the cliffs.

At the top of the lower of the two cliffs, it began to snow. For a few minutes I stood still; then I said to Phillips, "Curlie, my heart is broken." We had no more provisions to make another trip up the mountain, so this was our last chance. A snowstorm on the mountain meant that it would be utterly impossible to climb that awful slope, owing to its exposure to snowslides. To our intense relief it did not snow much, and the clouds seemed to be mostly mist. We resolved to make a dash for the north edge of the peak, which was nearer to us. I led the way with my ice axe, and Phillips followed hard after. The going was superb owing to the condition of the snow. The dense clouds of mist soon covered our hair and clothes with a frozen mass of ice. As we saw that the clouds did not bring the dreaded snow, we angled off toward the south and headed for the highest point of the peak, of which we caught glimpses now and then.

The upper of the two long lines of cliffs was passed. Small traverse cliffs of rock were constantly encountered, but we could easily get by them by keeping to the snow of the draws. So fearfully steep was that slope to the peak that for hundreds of feet, when I stood erect in my footholds, the wall of snow would not be more than a foot and a half from my face. There was no place to sit down to rest, and when we would get tired we could only lean forward against the slope.

Hour after hour of desperate hard work showed us the peak slowly drawing nearer, whenever we could catch a glimpse of it, but most of the time the clouds were so dense that we could see only a few yards, while the frozen sleet would cut our faces and nearly blind us, and only by constantly moving could we keep from freezing.

The last few hundred feet of the peak were the hardest of all. The snow was too dry and frosty to hold well. Cliffs of rock, with great overhanging bunches of snow cornice, were numerous and most difficult to scale.

All the time we spent at Mount Robson, the winds were west or southerly, and near the peak we found that those prevailing winds had driven the snow against the rocks, and that great overhanging masses of most fantastic crystalline formation had built right out against the wind. These were so dry and powdery that it was very hard to get along. Twice we had to climb almost vertical couloirs. At the very peak we found its razor-edge ridge and needle point fringed with a battlement of these snow masses that were almost impossible to climb.

Finally, floundering through those treacherous masses, we stood at last on the very summit of Mount Robson.

I was astonished to find myself looking into a gulf right before me. Telling Phillips to anchor himself well, for he was still below me, I struck the edge of the snow with the staff of my ice axe, and it cut through to my very feet. Through that little gap that I made in the cornice, I was looking down a sheer wall of precipice that reached to the glacier at the foot of Berg Lake, thousands of feet below.

Baring my head I said, "In the name of Almighty God, by whose strength I have climbed here, I capture this peak, Mount Robson, for my own country, and for the Alpine Club of Canada." Then, just as Phillips and I congratulated each other, the sun came out for a minute or two, and through the rifts in the clouds, the valleys about us showed their fearful depths. The Fraser lay over eleven thousand feet below us. Before I could take any photos, the clouds shut in again thicker than ever.

We could not build a cairn there, for all was steep cliff overhung with cornices of snow; to leave my country's flag there meant that it would be inevitably lost, or carried down the mountainside.

We did not stay long at the summit, for the storm clouds had swept in thicker than ever, and threatened to bring snow. We were nearly frozen, and had to get down out of the wind. The return trip was far more difficult and dangerous than the climbing up. We worked our way over the snow-corniced ledges, and through the snows of the upper peak. Then a few hundred feet below we made a cache of our records, and the Canadian flag, kindly donated by Mrs. Dr. George Anderson, of Calgary, in a natural cairn.

The going down was so dangerous that only one of us could work at a time. I would anchor myself as best I could, while Phillips would use up all the slack of the rope, then he would anchor. It was slow work, but a slip meant death. At last we reached Camp "Highest Up" on that knob on the west shoulder. It had taken us seven hours to get down.

Once more we got our tired and battered limbs in motion. Hastily packing our bedding, we climbed along ledges, rounded difficult passages, climbed down dripping cliffs, cut steps in icy couloirs, slid down a long snowslide, and then painfully labored down the cliffs of the north shoulder, in the dark. We reached Camp Robson, making the return trip in twenty hours. We were so tired out that we found it almost impossible to rest. Our feet were very sore from pounding them into the hard snow. But we had captured the peak.

The next day we packed our horses and started on the back trail for home. I had now only one horse, for the other one had caught swamp fever and died, and his bones now whiten under the cliffs of Mount Robson's north shoulder. We were about out of provisions, and we had hundreds of miles of trail to travel. For nearly two weeks we were short of food, living on what birds and gophers we could find, but our trip had not been in vain.

Others will doubtless someday stand on Mount Robson's lonely peak. But they who conquer its rugged crags will ever after cherish in their hearts a due respect and veneration for that rugged mountain.

With clothes artistically patched, and my feet all blistered, I got into Edmonton to find the city gay with bunting, and a banner that bore the legend "Welcome to your City," but I found that I was only an ordinary chap, back again to the everyday world, and that the city was giving honor to Lord Strathcona. And that Peary and Cook were monopolizing the public interests in the world of discovery.

The Mind of the Observer | Steve House

The dull white snow of late Canadian winter mirrors this morning's scudding clouds as Marko Prezelj and I ski for several hours alongside Wooley Creek. Eventually, we put the skis on our packs; finally, we crest Wooley Shoulder. I am ahead, anxious for the famously intense view across three horizontal miles straight into the north face of North Twin.

The north face of North Twin is as proud and honorable and mysterious as any alpine wall anywhere in the world. A mountain archetype, it bursts skyward from the very belly of the earth, gaining breadth with height and then like a stone wave turning concave and slim and sharpening to its bifurcated crest. I can see no obvious routes. All lines lead to steep ground, to big roofs, to blank-looking pillars. The patterns my eyes detect trend horizontally, tracking the stratified limestone that is so often the signature of the Canadian Rockies.

For several minutes I take it all in. Despite believing that I was prepared for the effect the face would have on me, I now realize I'm not. And where is Marko? My impatience spurs me to move again, so as not to have to confront the face anymore, but it draws my gaze upward to stare at its improbability, the lack of climbing possibilities, and my own arrogance at thinking I can climb it in winter.

My mind pulls up images I've memorized: Chris Jones, on page 6 of the 1975 *American Alpine Journal*, climbing steep rock in big boots and poor weather; a baby-faced Barry Blanchard and a honed-looking Dave Cheesmond from a 1986 issue of *Climbing*, printed before I had a driver's license, before I'd led a single pitch of rock or swung an axe into a frozen waterfall. These climbs, the only two climbs ever completed on the face, set the bar for alpinism in the Canadian Rockies. Their stories are ones of pure style and absolute commitment: difficult climbing on the backside of the Columbia Icefield, with little chance for retreat from high on the routes. The Lowe-Jones, which has repelled all attempts to repeat it, was likely the most difficult route in the world when it was established in 1974. It is alpinism's unbroken-for-twenty-three-years world-record long jump. My generation's best effort is still short of the mythical mark. But short on what, I wonder? Short on skill? On bravery? On heart?

Marko arrives, breathing hard from his exertions in the unsupportive snow. I watch his face as the lodestone of North Twin bends his gaze.

"Ta stena je en prav poshast," he states flatly. That face is a proper beast.

But "poshast" also connotes "gentle"—maybe a mangy, overgrown dog, but certainly not the fire-breathing dragon that I see. I spent a year climbing in Slovenia and have been on three Himalayan expeditions with Slovenians, so I expect to understand how this wall looks to Marko. Instead, I am stunned by his comment.

"Ja, je kar lepo steno, ne?" Yes, quite a nice wall, I say, trying not to let on. Marko turns to the immediate problem of getting off the shoulder and continuing our journey. I follow. We plunge down the wind-scoured scree to the snowy slopes below, strap the skis back on, and continue our journey toward the face.

| | |

Marko and I drove my rusty, shag-carpeted Ford van across the forty-ninth parallel into Canada three weeks ago. It is his first visit here, and we have climbed several wet and aging Grade 6 waterfalls along the Parkway and half a dozen difficult routes on the wonderfully sunny limestone of Yamnuska. Marko is clearly at home in these mountains, being as they are so similar in their peculiarities to his native mountains, the steep and often crumbling Kamnik and Julian Alps. It dawns on me, as I slide down-valley toward the wall, that the onus of these world-record climbs exists in my head but not in Marko's. He knows almost nothing about North Twin. I begin to see that if I can get us started on the face and the weather holds, we will find a way to the top.

Marko and I have a kind of pact, born of a shared distaste for posing and respect for the nobility of mountains. When we decide to go climbing, we go climbing. We grow serious; we don't laugh much once we start. We break when we have to, not when we want to. We go to work, and we work until we get the job done or until we are forced to accept failure. We try as hard as we can, and that often turns out to be harder than we thought we would be able to try. I wonder if Marko is playing this role now—not trying to make things, as we say, "tasty."

Marko carries the task at hand, preserving our fragile momentum. I smile to no one as I think how I love climbing with him.

We continue down-valley and cache the skis at the bench where we plan to circle back via the Mount Stutfield icefall into Habel Creek. After eating our last fresh bread, we pick up the packs again. A herd of bighorn sheep leads us down through cliffy ground to the valley bottom. Here we waver slightly as we are forced to crawl across interminable snow patches of breakable crust. We alternately pull and push each other across the flat snow, up the lateral moraine, across its crumbling crest, and down onto the mountain's glacier. Roping up, we skirt crevasses as quickly as our deadened legs allow. I alternately eye the seracs of Stutfield perched above us and the looming, but now comfortably foreshortened, north face.

The next morning we wake at 8:05. I am pissed: Marko, the one with the alarm, slept through the 5:30 AM revelry. We are camped below the biggest, baddest face in the Rockies, and here we are, oversleeping! I vent my frustration with hard and hasty words. Marko replies exactly as he should: with silence. He starts the stove, gets the coffee made, and starts packing while we eat the first ration of muesli and dry milk. There is no use now in trying to rush the necessary morning chores. We pack while we eat: food for four days, fuel for five. We have one synthetic sleeping bag, a five-by-eight-foot tarp, and a shovel blade that fits our ice-tool shafts. Extra clothing consists of a change of socks each and two synthetic belay parkas.

Just after 9 AM I ascend the one hundred feet of rope I managed to fix the night before. At the high point, I tie in, place a high nut, grab its carabiner, and pull. From a lock-off I place another cam higher. I repeat this a few times before the steepness relents enough to allow me to free climb. The rock seems to be made for tools and crampons. Thin cracks accept my monopoints; my picks slot into fissures too narrow for my fingers. When the crack runs out, I hook across small, flat edges and climb for several meters back to the left. For the first of many times I am thankful that we decided to bring leashless tools for the leader. My traverse brings me to the end of my pitch and the first of many hanging stances.

Marko continues the route by tension-traversing for a couple of meters to gain a patchy runnel of ice. As I watch his composure and control I am inspired to confidence and admiration and, perhaps most important, a feeling of momentum. After sixty meters he belays at the foot of the first and largest icefield. Here we unrope, and I punch off up the icefield.

As usual, we have agreed to climb with new-route eyes. We base our route-finding on what makes sense to us, not where we think others might have gone. This obviates mistakes that we don't wholly own and takes into account that both of this face's previous ascents were made in summer. We run up as much easy ground as we can; the physical realization of progress causes me to grin through heavy breaths.

At the end of the day Marko is fixing ropes at a stance when he finds the first sign of previous climbers: a red sling through an old nut. We have climbed much new ground today, but now we are joining the line of the 1974 Lowe-Jones route, which, by the way, is the only really logical way up from here. While Marko fixes the ropes and rappels, I start to dig a bivouac out of the snowfield. After a short while I hit rock, then continue to dig horizontally. An hour later we are comfortably drinking tea on our snow ledge underneath our small tarp. We sleep well, even waking up on time in the morning.

Marko has the first block. I belay, offer advice when asked, and otherwise keep my mouth shut. Marko climbs, and climbs brilliantly. He hooks and torques and pulls sideways on his tools and edges his crampons on the accommodating limestone. He leads a pitch for what must be three hours, and when he yells "Off belay," I already have the big pack on. As I follow, I understand what took so long: the pitch, which brings us to the top of a steep headwall that must be George Lowe's "A3–A4" pitch, consists of thin aid climbing with big-fall potential. Marko is through for the day, which is fine with me, since now I am hungry to lead.

I storm up moderate free climbing to reach a block beneath a roof. The long, squarish, black block appears to be just barely there, and I slow my headlong progress.

Some may think that alpinists are arrogant and foolish, seeking danger and reveling in risk. But the struggle, while possibly deadly, is not combat. The mountain is passive. Ice and stone are inert and more analogous to a canvas than to enemy forces. Alpinism is a set of actions that are created by, and therefore become, me. Me: a human being, a member of society, a mature ego that acknowledges an external reality, one that includes many, many shades of life as well as of death.

At thirty-three I am rid of any delusion that I have to prove anything to anyone. But now I sense an emotional province lying before me. I acknowledge risk as a necessary fuel that burns as knowable fear, moving me beyond the banality of the black and white. Right now, I understand that I could disturb this rock and kill my partner, and therefore myself. That is an observable reality. Below the surface of this reality churns the sea of I that is so affected. That I cannot control or predict these effects no longer frightens me. I've been here too often. I accept who I am, and who I will become, unconditionally. Anything other than equanimity in this moment will almost surely dislodge the block onto Marko's belay.

I climb a crack to the right of the block, use some French-free moves, pull the roof to the left, finish the pitch with a tension traverse, then make a hanging belay with what's left of my gear. Marko follows the pitch and kicks the block. We both watch quietly as it makes a curious half-spin before skidding and scraping against our former belay stance.

Then, as if acknowledging its audience, it performs a noiseless swan dive to the icefield some eight hundred feet below.

|||

Thirty minutes after sunset I finish the third pitch of my block at a thin crack in a steep headwall. Fixing the ropes, I descend to Marko's stance, which, being the size of one boot, is the biggest ledge we have seen since morning. With some chopping and prying we enlarge it to the size of three, maybe four, butt cheeks. Marko sets up the stove; I ascend twenty feet up our fixed rope to another snow patch and scoop snow into my empty backpack. We hang in our harnesses in the darkness and melt snow into water and convert water into lukewarm tea, soup, runny mashed potatoes, and, eventually, lukewarm tea again.

While Marko packs the stove for the night, I sit on the ledge to change my socks. Stripping the damp sock off a clammy, tired foot, I pull the now-dry sock of yesterday out from between my long-underwear top and my fleece jacket. The dry sock goes on and the wet sock replaces the dry one in the depths of my layers. Carefully I replace the inner boot on my left foot. Next I unclip the outer shell of my boot from the anchor, and, with my bare index finger firmly hooked through a loop attached to the back of the boot, I pull it on. Just as my heel is about to snap into the shell, the cord held by my index finger rips.

The boot recoils from my foot and suspends itself, floating for a long moment in the tractor-beam glow of our headlamps. Then it is gone. There is no noise. There is absolutely nothing to see.

I am acutely aware that everything around us is exactly the same as it was a moment ago. But everything about our situation is incredibly different. Even my best self-flagellating curses ring hollow and futile against this dispassionate amphitheater of rock and ice.

There is much stern silence from Marko and finally some curt discussion. We acknowledge that it will be easier, quicker, and safer to continue to the top of the face than to descend. Of course this means that Marko will have to lead everything. I will need to follow difficult traversing pitches without a crampon on one foot. We will be forced to descend from the summit by crossing the expansive Columbia Icefield to the Athabasca Glacier to eventually arrive at the Icefields Parkway.

We quietly rig our tarp overhead, squeeze onto the ledge, and, with our feet on a backpack, pull the sleeping bag over ourselves. No more socks are changed this night. The bivouac seems long. Both of us are restless in the uncertainty of what tomorrow will bring.

||||

At 5:00 AM winds near the summit cause spindrift to dump onto our ineffectively rigged tarp. Snow starts to accumulate in our sleeping bag. In the space of a three-word conversation we decide to abandon our austere spot.

I begin to pack our remaining supplies as Marko ascends the fixed rope. Because we are unable to use the stove in the morning spindrift shower, we start without food or water. I wrap a prusik onto the rope, simultaneously hoping that this day will work out and understanding that my hopes don't count for much.

Marko starts another pitch with a short tension traverse to the left and then climbs horizontally for sixty meters. I follow by leaving a nut and lowering myself out on my cordalette. The inner boot on my left foot is lined with two plastic bags, while the outside is wrapped with athletic tape to protect it from abrasion. I climb carefully with the pack, glad for Marko's many pieces of protection as I hop and hobble toward him.

The next pitch is a very traversing rappel, which Marko protects like a lead with many directional pieces for me to remove as I follow. He belays the free ends while I slowly lower myself out, scraping with one crampon and smearing on any exposed rock with the quickly wearing toe of my inner boot. My heart is brought to a lurching stop when the last directional fails as I'm removing the second-to-last piece; I swing out and down across the face before Marko's belay arrests my momentum. I continue to him, clip in, and pull the ropes. Ten meters from the end of one rope the sheath is completely severed and the core slightly damaged.

Marko reracks for the next lead. I tape up the ruined rope and give him the good end. This time I lower him down thirty feet to the left, where he can gain the large ice gully that marks our exit from the face. Much to our consternation, the ice gully is completely devoid of ice. I follow Marko's lower by rapping off our largest cam.

When I reach the belay, Marko asks, "Did you rappel from the nut?" His face bends into a smile. He knows what I did. I know he would have left the nut.

"No, I left the cam. It's heavier," I say, emphatically. "The top is a long way from here and the road much, much farther beyond that."

Marko shakes his head. His Slovenian mind fails to understand my American logic, where cost is less important than comfort.

As he leads a long and difficult mixed pitch up patchy ice and steep crack systems, I can see the fatigue, hunger, and dehydration in his movements. He is no longer quick and sure and fluid. Pumping out, he hangs from a piece to recover strength before continuing to a belay, which he reaches with a single screw. This he places in a dense, eroded piece of ice. After yelling down his predicament, he pulls one rope up through his gear and lowers the end back to me. I remove the two screws of the belay anchor, tie them into the end of the rope, stand on my one crampon, and grip my ice tools while he builds an adequate anchor.

Scraping and tugging and hopping, I make my way up the pitch. I am pulled down by fatigue and the weight of the pack, but up is salvation. I flash back to just a few days ago when success was going to be a new route in perfect style. The idea hovers in my mind like my boot shell in the soft glow of electric light. It seemed so close then, so possible. Now I am happy to be climbing toward the exit from this face. My precious success has narrowed to simply surviving this journey on a wall that in the North American mind is haunted by the living ghosts of the climbers who passed this way thirty years before.

Another hanging belay, but this one is different. When Marko disappears out of sight twenty meters above me, the rope starts to move quickly. I join him a few minutes later; we are on lower-angle ice, and we are both smiling.

I eat snow and the occasional Gu pack and follow Marko up pitch after pitch of moderate, tedious climbing. One crampon is lashed to my unsupportive innerboot with parachute cord; I mostly hop about on my right foot, taking the time to chop little steps for my left foot when my right leg pumps out. I try to be consistent, but I can't be fast.

Eventually we gain the small saddle between Twin Tower and North Twin and start walking together along the snowy ridgecrest toward the North Twin summit. Our arrival holds no emotion other than relief at finding a suitable bivouac beneath the summit cornice.

We're quite thirsty after a long day without water, so we cook until late at night. I fall asleep with my gloves drying on top of the pot and am awakened by the smell of smoldering nylon and leather. Despite our fatigue we both sleep fitfully, my body tucked rightly against Marko's for warmth. We each sleep only when the other dozes off; periodic, deep coughs violently disturb any rest. The night seems extraordinarily oppressive, but keeping warm occupies so much of my attention that dawn comes sooner than I expect, and I drift into a short, restful void.

In the morning while making coffee, I program coordinates into our GPS for the new descent via the traverse off the Columbia Icefield. At 10:00 we start over the summit of North Twin, down the southeast ridge and onto the icefield. All day we stumble along with me in the lead. I am more experienced at navigating with these electronics; I can also do penance for not leading yesterday by breaking trail all day today. The damned GPS counts down every single meter of our progress, and when I look up from the insidious countdown I lose reference almost instantly and start angling off course.

After nine hours of nearly continuous walking we reach the Icefields Parkway. It is well over an hour before we succeed in thumbing a·ride in the dark the ten kilometers north to our waiting van.

| | |

Late on a bright sunny morning I awake in the home of Barry Blanchard and Catherine Mulvihill. I tumble downstairs to a cup of Barry's French-press coffee; after that, the three of us and Marko walk up the street to a café. I drink more coffee, eat pastries, and consume an egg-and-potato dish mounded high onto an extra-large plate.

On the way back we meet two keen alpinists loading up their car for the Icefields Parkway. They've gotten our story from Barry the night before and are visibly fired up about our success. They jabber about climbing leashless in the alpine and slaying dragons and say flattering things that I'd rather not hear. Marko stays quiet and throws sticks for their dog. I am at a loss for words. I try to return their good will and say something encouraging about their objective, which they don't specifically disclose.

A day later, while driving south through the budding hills of Montana and Idaho, it occurs to me that what I wanted to say to them was something like this:

| | |

Our sole intention was to try to climb the north face of North Twin in winter by whatever path seemed most logical and with the clear understanding that we might not climb anything at all. There were other attractive routes in the range that we could have attempted to climb that week, some old, some new. But we decided to go for the highest, ripest piece of fruit we could see. In hindsight, the critical decision was that we would climb up into the tree in the first place.

Alpinism, when spoken about, is already dead. It lives only in the moment of action. It is alive in our observations, our judgments, our decisions, our movements, our successes, and, more often, our failures.

My climb with Marko is over. Learn something from it if you will, but you might be better off without the knowledge. I am not advocating that you ignore the lessons of the past, but neither can you allow yourself to be chained by the weight of what happened before you. Don't limit yourself by mythologizing the past.

Go, finish packing. When you come back, what you remember will already be different from what happened. Perhaps a part of the experience will have become a part of you, for a lifetime or longer. But you will not be able to share your I with me any more than I can share my me with you. North Twin is part of me now, just as indescribably and just as certainly as it is part of the other five men who have climbed its north face.

Today may be your day. Go.

The Serac | Arlene Blum

I reached my first mountain summit as a student at Reed College in Portland, Oregon, after John Hall, my handsome chemistry lab partner and a climber, asked me if I wanted to climb Mount Hood one starry night in 1964. When I put on my daypack and headed up, I began breathing so loudly that John later confessed he had wondered if I would make it out of the parking lot. So John taught me the rest step: Step, breathe, relax. Step, breathe, relax. Slowly and steadily, my body adapted to the unaccustomed exertion, and I began to feel peaceful and strong. As the golden light of morning traveled from the top of Mount Jefferson to the other Cascade summits and finally to us, I fell in love for the first time. I was in love with John, with Mount Hood, with mountains, with life.

John and I climbed Mount Hood that day and then many other Cascade volcanoes by increasingly challenging routes. Soon I wanted to go on longer expeditions to high distant peaks and heard about an upcoming expedition to Mount Saint Elias in the Yukon Territory of southeastern Alaska. This remote eighteen-thousand-foot-high mountain is the fourth highest peak in North America, and had been ascended only three times previously. The Saint Elias region was notorious for high levels of precipitation, bad storms, unstable glaciers, and avalanche danger.

The two young organizers of this expedition, both students from Corvallis, Oregon, were at first enthusiastic about my being part of the team. Then, Bill Hackett, a very experienced Alaskan climber, joined them and vetoed the idea of having a woman along. I was surprised, but accepted this rejection with equanimity. I wasn't sure that I was ready for Mount Saint Elias, anyway.

Later in the summer, Ted, one of the Saint Elias organizers, invited me to join him and two of his friends for a climb of Sandy Headwall, a moderately difficult route on Mount Hood. As the four of us drove toward Mount Hood on a sunny July afternoon, we looked straight at the Headwall, which looked adequately steep to me. Ted exclaimed, "That route looks too easy to bother climbing. Let's do Elliott Headwall instead." Elliott Headwall, one of the most difficult routes on Mount Hood, was considered objectively dangerous unless ascended during the night in the winter when the slopes were frozen solid.

"It's supposed to be risky this time of year," I suggested.

"Oh, that's just for the turkeys." Ted was confident. "Let's go for it."

He drove us around to the north side of Mount Hood, and we hiked in to a little cabin below Elliott Headwall, where we spent a restless night. I lay awake, anxious about the next day's climb.

The sun was already hitting the vertical ice cliffs of Elliot Headwall the next morning as we reached the glacier below, an expanse of broken forms and shapes like a huge ocean suddenly frozen into glistening ice. I saw wondrous blue and green ice walls and enormous shining seracs—white towers. As the sun touched the glacier, it was transformed into a magical landscape of sparkling jewels. Awed by the beauty and my companions' certainty, I did not have the confidence in my own judgment to voice my belief that we were climbing too late in the day and at the wrong time of the year.

Ted and Sandy, the two more experienced climbers, roped together and headed up rapidly, leaving me with Greg, a friend of theirs with little climbing experience. As he moved slowly up the glacier toward Elliott Headwall, I followed him with growing concern. With care, we crossed a frail bridge of snow above the bergschrund, an enormous hundred-foot-deep fissure in the ice. Above the bergschrund, the ice slope steepened as we ascended Elliot Headwall itself.

About six hundred feet higher, our progress was slowed by a short steep ice wall. Greg moved in slow motion, as I impatiently safeguarded his progress with a belay from below. Our two companions had disappeared above in the distance.

When Greg reached the top of the ice wall, he did not stop to give me a similar belay to protect me in case I were to fall. I didn't ask him for one, as it would be faster if we both moved at the same time and I was in a hurry to catch up with the others. The sun was softening the slope now, and I wanted to get up the headwall and down off the other side as rapidly as possible. I didn't realize how vital a belay could be in a treacherous place.

Suddenly my foothold slipped out. I yelled "Falling!" and plunged my axe into the snow to stop myself. I was just slowing down when I pulled Greg off the slope. He too began tumbling, pulling me out of my attempted self-arrest. Together now we were both bouncing down the precipitous slope. I somersaulted, landed on my head — fortunately I was wearing a helmet — and thought to myself, "You've really blown it this time, kid." A picture flashed through my mind of my falling hundreds of feet and ending up in a twisted heap in the bottom of the bergschrund, with myriad broken bones, if alive at all. It happened so fast there was no time for terror.

I felt a great jerk around my waist and found myself hanging by the rope tied to my waist harness. Miraculously, the rope between Greg and me had caught over an ice tower poking out of the face—the only such serac in the area. Our rope had sawed almost entirely through the serac, leaving only about an inch of uncut ice. Greg and I were dangling perilously on either side of the serac, our lives depending on that still intact inch of ice. Shaking with fear and relief at our miraculous survival, I quickly chopped out a platform in the ice face with my axe and stood there, gasping in tortured breaths of air. Greg, who had lost his glasses, helmet, and composure, inched carefully across the steep slope and joined me in my perch.

The other two hurried back down to our small platform. "That's the best fall we've ever seen!" they exclaimed. "We sure wish we'd had a movie camera. That was fantastic!"

"Let's finish the climb," they said.

"It's too late in the day," I insisted, although it was only nine o'clock in the morning. "With the sun on the ice cliffs, there could be avalanches and rock falls." Feeling in shock from our near escape, I couldn't believe their enthusiasm for what could easily have been a fatal experience. "I want to go down off this mountain right now. While we're still alive."

"The only safe way to get off this mountain is straight up to the top and down the easy slopes on the south side. There are treacherous avalanche slopes on either side of us and the bergschrund below," Ted insisted. "We can't traverse off, and up is shorter than down."

Shaken and terrified, I followed their lead straight up to the summit for the next few hours. The climbing was frightening: steep slopes of loose rock, ice, and mud. Rocks loosened from the snow by the sun pelted down on us. Several large rocks hit me on my head, but I was protected by my climbing hard hat. Miraculously the rocks spared my partner, who had lost his helmet.

Finally we reached the top and discovered that by accident we had gone up a route on the mountain that had not been climbed before. The others were very happy at our accomplishment, but I was mostly relieved to be on the summit unhurt and displeased with my own lack of judgment in not speaking up more loudly when I felt the climb was too dangerous. I had learned that it is very important to select the right companions and then listen to my own instincts about what is safe. For the first time, I realized that under some circumstances, mountain climbing could be a less than pleasant, indeed a possibly lethal activity.

Denali | Jonathan Waterman

In 1976, seven friends and I journeyed to Alaska. It was a huge leap of faith for a mountaineer not yet old enough to vote, and until our jet lumbered up into high altitude above Boston's Logan International Airport, I had never climbed above seven thousand feet. We were members of the Lexington, Massachusetts, Explorer Post, and as veterans of winter backpacks up New Hampshire's four-thousand-foot mountains, we fledglings planned to "conquer" Denali.

Most people refer to the mountain as McKinley, despite the Alaskan preference for the original native name. Although many names existed among the various tribes and visiting Russians, the Athapaskan natives who lived and hunted closest to the mountain deemed it Denali—the High One. In 1896, a self-assured Princeton graduate, William Dickey, renamed the mountain after a summer of prospecting for gold, performing a crude survey of the mountain, and drawing a map of the area. Since Dickey had recently argued with two Democratic silver prospectors who championed both free silver and William Jennings Bryan for president, Dickey retaliated by naming the mountain after his preferred Republican presidential nominee, McKinley, who championed, of course, the gold standard.

|||

The distances separating most Americans from their highest mountain fosters preconceptions utterly removed from reality. For instance, our scout contingent was so deluded as to believe that climbing a 20,320-foot mountain in the Bicentennial year of 1976 would pay tribute to our predecessors who fought in the Revolutionary War. Naturally, our final attack on the easiest route would take place about two hundred years after the Lexington minutemen fired on the British redcoats. Even if a few of our young team didn't champion the idea, the citizens of our town generously gave us thousands of dollars.

There are some expeditions, with even grander bank accounts, who use sponsorship to climb Denali for Women and Everest for Peace, and to explore Antarctica for the Environment. But most climbers scoff that mountain adventures could represent health concerns, corporate America, women's liberation, or Earth Day. Certainly, in June 1976, our crew of eight blithe Explorer Scouts didn't fully understand that climbing for anyone but yourself is making a mockery of mountaineering. However, our adviser back at the Boston Museum of Science, Brad Washburn, might have been one of the all-time exceptions: His sponsored climbs—which he shared with millions of people through his photographs, texts, lectures, and museum exhibits—at least advanced art and science.

Washburn was too busy making laser-detailed maps and taking artfully vivid mountain photographs to go climbing anymore. When our team of boys had shuffled into his office above the Charles River, he graciously pulled out his photographs and map. "Look out for these hanging glaciers here," he said with his thumb pressed tight on a contour line at eight thousand feet, "and don't even *think* of camping on Windy Corner; we didn't name it *windy* for nothing."

But the advice that Washburn gave to our team (and thousands of other climbers) was the least of his gifts to me. Washburn became my earliest role model. Although his stature and contributions to science seemed remote to someone who rejected a college education, his passion and dedication to Denali was my unmistakable clarion call. To an impressionable youth, admiration assumes a form of imitation. I wanted to be like Brad Washburn.

At the time, our team, flushed from visiting with the grand old master, did not have any idea that climbing Denali with a large group was a mistake. Decisionmaking for eight people would prove arduous, and like most large teams, our group dynamics became a bigger challenge than actually climbing the mountain. Consequently, we naively blocked the voice of the wind, the crack of avalanches, and the mountain's many moods. Having all attended a Himalayan lecture by the famed British climber Chris Bonington, we could do nothing but admire the siege-style tactics of his army-sized team on Annapurna; we did not know that being a large and well-supplied team in Alaska served only to insulate us from real adventure.

In Talkeetna, a hundred miles north of Anchorage, when bush pilot Jim Sharp saw us unloading our stockpile of gear—occupying half of an Alaska Railroad baggage car—he wondered how it would all fit into his skiplane. We stared at forty days of food for a twenty-day climb; a twenty-five-pound wheel of Jarlsberg cheese; twelve hundred chocolate bars; a spare ice axe, spare crampons, spare rope, a spare sleeping bag, and a spare ensolite sleeping pad; a fifteen-pound first-aid kit; two radios; five decks of cards; twenty-two books; twelve ice screws; ten pickets; eight snow flukes; and, of course, an American flag. We figured that we would each be freighting two hundred pounds of gear. After loading and unloading Sharp's pickup truck six times, we became concerned. Moving such a load fifteen miles and ten thousand feet up the normal West Buttress route was going to offer us all the joy of stone vassals bound for a pyramid.

| | |

On the glacier, a lone climber came skiing into our camp. It was the legendary Reinhold Messner, who had just completed a new route on Denali. The Messiah of Mountaineering amazed us; he had a small rucksack and a tiny bag of trash on back of the red sled he was dragging. He was also generous to a fault, giving us his leftover food that we didn't need, and his sled, which made us realize that we needed seven more sleds, in addition to a few porters.

I was awestruck and dim-tongued beside the well-known author of

The Seventh Grade and that brilliant treatise on climbing ethics, "The Murder of the Impossible." His prose was as direct and inspiring as the mountains he soloed. Although he was a handsome fellow, next to big strapping boys who had eaten meat and potatoes all their lives, he looked emaciated. I wanted to fix our hollow-cheeked, anorexic hero a fattening meal.

It struck me that Messner would now compose another essay about the advantages of mountaineering light and lean. Messner actually shook his head as he studied our mountain of supplies. If you were really listening, hanging on his every word like all good Scouts would have, you could hear him as he walked away from camp, muttering *sotto voce,* "You Americans disgust me."

He was right: Our ethics were obscene. For the following week, our green team marked the well-worn West Buttress route with caches of unneeded food and equipment—all to be picked up on our way down. The meeting with the Messiah started a ripple of dissension among our group, and every night we debated ethics and the concept of being fat, ugly Americans.

At 8,000 feet we cached the snowshoes, spare stove, spare ice axe, and spare crampons. At 8,500 feet, we bloated the ravens with dozens of cookies. At 9,200 feet, we sacked the first-aid kit. And finally, at 10,000 feet, we presented the ungainly wheel of Jarlsberg to the Japanese, who acted quite pleased and refilled our cups with sake until we all crawled off to bed. We later heard that they rolled the cheese off Windy Corner and started a colossal avalanche.

Twenty-five years earlier, the first climbers on the West Buttress route remarked, "This kind of climbing is about 90 percent trying to stay alive and warm, and 10 percent climbing." This team had camped at 12,900 feet, and a windstorm forced them to spend most of their time digging out their tents from Windy Corner—whose name was their creation. Their leader was Brad Washburn, who had advised us that shovels would be one of the most important pieces of gear we could carry.

While we were stormed in just below Windy Corner, digging out our tent with one of four ten-pound shovels, a solitary chickadee banged and fluttered against the tent walls. It chirped and wing-feathered the nylon with a rapid-fire desperation that made even the high-pitched wail of the wind seem trivial. I tried to bring the tiny bird in, to thaw the frost on its wings, but it flew off into the storm.

Athapaskan legends tell of the chickadee's (*K'its'ahultoona*) two-noted song as a lament for the passing of winter. It is believed that this song is an omen that the listener will soon cry over death.

In the morning I found the chickadee next to our latrine, curled into a coal-sized lump. Its underfeathers were softer than down against my cheek, and it smelled of sweet and distant roses. I held it up to my skin as if body heat could make a difference while I dug with my other hand. When the hole was two feet deep, I set it in without looking and quickly smoothed the snow back over.

The bird upset me. I was shaken about the graceful shell of feathers because its passing had alerted me to the fragility of life here, and if I was to spend any time on this coldhearted mountain, I would have to address the meaning of death. Maybe trying to understand death, I thought, would cast some definition on my own life.

At 14,300 feet we collapsed and gave our backs a three-day rest after two weeks of triple hauling and trailbreaking. Now that we were up high enough to transmit, we began flaunting our radios. Our leader, Bob Eaton, asked an Anchorage operator to dial our various moms and dads in Lexington. We made so many calls to our girlfriends that Eaton was forced to ban further transmissions.

Other climbers that summer radioed for helicopter rescues, to obtain weather forecasts, and to alert the media; radios provide mountaineers with the same swagger that gun-toting policeman practice. Although we did keep our friends and family informed, contact with the outside world depressed us. Mountaineering involves a necessary isolation, and, once broken, the lurid fantasies of showers, hot meals, and the opposite sex ravaged us as cleanly as a subarctic tempest.

|||

After recovering from pounding headaches at 14,300 feet, our intrepid Explorer Scout team continued its progress up the mountain. Certainly, the climbers who call Washburn's route "a cattle plod" have been deceived by severe mountain sickness or a whiteout, because walking the ridgecrest from 16,000 to 17,000 feet is the penultimate mountaineering experience next to summiting. On a good day, you can revel in a three-mile drop to the tundra below—a greater drop than most Himalayan giants. Or you can look east and see Mount Sanford, more than 200 miles away. Or you can meet legendary international mountaineers stumbling down after having suffered up high.

When the salt-and-pepper-bearded Don Whillans first met our group at 16,500 feet, we wondered if the Briton's pack helped balance his tremendous beer belly. Several years earlier, Whillans had summited on Annapurna with Bonington's team. This year, he had just finished an alpine-style climb up the West Rib route with two young partners—who were nowhere in sight. He talked about how much more splendid Denali was than the Himalaya, until he left me with some parting counsel: "Stay out of trouble, laddie." If intuition served me correctly, he was simply saying, "Don't die on the mountain."

|||

Up at 17,000 feet, we had built a spacious igloo. Washburn had told us that you build igloos because they don't flap in the wind, and "because you have to go outside to find out what the weather is doing."

That year more than five hundred ice axes pricked Denali (as opposed to four hundred climbers in 1975, and less than a hundred in 1969). In 1976 there were often lines waiting to climb the steep headwall at 15,500 feet; the trail seldom needed breaking, and the ubiquitous human feces mining the snow—snow we melted for drinking water—caused us deep distress.

Even the undisputed king of guides, Ray Genet, was astounded when forty clients signed up for just one of his climbs in 1976. Weaving around the two dozen tents at 17,200 feet, stepping over tent lines, Genet came to admire our iglooplex. We boasted of how Washburn was the real architect; Genet grunted a friendly approval. Although it offered the soundest shelter on the mountain, after one night Hayes and I retreated. We preferred the flapping nylon over the claustrophobic, stove-fumigated, blue glow of an "Eskimo hotel."

Numbed by cold and headaches, our team decided to go for the top. It took our unwieldy group hours to fix hot drinks and get dressed. When we finally began groveling up Denali Pass, we could hear Genet's booming baritone below, leading his group in morning calisthenics. As a lenticular cloud hovered like a flying saucer above the summit, I wondered how aliens would interpret beings who practiced jumping jacks in twenty below, then forced themselves to the highest points of their geography for no appreciable gain.

All morning long I whispered the mantra of Goethe: "Whatever you can do, or dream you can, begin it. Genius has boldness, power, and magic in it."

At 18,200 feet I could no longer feel my toes, so Dave Buchanan let me warm my icy feet on his stomach. At 18,500 feet we stopped the group to do it again; Dave grimaced in shock as I slipped my feet under his sweaters. My head pounded like a jackhammer breaking pavement. And at 19,000 feet we could no longer see up or down. Dave and I turned back, while the rest of the group wandered up in vain for another two hours.

Denali had whipped us. It was not so much a defeat as it was a kind lesson. If it had been a good day, and we had heeded Washburn's advice to avoid the lenticular clouds, we might have found it in ourselves to stand on top. If we had traveled lighter, we might have had more energy for our summit day. And if we had been two people instead of eight, we would have had four times as much fun and half the work.

Meanwhile, the Japanese waited patiently at 17,000 feet, six bodies politely entwined inside their two-person tent. When the storm clouds cleared and their sake ran dry, they reached the summit.

We camped at 14,300 feet, several hundred yards from the body of a climber who died from high-altitude pulmonary edema the day before.

Genet had tried to save his client by carrying him back down the mountain, only to watch the young man gurgle and drown in his own fluids.

I walked over to pay my respects to the stranger's passing. The dead man was wrapped tightly in an American flag so no one could see his death mask of surprise, the cyanotic lips flecked with frozen pink sputum and a face swollen with peripheral edema. A female companion stood weeping; the rest of the team celebrated up on the summit. Here, however, no one could speak. It was as if this pocket of the mountain had fallen to sea level: the air was heavy and listless and filled with the knowledge of what horror lay beneath the flag. Here on the frozen snows of Denali this twenty-one-year-old had actually drowned.

We spend our lives trying to evade death and its myriad of black mysterious faces, but unless we kick and shout back and fulfill ourselves wholeheartedly during our precious short time, death will stalk us until our days turn to mere condemnation. I thought of my grandfather stiff in his open casket and, stinking in a river, a bloated body I had found as a sixteen-year-old, but this corpse on Denali seemed so terribly clean and correct that I regretted the helicopter couldn't leave the body where it belonged: where the cold can fill your lungs like a steely ocean and where death waits in shadowed crevasse tombs or up in a unearthly violet sky so filled with menace that climbers know they are merely visitors.

To ignore death's possibility is to deny the most primordial of all feelings. Many climbers experience the undeniable and powerful dreams of plunging endlessly through space, of blood rinsing your face with the smell of copper, of running but not moving in front of a monster avalanche, or any of a hundred deaths so textured and memorable that they give pause to even our best climbs.

One of our team members had refused to climb higher than 14,300 feet because he had seen himself dying in a dream. Although he was plagued with what he perceived as cowardice for months afterward, I admired him for being more in touch with his feelings, more willing to express his fears and his respect for the mountain than any of the rest of us.

We began our retreat. Walking down with enough gear to balk a sumo wrestler took us four days. At 12,000 feet, ravens circled above us like vultures, as if word had gotten out that we had more food than any other group. The ensuing pack-lightening food orgies caused us all to gain ten pounds each. We dragged ourselves the last few miles to the airstrip, dreading the most dangerous part of our expedition. Sharp droned up the Kahiltna Glacier in his battered 185, dropped into a strafing dive, and before we could run for cover, a six-pack of beer plummeted out of the sky and landed ten feet to our sides.

| | |

Five years later, I approached Denali more gracefully. My lightweight and unsponsored climbs elsewhere in the world had served as an appropriate apprenticeship. By all rights, climbing on an unclimbed peak in the Himalaya (Thelay Sagar) and a virgin ridge in the Yukon Territory (Mount Logan) should have compelled me to go anywhere but the most crowded six-thousand-meter peak in the Americas. Initially it seemed a simple matter of settling the score from 1976; but after the climb, I had fallen prey to the same spell that Denali had cast over Washburn. Meanwhile, I trained by the widely respected Whillan's theory: curling multiple steins of beer and loading up on calories prior to the climb.

My partner from Thelay Sagar, John Thackray, was old enough to be my father, but when I phoned him with virtually no notice, he gamely agreed to meet me in Talkeetna. We had climbed together in New England, the Alps, the Himalaya, and Scotland.

| | |

After debarking, we were greeted by Sue Miskill. Her job was to brighten weary climbers down from the heights, pass them congratulatory beers, then summon their bush pilot on the radio. After she fixed us dinner, she gave me a small vial of cayenne pepper.

"Should I eat it, or what?" I asked.

"No," she said with a smile, "save it for the summit day, when it's really cold. Then sprinkle it on your feet."

I accepted graciously, thinking that Sue might know something I didn't, and tucked it away in a pocket.

On the first day, John and I climbed together up the fifty-degree ice couloir into a storm. Unlike the climbers on the nearby West Buttress route, we were secluded on the nine-thousand-foot West Rib. The days fell into a delightful rhythm of step-kicking, cooking, climbing, singing, and reading. We climbed side by side, dispensing with belays, chatting about the texture of the ice, the shape of a passing cloud, and the distant green blur of trees on the horizon. When the snowstorms pressed hard on our shoulders, we feared our tent might collapse, but our stormbound days on half rations provided a gift of acclimatization to high altitude.

Our packs contained the bare necessities. We ate gas-producing freeze-dried food, employed aluminum foil for a pot lid, shared one toothbrush, dug out from storms with a lightweight plastic shovel, and wore gamy neoprene booties instead of wool socks. As further concession to light packs, I slept in a down jacket with a flimsy fiberfill sleeping bag. Graham Greene and Stephen Crane novels provided both cerebral sustenance and toilet paper. The only discord of our climb arose when John used up the pages of Crane faster than I could read them. We reveled in abstinence from the material world, our shivering, and our altitude headaches.

We also became dependent on one another in a fashion that we shall not repeat with other men in our normal lives. We cooked for one another, shamelessly warmed our fetid and wintry toes on each other's stomachs, and confessed secrets that we would otherwise share only with our wives. Being alone on a subzero and windswept mountainside for twelve days reduced life to its simplest yet finest moments. We often spoke of a mutual friend who had recently retreated from here after burning down a tent. If ours had burned down, we would have continued up and dug caves. Our time together on the West Rib held a purity that we were afraid to let go of.

By the tenth night, we scratched out a tiny ledge between two boulders at eighteen thousand feet. The snow rose steeply above us in fantastic mushroomlike bulbs carved by the wind. One wrong step and one of these unstable platforms of snow would release beneath your feet and flush you three thousand feet down a chute that climbers had dubbed the Orient Express. Two Koreans had died here two years ago; three Japanese women died in 1972. John and I tiptoed through here as if padding across a minefield.

We awoke at four the next morning to cloudless, thirty-below weather and immediately started the stove. While John brewed sweet English tea, I dumped the cayenne pepper into our neoprene socks. After an hour we were moving, shouting at one another to be careful in the strange collapsing snow.

We agreed to move at our own paces to keep warm. After several hours, time seemed to abandon me as I frontpointed up the headwall that led to my previous nineteen-thousand-foot high point. I could barely contain my excitement. My feet felt like wooden blocks, so I danced a jig until the circulation returned to my toes in the usual biting warmth. The cayenne pepper had not yet acted.

The summit was mine after a short stroll, and I knew how Washburn felt in 1951, climbing quickly and lightly with his close friend. Tears ran down their faces because it was their last visit to a place they loved more than any plot on earth; Washburn knew that his career obligations would never permit him to return. I remembered a comment murmured by one of the 1913 climbers: "It's like looking out the windows of Heaven." And suddenly my cheeks were wet, too.

The high altitude, the lack of climbers, the cloudless warmth, and the utter uselessness of our climb to anyone except John and me—all these pitched me into a beautiful siesta, curled in a sunny hollow on the summit. A few miles away a skiplane circled and droned like an annoying mosquito, but I plunged into unconsciousness when I realized I was safe and secure, far from the clutches of any bush pilot.

I dreamed of staying on the mountain forever and holding court with my friends who visited in the summer while I roamed the high ridges with my lungs brimming over with frosted body fluids and my words dribbling out as unintelligible, bubbly breaths. The loneliness flowed into unbearable ache because even the stunning alabaster ripsawed skyline and pink orange clouds of a thousand shapes turned flat and ugly when I realized I was condemned to the mountain. I awoke in sheer terror.

Then I watched. I watched the green, beckoning tundra four miles below disappearing into a gentle curve of the earth, and I imagined the Bering Sea beyond like bluing infinity. I hung my legs out over the great abyss of the south face and contemplated the air rising and falling through the granite gorge of the Ruth Amphitheater. I knew then that our earth is really one big animal with me hanging on as a mere microcosmic flea. I could see it, I could almost feel it now, and I wanted to shout it to someone, but I was alone and John only a tiny figure wheezing along resolutely on the plateau below, so I gave myself to this new vision of the organism who lived and breathed and even tolerated us clambering on its back. When I looked out beyond the blinding white of the glaciers toward Talkeetna and budding of life and rivers and greenery as far as I could see, it was almost too true and too terrible to behold. Seeing the entire earth as an animate being can make you understand just how important our relationship is to the planet, but when you are sitting alone shivering above everything else in North America, it can also make you feel very small indeed. The wind blew a wondrous warm breath over me. Heat waves shimmered above the jade horizon. The sun winked through a passing cumulus. I had found a happiness beyond all time and ambition and breathing. I ducked back into the hollow, closed my eyes, and let sleep take me away.

When John arrived and woke me an hour later, I stared at him for a long moment, shaking off a deep and hypoxic stupor, struggling to recognize the man who had become my close friend during two short expeditions. We embraced. I was dazed, shivering, incredulous; I didn't want to leave. He knew somehow, and he brought me back to earth with a joke as we traded the camera and lingered to steal photographs. Finally, we had both read the philosopher René Daumal, who wrote, "You cannot stay on the summit forever; you have to come down again."

More immediately, my feet were burning—the cayenne had finally kicked in. I had to get down. Quickly.

Although I intended to descend with John, I couldn't stand the fire licking first up my arches, then below my ankles, so I ran pell-mell. At the fifty-five-degree headwall, my feet were throbbing, so I lunged down the ice and scarcely planted my axe. In the windslab area I jumped quicker than the unstable snow could pitch me down the Orient Express. I began cursing the potent spice of Base Camp Sue. After forty-five minutes of sprinting, I finally saw the tent heaving into sight. I plopped down on an ensolite pad, yanked off my boots, and thrust my bare, sweaty, reddened feet into a snowbank.

When John arrived, his face pinched in hot pain, he wordlessly yanked off his own cayenned socks and we laughed long and hard at one another. I threw our last freeze-dried dinner in a boiling pot of water, and John regaled me, in thick Scottish brogue, with stories of growing up in Glasgow. We talked forward and backward in time. The West Rib had not pushed our limits, but it had worked in all the ways that a climb is supposed to. We became friends forever.

El Cap Girdle Traverse | Chris McNamara

I run the rope through a biner on a No. 2 copperhead and shout to Mark, "Lower me!" A little bit fearful, a little bit psyched, I slowly descend the slightly overhanging granite wall. I grab the rope with my right hand and, using my left for balance, press my feet hard against the wall and begin sprinting back and forth across the golden face. A small sloping edge emerges and I thrust my body forward, left hand extended and latch on. Sweat begins to ooze from my fingertips as I fumble with the rack, remove a Talon hook, place it on a tiny granule of granite, and just watch.

It holds for five seconds before PING! The hook explodes off the placement and I lurch backward, skidding across wall in a helpless rag doll arc.

I try to regain control on the backswing, feet clawing desperately, but lactic acid in my legs is too much and I give up, gradually coming to rest below my last piece. I look across the two-hundred-foot blank expanse of rock to the next feature and then I look at Mark. He stares at me with mixed expression of impatience and empathy. Maybe traversing El Cap is as dumb as it sounds?

|||

Girdle traverses have enjoyed modest popularity in Britain but have only a brief history in America. Expat Paul Ross pioneered the first U.S. girdles, beginning in 1972 with a traverse of White Horse Cliff, New Hampshire, and he went on to make the first girdles of Cathedral and Cannon Cliffs. In the mid-1970s Ross may have been the first person to consider an El Cap traverse, but it wasn't until the 1980s that Bill Price led the first serious girdle attempt. Price started from the East Buttress with the intent of not only traversing El Cap but climbing many unclimbed features in the process. He made it to a spot near El Cap Tree before abandoning the attempt. After Price, numerous people drew up in their minds potential girdle lines, but no more recorded attempts were made.

For me, the girdle was born out of a desire to do a new route on El Cap. Years of reading books like *Yosemite Climber* and *Vertical World of Yosemite* left me aching to make my own addition to Yosemite's climbing lore. And if you spend enough time in El Cap Meadow with a high-powered spotting scope, eventually you find a way to link micro features that nobody has climbed before. Like Greg Child said, "The only thing more abstract than climbing up a wall is to traverse it from one side to the other."

In 1997 I had a new vertical route pieced together. I armed myself with hundreds of copperheads and a vast collection of thin pitons and hooks and marched to the base. Yet as I looked up the nearly invisible line and unloaded my mass of steel and aluminum, I was struck by the blasphemy of my act. Unlike the Nose or Salathé, this route would not sustain many ascents after mine. Fragile features would fall off, rivets would be added, hook moves broken then enhanced, and copperhead placements blown then retrenched. The route would become a line of fixed copper, steel, and enhanced hooks: what most modern routes will become after fifty ascents. I didn't want to be a part of this movement in aid climbing and walked away. By default, the girdle became my last chance to put a new line up on El Cap.

When first contemplating a girdle traverse, I briefly considered continuing Price's vision of a line that climbed many new features in a proud diagonal across the face. Yet the more I looked at such a line, the more daunting the project became. The logistics required would be unprecedented and the ascent might easily take twenty days. And who would ever repeat such an ordeal? I decided that the solution to the girdle's logistics lay in attempting the traverse as a speed climb. Instead of hauling hundreds of pounds of supplies sideways, I would leave the gear behind and climb in "single push" style. We would travel as light and fast as possible to make sure our time was spent climbing and not moving gear around. A partner might be hard to find, but whoever was game, it would just be us and the rock.

Going single-push style means taking a few gambles. If you bring too much food and water, you might go so slow that you end up not making a ledge and have to spend the night hanging in a harness. But bring too little food and water and you could end up mentally and physically crashing somewhere in the middle of the wall. But those little gambles are what make light and fast climbing worthwhile.

After two months of scoping both from the ground and from the wall, the girdle line came together in July 1998. Most of the terrain was familiar; I had climbed every established route that the girdle would share. The challenge would be negotiating the few blank spots between established routes where new climbing would be required. These unknown sections cast just enough uncertainty over the project to ensure a steady infusion of adventure throughout the climb.

|||

Marketing the girdle as "a grand tour of El Cap's finer ledges and pitches," I searched for someone who had the two requisite skills for such a long traverse: speed and creativity. Mark Melvin fit the description perfectly. When Mark led me up my first big wall, the West Face of El Cap, he forgot his rock shoes, and I assumed the climb was off. Yet Mark didn't see the fact that there were four feet and two shoes as a problem. At the end of each pitch he zipped the shoes down to me, except on the easier pitches where he would leave them with me and lead barefoot. Novel situations clearly don't faze Mark, but when I explained my idea for the girdle, he harbored some skepticism. Nonetheless, he agreed to give it a shot in early August.

While previous climbers dreamed of a perfectly diagonal girdle line, our line followed the biggest, friendliest features on the face. When pieced together, the jagged ups and downs of the line resembled the readout of a heart monitor. We began on August 4 on the East Buttress and traveled across easy free climbing and a few rappels until we reached the first pitch of Eagle's Way. From there we began an upward diagonal that took us as high as the Zodiac's Black Tower before we began a series of rappels back down toward Tangerine Trip.

When we reached the second belay on Lost in America, about five hours into the first day, Mark prepared to rappel by clipping the rope to a bolt and calling for tension. No sooner had Mark leaned back than he took a sudden five-foot static fall directly onto my Gri Gri. Shocked, we looked at each other and then the anchor. The bolt Mark was lowering off had sheared, leaving a rusted and pathetic steel stud. I had replaced hundreds of bad bolts with the American Safe Climbing Association over previous months and was aware of just how feeble many of them were. Still, I was not prepared for the ease with which this one broke. It was a sober reminder of how, as safe as you try to be, things still "happen" when you least expect them to. We rappelled one more pitch, and then climbed three more easy free pitches. Twenty pitches and twelve hours from our starting point we reached El Cap Tree and rappelled down to the ground and stumbled back to the all-you-can-eat for too much ravioli, breadsticks, and beer.

Returning to the ground between pushes posed an ethical dilemma at first. The purest way to girdle El Cap would be to haul all gear from start to finish, but this was logistically out of the question. Another approach would be to climb up various routes and leave food and water stashes, but this would have required "preparing" the route in advance, which was more contrived than resupplying between pushes. The drawback to rappelling to the ground was the mental inertia that had to be conquered. On the wall the climbing moved fast and painlessly, but as soon we touched the ground the momentum was lost and had to be regained with the start of each new push.

|||

Yosemite Valley is always hot in August, but we managed to pick the three hottest days of the year to start the second and most difficult push on the girdle. As temperatures climbed into the one hundreds we couldn't ignore the other climbers who had bailed off El Cap and now lay under the shade of trees on the banks of the Merced River. Neither Mark nor I were enthusiastic about continuing the traverse. We went about the morning rituals at half speed hoping the other would make up a decent excuse to bail. Not wanting to be the one suggesting we bail, I tried to get it out of Mark.

"Wow, it's hot. There's almost nobody on the wall. Are you still psyched?" I asked him.

"Yeah, it is hot. I guess I am psyched. What do you think?" he answered.

"Ben and Jerry's sounds good right now. But it's hard for me to just bail."

"Yeah, I guess we should finish this."

"Yeah, I guess."

So we unenthusiastically continued the ascent.

|||

The second push of the girdle would take us from El Cap Tree to Calaveras Ledge, across the Continental Shelf to El Cap Tower, and eventually down and across to Heart Ledges. Our first plan was to try this leg in a single push, but we changed our minds as we imagined spending a night hanging in harnesses in the middle of the steep and ledgeless Dawn Wall. We opted to bring a small haul bag with water and ultralight sleeping bags. The day began on the Atlantic Ocean Wall. After two quick A4 pitches we were faced with a three-hundred-foot stretch of new climbing to join the next established route. I began on what would be the crux pitch by hooking for thirty feet up and left to a copperhead. From there I began penduluming, face climbing, and hooking for ninety feet left across diorite to the base of a large rotten flake. I put a cam behind the flake and began testing when, to my horror, the one thousand pounds of rotten and sharp rock began to separate from the wall. I quickly removed the cam and looked back ten feet to my last piece of pro, a No. 2 knife blade. From there it was another forty feet to a small stopper and then another forty feet to a copperhead. I was in a fix. I stared at the flake for a few minutes in terror. Was this fear just blocking me from making a move well within my ability? Or was this fear the self-preserving kind that tells when you are about to get killed? Finally a wave of confidence (or stupidity) washed over me, and I called for Mark to give me fifteen feet of slack (to eliminate rope drag) and began delicately liebacking the flake for the most exciting fifteen seconds of my life.

At the top of the death flake I teetered left across more loose diorite to decent horizontal flake in which I frantically began sinking pins for a belay. I equalized three angles and gave one last hit to the last pin when the whole flake began to move. My anchor was separating from the wall. Enough already! I drilled an anchor bolt.

Another seven pitches of easy free climbing and rappelling brought us to the top of the Continental Shelf and our bivy. By eight o'clock the sun had set, but temperatures remained in the high eighties, and in an effort to keep cool Mark and I slept with no sleeping bags in nothing but our shorts. I had just gotten comfortable when I noticed the pitter patter of small objects against my body. I jumped up to discover hundreds of little brown bird turds covering my bare skin. A family of swallows lived right above our bivy, and there was nothing I could do about it. I lay back down with the hope that as night fell the birds would let up and catch few z's. We had no such luck. Every hour I would wake up, issue a few terse words, and brush off the turds.

We got an early start the next morning, eagerly abandoning our vulnerable position for the flawlessly vertical Dawn Wall. Mark led across South Seas and Mescalito's Molar Traverse to the Wall of Early Morning Light. Here we cruised across a classic Warren Harding full pitch of dowels to the last major unknown section of the girdle line.

From the start Mark had been concerned about this stretch. I had assured him I had it all worked out. Now as we sat at the belay, peering across the three hundred feet of blank granite separating us from El Cap Tower, I realized that I had miscalculated. Mark mentioned bailing, but I convinced him to let me have a shot at swinging over to the Tower. Thus began my rag doll pendulum performance. Five hours, one rivet, two anchor bolts, and four hundred feet of pendulums later we connected with New Dawn. Sighs of relief attended our belief that the main difficulties of the climb were over. We reached El Cap Tower by 4:00 PM and opted to bivy rather push through the night. Usually my friends cringe that I drink only two liters of water a day on a big wall. On this wall, with the anticipated heat wave, we brought five liters per day and luckily found more water on the wall. However, so intense was the heat that we were nearly out of water by the morning with another 100-degree day ahead. The fourth day began with Mark climbing the Texas Flake and Boot Flake. We continued up the Nose to Camp 4 where we reversed the Triple Direct to the Muir Wall and rappelled down to Heart Ledges and the ground. We were tired, but any real pain was dulled by the heat.

Sitting in the shade Mark said, "It's a shame we're seventy-five percent done, because now we have to finish. Otherwise I'd sit here and eat ice cream for the next two days."

"Yeah, it's too bad we didn't bail earlier, when we might have had a better excuse with the heat. Now it's clear that we can climb through the heat . . . or at least suffer through it," I replied.

| | |

We swam in the Merced River and refueled with all-you-can-eat salad and beer to prepare for the last leg. At 4:00 AM on the next day, (August 8) we began jugging up to Heart Ledges and moved quickly up the Salathé Wall. By 1:00 PM we reached the Roof, and I began moving left over the last two hundred feet of rock before Thanksgiving Ledge. I had led part of this pitch before and was convinced that it was the nastiest pitch on El Cap. The first forty feet was easy free climbing with poor pro that led to a large roof. Cams led across the rotten, moss-filled, horizontal roof cracks to a small ledge beneath the roof that formed a loose-block-ridden belly crawl. I hated the pitch, but loved the idea of being so close to the end of this endless climb. Usually El Cap is just fun and games. This was a different type of climb. There were moments of doubt, relief, pain, and exhilaration. The emotions moved up and down almost as much as we did on the wall. I was looking forward to more food and beer and less climbing. Mark then received the honor of releading most of the pitch to clean the gear.

Thanksgiving Ledge, a quarter-mile-long and eight-foot-wide weakness in El Cap, was clearly the key to the girdle. With only a few hours of daylight left we quickly moved across the ledge through a two-hundred-foot section of "5.8 bushes" to the west face finish. By 7:00 PM we had finished the final easy fifth-class sections and stood on the summit. After seventy-five pitches and 14,000 feet of movement (climbing, rappelling, walking) we had triumphantly conquered the illogical. The girdle is not El Cap's best route, but it does climb many of El Caps finest pitches. It is also not the worst route, although there are a few stinker sections. In the end the girdle was just what we expected it to be: long, obscure, and, most of all, adventurous.

Running on Empty | Peter Metcalf

Hanging from an ice screw just 150 feet below Hunter's summit plateau . . . I'm freezing. The blizzard has not let up all day and the light is fading rapidly. Once on the plateau we can dig in, but suddenly, halfway from it, Glenn stops his lead. Oh God, his crampon has broken. Clipping into his ice tools he yells that he will jerry-rig something. The storm is too intense for waiting. With Pete belaying I practically sprint across the rock-hard fifty-five-degree ice, forgoing as usual the time-consuming task of placing protection.

As I pass Glenn, he mumbles something about frostbite and fingers. I'm too preoccupied to respond and gather he means frostnip. Five feet from the plateau edge I nearly do myself in. With rapidly weakening calves, I attempt to smash through several feet of overhanging crud that I had failed to see in the flat light of the evening storm. While I pant, heave, and grunt, the back of my spaced-out mind almost laughs at the thought of ending it here just one foot from the climb's end. But as I collapse, exhausted on the plateau, I realize we are far from the end of this jaunt. There are still several miles of summit plateau to be traversed and the four-mile-long West Ridge to descend. Our bags are loftless, our food about gone, our ice screws down to three, and we all have some degree of frostbite.

This is already day nine of what we had thought would be a six-day alpine blitz. We are no longer in control of the situation. The best we can do is battle from a defensive stand. When and where had we lost the upper hand? Did we ever have it? Does one ever have it when doing big routes in Alaska alpine style?

I had viewed Mount Hunter's Southeast Spur on two previous expeditions into the McKinley area, and the route is as aesthetic as they come. When seen from Talkeetna, some sixty air miles away, the spur resembles a huge ice-encrusted Walker Spur. The previous summer I had done the Walker in a day and a half under very icy conditions. So double the time, add a day for the unexpected, two more for the summit traverse and descent, and, presto, six days was the reasonable (and highly stupid) time estimate I came up with for the climb.

Those Washburn photos had been so beautiful and the lines so elegant. All winter long, the three of us, Glenn Randall, Pete Athens, and myself, would ooh and ahh at them as we made our grandiose plans. Had we really been tricked by those captivating and benevolent-appearing photos? Or was it just wishful thinking so we wouldn't be scared shitless? Perhaps it was but a rationalization for our decision to bring only six days' food. Inside I knew it would take longer, but I also thought we could pull it off with the marginal food and gear we planned to bring. Now I began to wonder. But, better partners I could not have hoped for.

Talkeetna appeared to be fighting to break loose of the last vestige of winter when we arrived on the final day of April. We had waited and I had worried as nagging doubts sprang up from within—a result, in part, of memories from past climbs up here. There is something to be said for being naïve. I remembered my first Alaskan expedition, a new route on Mount Fairweather; I was only seventeen at the time. It was all anticipation—no anxiety. Now I'm ever so glad Pete is along. He's never been here and he is total enthusiasm; I can't help but feel reassured by his infectious untainted attitude.

Late that next afternoon we were flown in to the Tokositna Glacier, and even managed to waddle to the spur's base with our overflowing sack. That night I had a recurrent dream in which a friend from Boulder attempted to reach me with a tent. He never quite made it and we were left to save weight and go it with Gore-Tex bivy sacks alone. The next morning we awoke dumbfounded. It was clear, warm, and calm. I mean we were not in Colorado anymore. No waiting; hard to believe. I was so confident that morning I threw away a stick of margarine and a package of Rye-King from my six days' food. Now I can't believe my cockiness.

We were an inspired lot who cruised up the entrance gully to the spur's crest that morning in a bright sun. Once on the spur we belayed numerous steady mixed pitches as the weather rapidly deteriorated. It was nearly 5 PM when we came across a potential bivy site only two hundred feet from the start of the overhanging headwall. With a heavy snow falling, we called it quits. Two hours of work later we had chopped, hacked, and dug ourselves a tri-level bivy platform among the cornices. As the wet snowfall increased, we hurried through dinner and slid into the dubious comfort of our hooped bivy sacks.

The sullen gray of the third morning was acknowledged with nothing more than a few grunts and kicks attempting to knock a foot of new snow off our sacks. At noon we reawoke to the sensation of warmth and light coming through the Gore-Tex. The storm had miraculously vanished, leaving a bright sun and sky.

A precarious lead took us to the base of the headwall, which Glenn attacked without his sack. The rock on Hunter is some of the best the McKinley range has to offer, but the going was still slow owing to the veneer of snow and ice plastered even to the overhanging rock. Aid under these conditions is never quick, and with the onset of dusk we were forced to bivy on the headwall itself. But what a site it was! An hour's worth of chopping cleared one hell of a perch in the middle of the headwall, giving an airy big wall ambience.

Glenn's overflowing and almost annoying enthusiasm had us up at 4:00 AM on the fourth morning. Pete and I just lay still in the warmth of our bags while Glenn undertook the unpleasant task of getting a brew going. The orange glow of morning and a hot drink gave me a feeling of cocky self-confidence. The jumar up our free fixed rope warmed me sufficiently to come to grips rather quickly with the mixed terrain above. At the headwall's crest we got our first views of the upper route. It's hard to gauge size and conditions from a distance, but we naively thought to polish off the next section of the route, a long Latok-looking corniced knife edge, by late that night. Not too surprisingly our wishful thinking was just that.

Everything proved harder than we first thought. A little band of rock forced me onto some intricate and time-consuming A3. Some more rock pushed Glenn high onto a dollop of snow on the ridgecrest, which, like a poorly placed scoop of ice cream, rolled off with him on it. The result was a slightly shaken, but determined, Glenn. From then on we stayed low as we moved together across fifty-degree ice slopes, which went from being bare to having a foot of time-consuming crud overlaid. The climbing remained exciting as we weaved our way through, over, and around waves, fins, and headwalls, placing the odd screw or deadman when possible.

By 11 PM there was still no end in sight, but both daylight and our energy had nearly given out. With no natural bivy site in view, we were forced to start hacking away at the fifty-degree ice. An hour's worth of sweat excavated an adequate though tilted sleeping ledge. Three securely placed ice screws prevented us from awakening in Heaven and gave us anchors from which to hang gear. With legs dangling and headlamps glowing, we cooked dinner and reviewed our position. We had gone slower than anticipated owing to the hard climbing, but we still felt firmly in control.

Day five began as a repeat of the previous day's time-consuming climbing, but the weather was holding and we were making steady progress. Near the end of the day we approached the knife edge's juncture with the spur proper. After some enjoyable mixed and pure gully ice, we were almost at the spur. But the last bit was blocked by an exceedingly steep concave ice face and double cornices of rotten meringue overhanging vertical walls. It looked next to impossible and getting there even worse. The only hope lay in turning the corner one hundred feet lower. Glenn lowered me from a bollard as I cursed the loss of hard-won height and the dullness of my rock-abused crampons. The ice went, but it was tenuous—rock hard, steep, and leaning. We were still on it when the light went from dusk to black. With headlamps we moved onto rapidly relenting ground and hit the largest ledge of the climb—a huge snow block that slept all three of us without any chopping.

It was past midnight when we collapsed onto it. At about the same time the bright stars suddenly vanished and a wind sprang up. In just a matter of minutes we were engulfed by a full-fledged storm. Rather than have any more spindrift blow down our necks, we settled for lukewarm water to reconstitute our dinner and retreated to our sacks, praying that the storm would be nothing more than a passing squall. Our wishes went unfulfilled, and the next morning no one rushed anywhere. But the bivy sacks offered little comfort, so we prepared to depart. Pete then voiced his doubts about the prudence of continuing, especially so unquestioningly, and Glenn and I agreed. A few minutes of discussion resulted in the decision that we were still in control of the situation and that up was the way we should go. But deep within, seeds of doubt were cast.

"Interesting" ice climbing took us to the prominent hanging glacier at two-thirds height. There we had to cut round the left corner of the spur into the full fury of the storm while wind-driven snow nipped away at our faces. The ice face above appeared indistinct in the flat light of the storm, and small spindrift avalanches kept sweeping the runnel we wanted to climb.

Conditions had deteriorated rapidly. While small avalanches fell and the wind grew in strength, we argued the merits of descending back to the hanging glacier. Then the question of which way to move became secondary to just moving. I was becoming hypothermic as I hung from my tools and stood on my front points. We feared the psychological consequences of losing ground and jetted up the snow-swept runnel. A tricky-looking face whose top was hidden by an overhanging rib of crud lay above, so in went an ice screw as Glenn led on up. His rapid progress slowed, and then halted. Through the storm I saw nothing but a vague image—a precariously balanced figure hanging from a smashed-in ice axe chopping away at the overhanging crud at the rib's top.

My concern grew when the usually confident Glenn yelled down something about it not being possible. He added a few inches before coming to a dead halt. I was freezing. My duvet and the wild swinging of my arms succeeded only in slowing the cooling process, not stopping or reversing it. I had to move and screamed at Glenn that he must either get up or else come down so we could retreat. He responded that he couldn't reverse the crap that he had just climbed, nor could he get in any anchors to be lowered on. Our situation had become precarious. Both the climbing and weather had been underestimated, and I feared we might pay.

Glenn finally surmounted the rib, putting him, I surmised, onto relatively easy ice. But the rope continued to feed out agonizingly slow. The instant it went tight, I took off for the crest. Slowly a semblance of warmth returned. My goggles were badly frozen, and I nearly fell off the crest of the rib as I topped it. The rib was a bizarre, one-foot-wide fin of ice dropping off at nearly eighty degrees on its opposite side, which I had to traverse. Glenn, who belayed from a level blob of snow sixty feet farther up the fin, told me that the whole thing would shake and vibrate every time I placed my tools.

I was distressed upon reaching Glenn's belay. He had stamped himself down into an unstable-looking cornice since that's all there was. But his site did not offer the bivy potential that the late hour and continuing storm required. The cold prevented any idling, so I immediately took off on the intimidating slope that lay above. Glancing down on Glenn, I was shocked to see that his belay was nothing more than a dollop of snow that completely overhung the fin. Though I was none too thrilled about the unpredictable Swiss cheese I was on, I was glad to be off his stance. My apprehension grew when the rib I was aiming for turned out to be another of those one-foot-wide fins of air-filled ice. I was forced to climb the seventy-five-degree terror head-on. But my fear of falling disappeared as I devised a slow, rhythmic method of climbing the fin. A grim joy arose as all other thoughts were forced from my mind. Four hundred feet later, the slope began to ease and turn to snow. Suddenly, out of the gloom of that stormy night, a fairly low-angle snow crest appeared that held snow cave potential. I thanked the Lord.

Though we were wasted, the blizzard necessitated building a cave, and at 1:30 AM we moved in. The mental and physical relief of our first shelter since leaving Talkeetna was heaven, and it came just in time. The cave allowed us to relax while forgetting about our circumstances and the raging weather outside. By the time melting and cooking chores were completed, it was 3 AM. Regardless of weather, we decided to sit tight the next day. The cave's security was real, and with that in mind sleep came quickly and deeply.

"Day six—Alpinists held hostage," was my first thought as I emerged from our cramped quarters. I was suddenly struck by the absurd analogy between our situation and that of our American compatriots in Tehran. We all got a laugh from my comparison, but inside there was the unstated realization that we could no longer descend what we had climbed and that we really did not know what lay ahead. There was now only one way to go. That evening, a somber air hung over our less than half-ration dinner. We had to make the South Ridge the next day.

Anxiously, we got underway early, climbing through light clouds. The going was relatively mellow for a change—hours of Styrofoam-like ice. Then once again it was dull crampons on hard blue-water ice, some mixed stuff, and back to steep hard ice. The clouds had built to a general whiteout as I led onto increasingly funky ice, which transformed itself into another seventy-five-degree fin of rotten honeycomb. The climbing was now a nightmare repeat of that of two days before—a snail's pace of gardening and hand hammering in tools by their shafts. After an eternity I reached a horizontal knife edge. Suddenly my skeptical mind understood—we had climbed the Southeast Spur, sweet Jesus!

The next hour was a simple slog—the first of the climb, a joy. If the South Ridge stayed like that, we could be descending the West Ridge in the next day or so, as an optimistic scenario. For sleep's sake, perhaps it was fortunate that we were still in a whiteout.

Day eight was a magical but bitter cold morning. My hands and feet went numb in minutes. Any hope of warming the extremities through rapid movement vanished when Glenn came up against a pinnacle of overhanging garbage. It was an hour and a half of wild swinging by both of us before he was up, and my jaw dropped out on reaching him. Over his shoulder lay more than two hundred feet of the narrowest, most jagged corniced knife edge I had ever seen. The consequences of a fall, which seemed likely, were beyond thought. The Happy Cowboy Pinnacles—that's what they were called on the first ascent. I could understand the cowboy, but not the happy.

The double-corniced crest was less than a foot wide, with vertical sides dropping off thousands of feet in either direction. Pete became a human belay anchor as I gingerly hopped onto it in straddle position, crampons biting both sides of the hollow crest as if I were spurring a bronco. One axe shaft went straight down while I chopped away at the unconsolidated cornices in front; praying all the while that the fracture line didn't cut back under me. For two unprotected hours I repeated that tedious process until I reached the safety of a snug col. With a sigh of relief, I screamed, "I'm alive. I'm alive!" finding it hard to believe that the whole thing hadn't collapsed with me on it.

It was late when we reached the final steep face of the South Ridge, so we dropped down on the east side and dug a cave. None of us were overly motivated, so we ended up with a hole that fit only 75 percent of our bodies. Hell, it seemed good enough. Talk was minimal and the mood somber. We were low on food and would need good weather to get across the summit plateau. Halfway through the night, blasts of wind-driven snow began stinging my face, forcing me to pull the bivy sack over my head. I fell back to sleep alternately praying and cursing.

I awoke on day nine buried under a foot of snow. Pete was so uncomfortable that he bailed out into the storm. Our lack of food and shelter dictated that we climb regardless, and it was obvious that things were looking a bit grim. My feet numbed out instantly upon hitting the mixed face above the col, where I was subjected to the full force of the storm. It was a damn blizzard. I don't believe I had ever been out in, let alone climbed in, such fierce weather. Insanity! Futilely I shouted up to the others but resigned myself to continue moving together. My apprehension subsided on reaching the sixty-degree water ice above, since it was easier to stay in control than on the mixed ground below.

But progress was far from quick. For every vertical foot climbed, we had to traverse at least three or four feet to the left. After several grueling hours out front, Glenn established a belay at an island of rock below a headwall. How far? We surmised it might be only a pitch or two to the summit plateau. Pete headed up an ice gully and disappeared over the headwall. A sudden pull jerked Glenn against his anchors. Pete had fallen, but communication over the storm was impossible, so I soloed up for a look. Pete was all right, after having gotten too high on the fragile crest which broke off with him on it. But there was as much ice to climb above as there had been below, only steeper.

I returned to Glenn with the depressing news. It was a mixed blessing that we were down to three ice screws. If someone fell while we were moving together, it was unlikely that one screw would hold. Yet, the blizzard was so intense that we would have frozen while waiting for the leader to place protection.

Later, Pete arrives in the growing gloom and belays Glenn while I start digging in for the dual purposes of immediate warmth and a night's shelter. At 1:00 AM we crawl into our cave. For the second night running, Pete offers me his abdomen to thaw out my numb feet. While Glenn calmly mentions his frostbitten fingers again, I shine my headlamp in his direction for a look. I am so shocked that I am unable to hide my surprise. His fingers are solid white from the first joint up. Unconvincingly, I tell him not to worry. But, inside I am concerned. With his frozen hands and a broken crampon, not to mention no food, a frostbitten foot, and the continuing storm, the West Ridge will be no picnic.

During the night Glenn's hands thawed and are now covered with large purple blisters. The storm, God bless, has sunk below us and into the distance. I spot our escape route—the four-mile-long West Ridge. Fussing with snowshoe straps, I admire Glenn's indomitable spirit. Even with blood oozing through and freezing on his Walker woolies, a smile breaks his lips as he refuses any assistance. The hoped-for dash across the plateau turns out to be a masochistic endurance test. We are barely underway when the clouds rise and once again we are engulfed in a storm that freezes eyes, glasses, and goggles. If it were not for the compass bearing and Glenn's yelling from the rear, I would be going in circles. But by late afternoon we are no longer certain of our position and the storm allows no idling. Once again we dig in and eat our final half dinner. My frozen toes refuse to warm and I spend the night wriggling them in my now worthless down bag. We worry.

The night is not restful and the hot water for breakfast does little to fortify me. This is rectified mentally by blue skies and physically by Dexedrine. God must temporarily be on our side, for we find a quick route through the serac barrier that guards the West Ridge. We downclimb some easy ice and then start charging down steep snow slopes. Each lost foot raises our morale. For the first time in days I'm actually warm and savor this minor miracle. We stop and attempt to administer first aid to our lifeless bags. But no sooner are they pulled open than the wind picks up and covers them in spindrift, mocking our efforts.

The snow slope leads us to a thin ridgecrest that suddenly gives way to a sixty-degree water-ice face. We guess two or three rope lengths to the col below. Pete is wasted; Glenn has frozen fingers and a broken crampon; and our two remaining screws rule out rappels. The responsibility falls to me, and the expected two pitches turn out to be eight or nine. I lower Pete and Glenn, who establish a belay 160 feet below, and then I downclimb. After the second pitch, I no longer feel alone while descending. I sense the presence of another force or spirit—a fourth member with whom I am in perfect contact. Perhaps this is due to the feeling of detachment my still alert mind has from my weary body. Whatever the reason, I refrain from mentioning it when I reach Pete and Glenn for fear they will think me crazy.

The hours fly by like minutes, and our long-awaited arrival at the col coincides with the sun's departure on the western horizon, killing any hopes of drying our bags. The night is calm and still, superficially tranquilizing our inner anxiety. Several thousand feet below lies the Kahiltna Glacier landing site with over a dozen tents—alluringly close, yet infinitely far.

I lie awake most of the night attempting to stay warm through rubbing in my nylon sheet bag. I awake exhausted, and neither hot water nor drugs has any effect. We pack rapidly, for clouds are racing in with the appearance of another storm.

Pete leads a moderately steep ice pitch out of the col, and the storm breaks when he is less than halfway up. My feet go numb in the blizzard despite wild jumping. The hopes of last night dissipate as we run it out on empty. After three hours the storm miraculously vanishes. Some spirit must be watching. We pledge ourselves to getting off that night, but our wasted bodies seem unable to carry out the mind's promise. After numerous rock rappels, downclimbing over beautiful terrain, and jumping off cabin-sized collapsing cornices, our bodies call it quits while our minds worry. The weather is once again turning, and we can see heavy snow falling below.

The night is relatively warm, and the foot of snow that buries my bivy sack gives me enough insulation to remain comfortable. For the first time in three days I actually sleep decently. But it is still snowing heavily when we awake, so we even dispense with our hot-water breakfast.

As we get underway I give up predicting when we will be down. Visibility is close to zero, and navigating the final icefall will be dangerously hard in such conditions. We curse our inability to have escaped last night. As we feebly stumble about in the blizzard, I feel close to exhaustion, yet we still manage to bullshit one another on how we can dig in from here to eternity if need be.

A break in the weather comes just as we need it. The exit suddenly becomes apparent, and I get inspired. Practically running downward, I nearly pull Glenn and Pete, who don't seem reenergized, off their feet. Glenn loses my tracks in the whiteout and takes a six-foot freefall off the top of a serac. Icefall danger or not, I slow up. Suddenly there is no more downhill, only a ski track and a vast expanse of flat white stretching endlessly to the north and south. But there have been too many hard knocks for us to relax before we are actually at the landing site.

Three seemingly endless hours later we trudge into the Kahiltna airport community. I yell for a friend, Charlie Fowler, who appears from a tent. I call again and get no recognition. Charlie walks closer and asks, "Who's that?"

I'm shocked. Do we look as changed as we feel? "Charlie, it's Pete." We all embrace, laugh and talk. As beer and fresh fruit are generously given out, I feel as if I could cry.

Several other climbers kindly offer us their seats in one of two planes that are attempting to get in the air during a break in the weather. They have already waited several days, but are willing to wait longer. We accept their offer, and ten minutes later the two planes drop from the clouds. But the hole that gave them entrance is rapidly closing, and they yell for us to hurry. Others rush our gear into the plane, and suddenly like commandoes being whisked out of enemy territory, we are airborne. The ceiling drops all too rapidly as each succeeding pass closes as we near it, but with a gunned engine we just manage our way out on the third try.

Talk of flash and crash. I can't believe it's over. But gradually I realize it's not; it's just beginning. My life is forever altered by an enigmatic experience that will eternally bond the three of us together and by an adventure that no one else can ever begin to understand.

Epilogue

The morning after returning to Talkeetna, the three of us checked into the frostbite clinic at the Anchorage Hospital. We spent varying degrees of time there for treatment. Pete had a two-day stay; I got away with a week and several more on crutches; while Glenn stayed several weeks and in the end lost the tips of three fingers.

Several months later I contemplate Hunter and ask, "Did I find what I was hoping to or was that an unanswerable enigma to begin with?" The thoughts and feelings are many, but one discovery is for real.

"All my life" he said, "I have searched for the treasure. I have sought it in the high places and in the narrow. I have sought it in deep jungles and at the end of rivers and in the dark corners—and yet I have not found it.

"Instead, at the end of every trail I have found you awaiting me. And now you have become familiar to me, though I cannot say I know you well. Who are you?"

And the stranger answered—"Thyself."

—JACK LONDON

Six Pounds of Lard | Karen McNeil

Excited and sleep-deprived, we imagined what we saw up ahead to be the jagged, rocky coastline of Greenland—the mountains we were coming to climb. As the *Vagabond* sailed ahead it was soon evident that the rocky coastline was actually our first iceberg sighting. These huge masses of ancient ice had slowly made their way down a flowing glacier that had abruptly severed its tie with the ice like an umbilical cord when a fjord was reached. Eventually the ebb and flow of the ocean's tide carried the frozen beast out to the Greenland Straight where it would play trickery on our weary eyes.

Twenty-four hours previous to the "berg" sighting I had been jolted from a deep sleep in the bowels of our boat by the sounds of our forty-seven-foot yacht apparently being torn to shreds. The *Titanic*-like moment roused me from the preferable position of lying down to a more upright seminauseous state. Upstairs my moment of terror was quelled when I saw the ice flows hitting the steel hull of the *Vagabond* to be pillow-sized and quite harmless. Proceeding in a northwest direction, leaving Reykjavik, Iceland, behind and aiming for Tasiilaq, east Greenland, we encountered more frozen salty water in the form of ice floes. During the day the floes gradually became bigger. The larger floes seemed to be no problem for the *Vagabond*, which effortlessly pushed them out of the way.

I felt seedy for the majority of the crossing, yet I found the sailing thrilling. Each piece of ice or floe seemed more beautiful than the last piece. My finger continually depressed the shutter button on my camera.

I had invested hundreds of hours on the Internet finding a yacht and arranging to sail to Greenland rather than using the more conventional method of flying. Now I was extremely pleased with my choice. I did not know the best part was still to come.

We sailed into more densely ice-covered sea. All hands were called on deck to help steer the boat. Using eight-foot-long aluminum gaff hooks, the five crew and three climbers took turns either pushing our yacht off a floe or pushing the pond-sized floe out of our way. Working around the clock, we experienced sunset and sunrise within two hours of each other. Around 11:00 PM the tired sun slid below the horizon under a milky, pink sky. The Greenland Straight lay perfectly calm, allowing our vista to be reflected in the flat water. Off in the distance, white bergs glowed yellow at their tips. When the sun reappeared hours later, the fiery red ball replaced a twilight that had hovered since the sun's departure.

Hours after sunrise, the *Vagabond* was stopped dead in her tracks. Seven nautical miles from our destination a wall of ice barred our entrance to the harbor. Some 95 percent of the water's surface area was covered by ice. Each time we tried to find a passage through, the ice would hit the boat, causing the *Vagabond* to shudder and creak. At times the yacht tipped over sideways. This was especially exciting if you were high in the crow's nest scouting the route ahead. With each attempt at a passage through, strong offshore currents carried the *Vagabond* farther off course. We were forced to retreat to open water and sheltered behind an iceberg that the *Vagabond*'s instruments measured to go one hundred and forty-one feet below the water's surface. We were helpless and at the mercy of the ice pack. Feeling overwhelmed, Eric, our captain, spoke into the radio asking for assistance. A distant crackled voice asked questions and then agreed to help.

The *Kista Arctica* appeared to glide swiftly over the sea of chaos. As the tiny red dot grew nearer, we watched car-sized chunks of ice effortlessly being spat out of the way of the icebreaker. The ocean below was momentarily freed from its icy captive. The icebreaker steamed ahead at her slowest speed of ten nautical miles per hour. This happened to be our fastest speed. The *Kista* aimed straight for our starboard side.

Seventy feet above us the crew aboard the *Kista* came out to watch the suspense-filled moments, knowing everyone aboard the *Vagabond* were completely at their mercy. We were all aware that there was no room for error. At what seemed the last possible second the icebreaker swiftly turned away from our yacht, leaving a path of open water for us to follow closely behind.

Tasiilaq, with a population of fifteen hundred people and another fifteen hundred in its surrounding municipality, is the largest community on Greenland's east coast. The name literally translates to "that which looks like a lake," after the fjord which the town is placed beside. Originally the area was known as Ammassalik after the delicious, tiny fish abundant in the fjord. When an elder from the town with the name of Ammassalik died, the name was changed, as it is disrespectful to speak the name of the dead. Coincidentally the name of the fish was also changed.

The *Vagabond* sailed into Tasiilaq harbor on one engine. We followed stern of the *Kista Arctica*. Most of the townsfolk lined the harbor and fired guns. Their excitement lay not with us but with the icebreaker we followed. Deep inside the hull of the *Kista* were containers of fresh food that would soon be merchandised on the shelves of the town's two supermarkets. This food carried by the icebreaker was cheaper than the winter supplies that have to be flown into the tiny town when the nearby harbor is frozen over with ice.

Eighty percent of Greenland's population is Inuit. Subsistence hunting and fishing remain popular today with the majority of Greenlanders, who struggle to make a living. Stepping onto the first solid land in four days, I still felt the swell from the ocean. The fishy, pungent aroma of whale blubber and seal fat, along with the sweet, sugary smell of fresh Danishes wafted up our nostrils. Close to every house chained huskies rolled in fine dirt and pulled on their steel restraints. The sled dogs barked in a frustrated way at everyone who passed by. Houses were small and boxlike; each was painted a bright vibrant red, blue, purple, green, or yellow.

Our mission while in town was to buy food and fuel for the five weeks we would spend climbing in the mountains and meet our photographer, Dave, who had flown in from the capital, Nuuk. On any expedition climbers exert a lot more energy than in their everyday life. Therefore, it is imperative that you double the number of calories you usually eat at home. The usual staples of pasta and rice filled our shopping carts, along with Danish cheese, crackers, soup, sauce, and six pounds of butter. Being from New Zealand, where lush, fertile pastures produce some of the best-tasting butter in the world, I find I have a weakness for the spread. I love the soft, pale, yellow, fatty food that belongs in its own food group. I thought the amount we had purchased would be barely enough for me, let alone everybody on the trip. Feeling its heavy, compact weight that we would have to carry on our backs, we had to put a stop somewhere. Special care was taken to ensure that the butter wasn't damaged as we reloaded hundreds of pounds of food into the hull of the *Vagabond*.

III

The mountain range we came to climb was spectacular in photos, with needlelike spires rising into the sky; so it's funny that we walked right past it while hiking into an established base camp. From the bow of the *Vagabond* in Tasiilaq Fjord I eyed the massif, immediately knowing these were the peaks we had come to climb. While researching Greenland I found an article in a climbing magazine that had the same photographic image as what I was now looking at. Somehow this image became fuzzy as we wandered by the peaks, but all that was lost was a little pride and a night camped out farther up the valley toward a pass.

The area we eventually selected for our base camp was perfect for spending a month out in the wilderness. Raised higher than the riverbed was a luscious green vegetated oasislike area. Behind our tents were large boulders that we could cook on and then stash our food in their depths. After cooking a meal we would barricade the entrance to our food cache with smaller rocks. This would prevent the sly foxes from stealing our precious food. Closer to the river were two tarns filled with fresh cold arctic water and tiny elusive fish the size of goldfish. Our base camp was so green compared to the stark rocky mountainous landscape surrounding us. It was ironic that we had found such greenness in Greenland, a country that hosts an icecap 1,834,000 square kilometers. Breaking up the monotonous brown desert of rock surrounding us were the bright pink blossoms of the national flower, Niviarsiaq—or "the young girl"—which grow in gravel and stony ground. The banks of the river running down to Tasiilaq Fjord were littered with the vibrant, happy-looking bushes.

Ironically, days later when we were halfway up our first route in Greenland, we were dehydrated and had a quarter liter of water between the four of us. Glaciers and rivers surrounded us, and yet we were without water. Embarrassing for me, my bottle was bone dry, and yet I was the team member who had preached the values of staying hydrated on a long climb! From our reconnaissance, we had chosen the highest peak in the massif for our first objective. With no information about the mountain, we didn't know if it had ever been climbed or what getting to the top entailed. In an afternoon, we climbed five pitches and fixed two 7.8 mm ropes down to the glacier. With this in place we felt sure that we would have a head start on the climb when we began.

With these smaller-diameter ropes we felt a lot of spring each time we pushed up our jumars and weighted the ropes while ascending the fixed lines. This effort, along with the blazing sun that shone down on us and the glacier below, made for thirsty work. The glacier radiated heat back to the mossy black lichen walls we were trying to ascend. Tired from the jugging and feeling sweaty, I thirstily gulped back my water and neglected to refill my bottle at a cascade we passed. Enjoying the splash of the water on my hot body, I was somehow not thinking about hydrating. Only Andrea remembered that detail!

Geologically, Greenland is old, and the majority of her rock is granite. The peaks on the east coast in general are higher and steeper than those on the west coast. However, the rock on the east coast of the country is younger gneiss. Gneiss is composed of the same minerals as granite and is broken up by lovely parallel cracks.

From the top of the fixed lines we scrambled ropeless for two hundred meters. When the rock became steeper again, we donned the rope and concentrated on finding a route to the top. The climbing was engrossing, and we weren't aware of the day passing. Around 10:00 PM one of us noticed that it was dusk and therefore it must be nighttime. The northern latitude of Greenland and the closeness to the summer solstice meant that here we would experience no dark hours. The "lightness" played trickery with our minds, and we didn't feel sleepy. In the dusk we did feel colder. We continued to climb through the night and into the following day.

Head-on the summit tower seemed impassable, even to Katy, who has a natural gift for rock climbing. It was around noon, twenty-six hours after taking leave of the glacier below. A pathlike ledge crossing under the tower was discovered. Traversing around a corner we walked onto another oasis. Hidden from the sun in a rocky depression was a small patch of snow. Feeling lethargic and dehydrated, we collapsed to the ground next to the snow patch to eat a little food and regroup. Although the climbing was physical, our bodies didn't feel hungry. This would come later when we were down and feeling more relaxed.

While we sat, Katy spied the snow patch dripping and ingeniously placed a wide-mouthed water bottle under the slow-paced drip. It was torture to watch the infinitesimally slowly filling bottle . . . drip, drip, drip, drip. When the bottle was half-full we each took a swig of the deliciously cool snow-melted water. It took a huge amount of restraint not to selfishly gulp down all of the precious liquid.

After a half-hour pit stop we got going again. From the snow patch we followed a snow slope to the base of the rocky summit tower. As we arrived at the rock and felt its smooth texture beneath our hands, I realized that a rope had been left beside the snow patch. Selfishly, I volunteered to go back and retrieve the forgotten rope. While Katy began to lead up on the rock, I scampered down the snow, licking my lips. My body almost shook with a guilty joy as I gulped more water from the bottle, which I refilled with the remainder of the precious liquid after

I had my fill. My teammates were grateful when I handed them more water to drink.

| | |

On July 16 at 3:00 PM we reached the summit of Trillingerne Peak. It had been 30.5 hours since we began the journey. Clouds had filled the blue skies and snowflakes swirled around our shivering bodies. We looked down to the fjords where glaciers flowed right into the water. The bays were littered with thousands of pieces of white broken glacier now being pulled out, then in, by the ocean tides. Surrounding us were hundreds of summits. I wondered how many, if any, had been climbed? I couldn't ponder this thought for long as there was no easy way off the mountain. We agreed to rappel the sixteen pitches we had just climbed.

During the descent, Andrea, feeling hungry, devoured dehydrated soup in its dry state. Later we all came close to hallucinating or actually imagined things that weren't. It had been a long haul getting to the top. Fortunately, on the descent we came upon a small puddle of water in a concave rock. Using a straw, we were able to drink some murky liquid. Eventually we rappelled through a raging torrent of melted water. Here we were finally able to get our fill.

Two pitches above the glacier our little ropes decided to jam. It became a test of our patience and ability to "deal." Twice Katy jugged the lines to fix the problem. Only after the second time did she succeed and free the ropes. We descended to the glacier, where it felt weird to walk. Forty-four hours after setting out to climb our peak we stumbled down to our gear. After melting snow and making warm juice and eating tinned kippers, we slept soundly. Six hours later and feeling rested, we were able to contemplate the descent back to base camp.

The three-thousand-foot descent from the glacier bivouac to our base camp crossed through many different terrains. First was a glacier. Part-way down, I fell arm deep into a crevasse. Daring myself to look down, I saw a huge dark chasm hundreds of feet deep that appeared to go to the center of the earth. With my arms splayed away from my body to prevent myself from falling deeper into the slot, I swung my legs back and forth to gain momentum. Eventually I was able to swing my pack-laden body out of the hole onto more solid, safer ground.

With adrenaline coursing through all of our veins, we hurried off the soft snow and descended the rock slabs that took us to the top of the lateral moraine. From its apex we descended a sandy soft path formed from our few trips back and forth. The trail was littered with unstable rocks. The rocks were rounded from the glacier and then spit out where the glacier terminated or retreated.

The climate on Greenland's east coast is influenced by low-pressure areas that are formed over the North American continent and the southern part of the jet stream. These pressure areas often bring strong winds and a lot of precipitation to the east and southern coast. However, during this summer season we had been blessed with continual warm sunny days. In the five weeks that we climbed in Greenland, we experienced only three days of rain. This unusual warmth resulted in the rapid melting of the glaciers surrounding us. Nature's quiet was replaced by the roaring glacier that sounded like a freight train always passing through our valley. In turn, the river was swollen with glacial meltwater, which had overflowed onto the surrounding valley floor. Crossing the raging tributaries was difficult. We needed to retrieve more food supplies to replenish our starved bodies. The extra food was stashed seven kilometers down the valley, closer to the fjord.

The fourteen-kilometer round-trip resupply mission was challenging when dealing with the flooded river. But the discovery of a impostor among us was completely devastating. I gently pulled back the golden foil wrapper of the first pound of butter only to discover white pork fat. The four of us stared disgusted and dismayed at the rectangular block. To be sure it was lard we all tasted it, each quickly spitting out the slippery contents. We couldn't have brought six pounds of lard instead of butter? An investigation into the second and third pounds provided us with the same answer . . . lard, yuck!

The lard sat in our supplies for several days, being used only when absolutely essential. Then something changed . . . Maybe it was the magic of Greenland or the success, stress, and weight loss our bodies endured from the physical exertion. Overnight we all began to crave the delicious salty-tasting lard. Katy, Andrea, and I creatively thought of ways to include the lard in our cooking. When Katy made donuts, we fought among ourselves to scrape through the hot fat for remaining tidbits of flour and sugar gelled together with pork fat. We'd reuse the fat to make more donuts. We cooked rice and then soaked it with the lard. Still we craved more. One by one, our six pounds of lard disappeared. Dave left to kayak back to Tasiilaq. We climbed a further two routes and experienced the reappearance of darkness. I found that I had missed the nighttime. At first it appeared for two hours. I saw stars. We picked berries and ate them along with the fat. There was still time to climb, but our skinny bodies begged for more food and a holiday from climbing. We left the mountains and caught a ride back to town on a fishing boat. The kind people waited six hours for us to ferry all of our loads down to the shore. The ride back to town on the small motorized boat was cold. I stared back at the peaks we had climbed.

|||

Waking early the first morning back in town, I eagerly slipped down to the supermarket while the other two slept. I arrived back at our sleeping spot with freshly baked Danishes among other tasty treats that we gorged on trying to please our hungry bodies. That night we ate whale steaks at a local woman's house.

We left Greenland skinnier than when we had arrived, but we all felt content; Greenland had treated us well, lard and all.

A Day Alone | Barry Blanchard

He had slept in the back of his pickup with the windows cracked one-quarter of an inch and two candles burning on the small shelf of the canopy. The candles had warmed the canopy considerably but were too small to burn all the night, and their flames had shrunk until they were small blue spheres that sat lightly on the blackened wicks like fragile flowers. They sank into the pools of wax like fragile flowers sinking into water, small lights conceding to the darkness. They died within minutes of each other.

Outside, the ice overlying the reservoir thickened and groaned as it battled the taut current below. Like broken slate, plates of ice uplifted along the shoreline, and every hour pressure forced explosive shifts in the ice that cracked through the arctic air with all the clarity of a rifle shot. Rolling in semiconsciousness he saw black-and-white footage of tank barriers: concrete, geometric, impassable.

|||

He woke to darkness and cold. The tip of his nose and his cheeks were numb as though they'd been in contact with algid metal for the hours that he'd slept. He pulled his face back into the sleeping bag and slid his gloved hands up and enclosed his face in them and flooded the vault of his hands with warm exhaled breath. He did this until he felt the blood and life return to his face, then he pushed his head outside the bag. The cold slapped him and he felt a heavy and lethargic urge to retreat back into the dark enclosed heat of the bag, there to curl up and not move. A beat passed and he wrestled a determined hand past the closure of the sleeping bag and twisted on the headlamp where it lay snug over his toque. His breath rose in mist in front of his face, and light glowed silver from the frozen breath that glazed the portal of the bag. His frozen breath. Further he saw the death pools of the candles puddle on the sill of the canopy, their stature defeated by heat and gravity, then gelidity. An aloneness rose in his throat and with it an instant of sadness that compressed lines into his brow and floated his eyes in an outline of tears. He allowed the sadness to sweep him beyond lonesome to a place where he saw he had left the planet and was slowly rotating in the black void of space, arms and legs outstretched in a star, his image shrinking. The sadness scared him here, and he clenched his eyes and hauled himself back to his resolve to climb.

He found the bag's zipper and opened it in jerks, having to pull jammed nylon from the slider every foot or so. Raw cold bit through his liner gloves, and he cupped his hands to his mouth and blew warm breath into them, then scraped around the open bag to find his outer gloves one at a time. He had slept in his underwear and pile.

He knew that to be warm he had to get into his feltpack boots and parka and then into the cab of the truck. Leaving the ice tools and pack in the back would keep them cold so that snow would not stick to them when his passing scraped the snow from the trees later in the forest. His climbing boots and outerwear were already in the cab. They would warm up on the drive when the engine was hot and the heater blasting.

As he pivoted off of the tailgate the hair inside his nostrils bristled rigid with frost; the skin on his face, thighs, and groin contracted in horripilation. He spun and heaved the tailgate up and eased the canopy window down—he always expected it to shatter in this kind of cold.

| | |

He paced outside as the truck idled to warmth and threw his arms through full circles to force blood down to his hands. Brittle snow crunched under his bootsoles like deep gravel. Elongated shadows stretched from his feet and lost themselves in the reach of the headlights. Surface hoar sparkled along the light's edge like a border of jewels, or, he thought, like the last stars that stand guard between living space and the void.

Slowly, wet stains spread up the frozen windshield. When the stains had grown to eye level he climbed into the pickup and coaxed it into gear and pulled onto the road.

At the Stoney Indian Reservation he crossed the Bow River, and the dark forms of the immobile vehicles and of the solemn and unlit Indian shacks passed by his panel window like slow grazing bison, and he thought of how his people—the Métis—had once been buffalo hunters. He imagined his grandfather hunting in winter in the Qu'Appelle Valley seventy years after the buffalo had gone. Galoshed shin-high moccasins punching holes into the brittle snowpack or trenching furrows through waves of drift that clung to the lees of the coulees, knotheads of ice clinging to the rough home-tanned leather and growing to the size of marbles through the day. Then he saw the photograph of his grandfather going to war in the uniform of the South Saskatchewan Regiment, and he thought about how men had fought a war and worked in the bush or even climbed mountains dressed in cotton and wool and leather. Pressing his hand over his thigh he felt the slickness of the pile salopettes and how cleanly they slipped over the silken underwear that were not silk but synthetic material made to be silk. These modern clothing systems gave him an advantage, yet he realized that when he wasn't climbing he preferred to dress in cotton and wool with leather boots or moccasins. He felt closer to his grandfather that way.

He drove in silence, playing neither the tape deck nor the radio. The smooth and efficient hiss of the truck was muted by his imaginings.

Breaking the forest at the top of the big hill he saw the full frontal escarpment of the Rockies; and the whole of it, the forests footing it, its borders of snow, and the sky above, immersed in a shallow blue light of the brumous dawn. He pressed the pickup into four-wheel drive and braced his hands against the steering wheel as the truck walked unevenly down the steep and rocky grade. The pickup always felt like a horse to him here as it shifted left to right, the tires riding high over boulders, then gutting down into ruts.

He stepped out of the pickup at the boundary to the national park. The border saw-cut three meters wide up both flanks of the valley for as high as there were trees.

|||

Climbing boots and outerwear on, he started down an old road to the Ghost Lakes.

Dominant west winds, hauled earthward by gravity and squeezed between the shoulders of the Palliser and Fairholme Mountains, had raked hard at the dehydrated and cracked bed of the second Ghost Lake. Over time the wind had pried loose grains of dirt and bounded them over the lake bed, or borne them aloft, to deposit in the lee of the lake's eastern shoreline. Here the wind sculpted the earth into dunes. It was the only place in Alberta he had ever seen dunes. Now scythes of dirty snow clung to the dunes and extended their taut lines. Lines of wind visible on the land—to him, as abrupt and clean as a saber cut, as beautiful as the sickle moon.

The melding of color from earth to snow was so perfect that he could not differentiate between them, at least until he punched in knee-deep and saw the pure white basements of his footfalls. He sank little into the dunes, striding down their western flanks with extended scree running steps. He passed stunted and leaf-bare trembling aspens, their trunks engulfed by the dunes and what was left exposed dusted dirty gray by the wind. A branch clawed at his upper arm but snapped immediately against his passing, the core of the branch alive and yellow but frozen brittle, the skin of it like brindled bone.

Coyote tracks were preserved in the dust of the lake bed and in the cement-colored snow that bordered it. The coyote's crossings were numerous and, to the man, haywire, erratic, and seemingly purposeless. The man knew that it hadn't blown in a while. Not since the invasion of the arctic air mass, maybe longer.

He first heard, then saw, the great wind. A distant rumble reverberated against his sternum; an anomalous cloud rode the surface of the Devil's Lake. The cloud advanced and the rumble exploded to a towering roar. He saw trees upslope bend crazily, releasing silhouettes of dust that instantly blurred into the wind. One tree sparred with a loud crack and its top twenty feet was hauled away on an angle and the fractured trunk snapped back into the wind, its core flesh white and jagged and swaying in a structural tension.

Then he was smacked full front by a screaming wall that bowled him off his feet and thumped him down hard into the dirty snow. The abruptness of the blow defeated his reflexes, and he trenched into the snow back first with no hands extended in protection. His lungs burst out and dirt and ice shards hacked at his face. Panicking for air, he rolled to his front and hauled his arms to his head. Now that he was able to draw breath, the wind stuffed dirt and snow into his throat and he hacked and swore and struggled to rise. The Chinook buffeted him about like a puppet, putting him to his knees twice before he finally got to his feet a full five meters from where he'd gone down.

| | |

He could breathe now.

| | |

As the wind's warmth flooded over him his face grew slimy with slush, and the breastplate of frost he'd grown since leaving the truck cracked and fell away in small plates. His eyelashes no longer bonded together when he clenched his eyes, and the hood he had on all morning suddenly felt hot and claustrophobic. He ripped the hood off and faced the wind. Water teared across his face and pooled in his ears, and he pulled the toque from his head and laughed and leaned his shoulder into the slapping hand of the Chinook.

Reaching the side valley of the climb was an act of will. He continued against the Chinook because he didn't know if he could. The wind pummeled him constantly, forcing him to calculate each footfall as a thrust for balance. Leaning heavily on the ski poles, arms fully extended like outriggers, he felt like he was wading a thigh-deep river; then the wind would back off and he would stagger and fall into where the wind had been.

| | |

He wondered if by continuing he was expressing courage, arrogance, or stupidity. Finally he decided that he continued because it was day and, therefore, his time to move.

By the time he reached the ice he had fought his way out of a pile jacket and vest. He stowed both into his pack by force, the wind pulling at them like a desperate thief.

The first plant of the axe released a starburst of ice shards. The wind swooped all the shards into the vortex in front of his face. He panicked about taking a piece in the eye and shouted to himself: "No! Not in the eyes, Pelletier. You can't take it in the eyes!" He stepped down and unslotted the tool. He pulled goggles from the top flap of the pack and turned into the wind to put them on. He kept the lenses sheltered in his gloved hands; they had to be clean to work. Rose tinting gave the sun a beautiful halo and outlined the clouds with a prism of oily blues and reds. High above he saw the tidal edge of the Chinook, a three-layered standing wave that ran south to the horizon in a series of perfect arcs and troughs.

He climbed. The Chinook harassed. It pushed him hard one way, then oscillated to slap at his opposite flank. There was always an eerie instant of calm between the changes as if the wind was loading up and deciding where to land the next blow.

He told himself to stay wide. That if he was stable the wind couldn't take him off. A lie, but one that gave him hope.

The final pillar gave him pause, and he shifted from one frontpoint to the other for long minutes, considering twisting in a screw and beginning the problematic rappels into the wind. Retreating.

He soon passed the point where it would be possible for him to downclimb. Getting real placements took many swings of the axe. The waterfall wore a facade of icicles the size and shape of church candles. They hung like wind chimes between finned and exfoliated roofs of ice and the corresponding flat floors. The icicles gave no support and clearing them with the head of the axe broke them off in their entirety. The ice tumbled toward his face, piled up on the small floors like toppled columns, or bounded off his other tool, ringing a tuning fork vibration down the shaft and into his hand to initiate the breathtaking intellectual fear of dislodging that tool—his one pick of security. His forearms were tiring, and fear now heated his climbing and pushed on him to move, to get his body out of threat.

Then the Chinook backed off completely, and he felt the pounds of weight that the wind had been supporting sag onto his locked left arm and he knew that he was going to get hit hard. He swung his right tool in desperation, and the head of it collapsed into a splinter of shattering icicles and the useless window behind. Then the booming wind hit him, grabbing inside and spinning him through a half-rotation so that he faced out from the mountain, both feet and his right tool clawing uselessly at the air, like an insect turned over, and solely the left tool holding him on. "Fuck!" he screamed, and the wind let up. In blind animal fear he kipped back to face the ice, body fully extended, hung from the left tool in a dark poet's enactment of the route's name: the Lacy Gibbet—a hook gallows used to display the bodies of the executed.

Reflexively he kicked and hacked for purchase. The right crampon stuck, the left clawed and skated blindly. He bludgeoned the right tool at the window and on the third flail felt it stick, but heard the ice crack deeply and saw the plane of the fracture radiate to his left tool. Fear. Far beyond the fear of falling now, the man's hard-wired imperative to survive. This fear flooded his blood with fire, the command to flee shouted out at the cellular level. He shook now in a vibrant and clear tremor, and he knew that if he swung madly the ice would shear off and he would fall and die.

With quivering thrusts from the heel of his hand he coaxed the left tool out. Immediately he barn-doored right and flagged his left foot behind him. The crampon points tapped the ice surface in a desperate Morse code. He swung and swung the left tool, his hand near useless, the muscles in his forearm extending into total failure. He swung. The tool fish-tailed in his hand. He cried. He swung again. The pick sunk. He heaved his left foot back around and kicked it trembling into the ice. Tears ran in small streams from the corners of his eyes down the lines of desperation and regret furrowed into his face.

Gently he lifted out on the right tool. It unhooked with no resistance, for the teeth of the pick had not bit. But the hammer hung up in the window and when he pulled on it more the failed slab skated away with a sick clunking sound. The slab hit him in the chest and pushed a prayer from him. "Please, God, no," he prayed. The ice grazed his chest and crashed away over ledges to thump a crater into the snow eight hundred feet below.

Blindly he found a sling on his right side. He brought it up to clip to the left tool. The right tool flayed about his eyes, the sling too short to reach his harness, his left hand open and dead now, encircling the tool because of the taut wristloop and the pressure between the shaft and the ice.

Catching the right tool, its wristloop hopelessly twisted, he swung; and perhaps providence guided the tool's solid stick. He pulled and kicked up and bit at the left wristloop to find the slider and open it. His left hand hung dead at the end of the trembling limb. He wrestled the wristloop to his elbow and hooked it there, biting into his jacket at midforearm. Desperately, he thrashed to find the sling and clip it into his harness, then to catch the right tool and resink it into providence's placement.

|||

He fell onto the security of his harness. Breath raged from him. He shook violently. His tears flowed freely and the Chinook smeared the tears across his face.

It had been one minute and twelve seconds since the wind had hit him.

|||

Fits of shaking seized him with the regularity of a woman's labor. Over time the intensity of these events waned and he was finally left limp and spent, a man destroyed.

He raised his head slowly. He was very tired now. He went about the tasks of getting in a screw and clipping to it and of threading two Abalokov anchors into the ice. He threaded 5.5 mm spectre through the anchors and fixed the spectre rope around itself via a knot and small locking carabiner. Sixty-five meters of the spectre was rescue coiled in the bottom of his pack; it would support his weight on rappel on the small end of his figure eight. Into the small locking carabiner he clipped an end of 4 mm perlon. The rest of the perlon — sixty-five meters — was placed into a stuff sack clipped to his right side. He would pull the spectre down with the 4 mm. Easing onto rappel, he took one last look at the Abalakovs and the bright purple cord he'd slung them with. He laughed, and shouted into the wind, "Oh ya! I'll be backing off!"

|||

Leaving the side valley, he cut out of the drainage and onto the exposed grass and low growth of the south-facing side slopes. The ground gave softly to his boot edges. Lower, he saw that the Chinook had taken the main valley down to nude brown earth.

He found the ram's skull halfway down to the main valley. The ram had been old, his horns curling to a near full circle, the husks of them incredibly heavy, coarse, and deeply ribbed. The husks grated away from the weathered bone beneath and pressed into the ground, vacant cornucopia.

He strapped the ram's skull under the top lid of his pack and continued down.

Two hours later he walked into the meadow where the pickup was parked. Shallow pools of water had collected in the low-lying places, and the Chinook, now blowing firmly but without violence, corrugated the water's surface.

|||

That evening he cooked on the tailgate and in the lee of the pickup, collecting water from the shallow pools with the lid to his pot. The ram's spirit surveyed through an empty eye socket from the shelf of the canopy beside two pools of candle wax. That night the man would sleep again in the back of the pickup and, perhaps, tomorrow he would climb.

2: caretaking

When I was a boy in New England there was an Indian who cried on TV. He looked across the noble landscape and saw bottles, papers, tires, and trash across the ground, until a tear trickled over his craggy cheek. It was affecting—if you saw it then, you recall it now. And the slogan, "People start pollution, people can stop it," says that nature needs our attention, not our debris. What a productive simplification. Climbing literature is energized by a similar conception of people as either saviors or scapegoats, and throughout that literature we see an earnest and devoted attention to conservation.

I think climbers underestimate their significance as environmentalists. One small example is that each spring climbing areas across North America host a crag cleanup where a day or a weekend is spent in the important work of trail maintenance, trash removal, and general battle on behalf of the local crag. This initiative succeeds because we climbers are happy to see ourselves as caretakers of the environment. Barry Lopez has written that—for better and worse—our culture considers nature a "grand garden," and his phrase distills the gain of a beautiful place to live, and the loss of a wilderness condition to thrill. Not that thrills are absent in Joshua Tree or Little Cottonwood Canyon, only that they are places wild by legislation and not by fact.

Caretaking is the second of my three categories of climbing, and in it we see some of our culture's greatest achievements. The American system of national parks, for instance, was founded on the pragmatic conclusion that people need a dose of wilderness to be as hardy and democratic as Teddy Roosevelt—hence Yellowstone, Yosemite, and the Adirondacks. One nineteenth-century U.S. senator called Yellowstone "a great breathing place for the national lungs." The grand effort to preserve millions of acres in national parks assumes that if you want wilderness amid modernity, you need to maintain, to support, in short . . . to caretake.

The Sierra Club is one of many worthy organizations who have made this their purpose thanks in part to climbers like John Muir and David Brower. Their slogan, "In wilderness is the preservation of the world," indicates nature's role as a restorative to the modern citizen, and demands that we citizens maintain that same wilderness. Across the border, Alpine Club of Canada president William Foster argued in 1922 for climbers to "devote more attention to the conservation of our great mountain heritage, as undoubtedly the present tendency of this very commercial age is to lose a proper sense of proportion and alienate, and even destroy, area of natural beauty which can never be replaced." For both the Sierra Club and the Alpine Club of Canada nature was (and is) a vulnerable realm to be defended and admired—an object to be preserved for the health of the active subject. So climbers are in the vanguard of efforts to protect North America's wild lands.

This focus on protection links caretaking to the great division in American environmental history between *conservation* and *preservation*. The split occurred in the 1890s when the United States began to denote national parks and especially "forest preserves," and echoes across the century in today's wilderness debates. Conservation is the "wise use" of resources, their stewardship for planned development and sustainable-consumption civilization. Preservation, on the other hand, is the effort to treat wilderness as an inherent good with no need to pay its way in dollars or cents. Preservation is biocentric whereas conservation is anthropocentric. Preservationists from John Muir on reject utilitarian values and advocate for a natural world unaltered by humanity. Conservationists from Gifford Pinchot, first chief of the U.S. Forest Service, to the contemporary Forest Service say preservation is unrealistic and unsustainable in modern life. It's the difference, some say, between romantics and pioneers.

Caretaking in climbing is like conservation because it treats the mountains as a resource. The Sierra Club, the Access Fund, and numerous local climbing organizations from Castle Valley, Utah, to the North Cascades to the Gunks, have achieved great things since climbers believe that the preservation of alpine wilderness is the preservation of a vital resource both for recreation and for society's well-being. In this sense, mountains are protected as more than an effort to stop development; they become a medicine chest from which climbers may withdraw doses of vigor. This outlook is expressed in individual climbing narratives that describe the mountains as a place where the best part of oneself is found, or where the picturesque wild revivifies a life rendered staid and docile by the crowded comforts of town.

Conrad Kain's story "The First Ascent of Mount Robson" tells of this great guide's trip up the massive face that now has his name. Notable here is Kain's attitude to nature as a place where a guide shares his spirit, and in particular his sense that these mountaineering exploits are intended to preserve and protect nature. Indeed, one of his charges is the young William Foster, later Alpine Club of Canada president, and Kain is clear that he values Foster as a "nature lover," not just a climber. Another chapter to look at closely was first published in a climbing catalog. Doug Robinson's "The Whole Natural Art of Protection" is a classic essay that asserts the satisfactions of rock climbing in an environmentally responsible style. His more recent introduction clarifies the stakes for Yosemite crack addicts and wilderness lovers alike. This essay is a fundamental statement of climbing's caretaking awareness in the era of the Wilderness Act and Rachel Carson's *Silent Spring,* and it charts a way forward both ethically and athletically. Gary Snyder has long been a poetic speaker for the natural world. Here, his prose poems describe alpine days and, especially, the vivifying, enlightening charge of wild experience. Across these readings there is an appreciation not only for high nature, but for human responsibility to it. The reading starts with Mark Jenkins's consideration of Europe's receding glaciers and the story they tell climbers of global warming and loss.

In Denial | Mark Jenkins

We'd heard rumors that the Alps were decomposing, but we ignored them. Europeans can be so querulous, so theatrical, waving their arms as if the sky were falling. John and I had been planning this trip for half a dozen years and we weren't about to change our minds.

Any mountaineer worth his weight in crampons eventually visits the Alps. It is the climber's hajj—a pilgrimage to the birthplace of the sport. But for John, this particular journey meant considerably more.

Born John Presley Harlin III, he is the son of John Presley Harlin II, who died on the north face of the Eiger—the macabre "Mordwand" (Murder Wall)—in March 1966 when his rope sickeningly snapped and he fell four thousand feet. John was ten years old. Harlin II is still remembered in Switzerland (a country where mountaineering is as much a part of the culture as basketball is in the United States) for his boyish charisma and numerous first ascents. Not surprisingly, the north face of the Eiger has haunted Harlin III for four decades. Although an accomplished climber and editor of the *American Alpine Journal*, he had never attempted it.

So we came to climb the Eiger. Get it over with. But we were too late.

"The Eiger has changed completely," exclaimed Nicho Mailänder upon our arrival. Friend, fellow alpinist, and peerless Munich climbing historian, Nicho is the originator of the Tyrol Declaration, a pioneering international treatise on mountain ethics. The Eiger is not the mountain it used to be. To climb it this summer, particularly, would be very, *very* dangerous.

Nicho proceeded to crush our big plan like an aluminum beer can.

"Just like most of the traditional ice faces in the western Alps, the Eiger per se no longer exists. This has all happened in the last five years. There used to be three main icefields on the Eiger. These have all but vanished. In their place are slick, fifty-degree limestone slopes covered in rubble — rubble that tends to slide off. Who wants to climb rubble?"

Mind you, Nicho is a somber German, inherently prone to understatement.

"As early as June, the Eiger was so devoid of ice it looked like September," he went on. "No. I'm sorry, but nowadays, the Eiger can only be safely climbed in winter."

Given that over thirty climbers have died on the Eiger, "safely" is a relative term. So much for the Eiger. It was almost a relief. John and I went directly to Plan B: a new route on the fabled Fréney face of Mont Blanc. Mont Blanc is the highest peak in the Alps and the Fréney face its most difficult wall, but psychologically, without the ghosts to contend with, it would be easy in comparison. But when we got there, the response was the same.

"Il est suicide!" decried the French caretaker of the Franco Monzino hut, a fortresslike hostel on the Italian side of the massif.

"Mont Blanc is ruined," he said, wagging his big head mournfully. The crevasses were hanging open like the mouths of a thousand dragons. The summit snowfields were running with water, setting off waterfalls of stone. The couloirs formerly used to access the climbs had melted out.

Now desperate, and being mountaineers after all, men whose best assets are a bad memory and balmy obstinacy, John and I decided to go up and have a look for ourselves. Hence, with a foul weather forecast in hand, we departed the Monzino lodgings laden like Egyptian camels—over a week's worth of food and fuel, a complete wall rack of climbing gear, pitons to micro-cams, ice gear, bivy gear, and none other than Jacques Barzun's enormous tome *From Dawn to Decadence: 500 Years of Western Civilization*. Within an hour (okay, maybe it was more like five minutes) we were hating our rucksacks.

Throughout the day, scrambling vigilantly up into the clouds, we heard rockslides thundering all around us, but we didn't know their origins until we reached the intermediary summit of Punta Innominata. From there we had an interstitial view of one of the two southern walls of Mont Blanc: the Brouillard face. Rivers of stone were cascading down its countenance, the normally white glacier at the base carpeted black with debris.

"He was right," I said pitifully.

John nodded. "But the Fréney face might be just fine. We'll get a good look tomorrow from above the bivouac hut."

At this point, I don't know if either of us really believed this—but denial is a powerful thing. I do know neither of us was prepared to give up.

But we should have been.

III

This past summer in Europe was the hottest in recorded history. New highs were set north to south, east to west. In England the mercury shot above 100 degrees for the first time ever, this in a country accustomed to wearing tweeds even in July. In Switzerland the temperature spiked at a Saharan 107 degrees. From the Netherlands south to Italy, deaths of the elderly, due largely to dehydration, skyrocketed. France alone attributed some 10,000 deaths to the excessively prolonged heat wave. Over 200,000 hectares of forest went up in flames in Portugal; 30,000 in Spain.

The Alps, the highest and thus normally coolest region in Europe, were not spared. In mid-July several massive rock towers collapsed on the Matterhorn, stranding some seventy climbers and temporarily closing the mountain. In early August a series of enormous rockslides swept the typically quite climbable west face of the Dru. By mid-August, the three customarily safe snow marches up the Mont Blanc massif had become death traps—the Grands Mulets route threatened by collapsing ice cliffs, the Traverse route across Mont Blanc du Tacul menaced by a labyrinth of yawning crevasses, and the Goûter route subject to treacherous rockfall. After two hikers were killed by falling rock before even reaching the hut restaurant near the Goûter route, the Chamonix guides stopped taking bookings for Mont Blanc by any route whatsoever (there are over a hundred), effectively shutting down the historic peak for the first time in 217 years.

Mont Blanc is the indisputable geological father of mountaineering. Recognized as the highest peak in Europe by the mid-eighteenth century (4,807 meters, 15,770 feet), in 1760 Professor Horace-Bénédict de Saussure of Geneva offered a reward of twenty gold talers for the first ascent. The concept of actually climbing this shimmering white behemoth of groaning, octopusal glaciers was so beyond the imagination of most humans that no one even took him up on the offer for fifteen years. It would require ten more years and an equal number of attempts by various nascent mountaineers before Michel-Gabriel Paccard, a medical doctor, and Jacques Balmat, an opportunistic crystal hunter, reached the summit on August 8, 1786. They had alpenstocks, but neither crampons nor rope, and bivouacked in the snow with only wool blankets.

Yet the embryonic sport of mountaineering must have struck something instinctual, because in the following decades ascents became common and coveted. The first woman to summit Mont Blanc was Chamonix native Marie Paradis in 1808. The first mountaineering catastrophe occurred in 1820 when five guides were swept into a crevasse by an avalanche, three dying. The first organized mountain guides company was founded in Chamonix in 1821. Ascents of all the satellite summits—Grandes Jorasses, Les Droites, Petit Dru, Aiguille de Grepon—were accomplished in the following half century; the innumerable and inevitably famous hard routes were put up on these same spires during the twentieth century.

Today, the vast, intricately incised Mont Blanc massif remains the cradle of mountaineering.

As long as there's snow.

| | |

Following a snug night in the Eccles bivouac hut, John and I scampered up the slag heap of steep talus to Punta Eccles, a prominent pinnacle on the Innominata ridge, and sat there with the monocular. The entire southeast side of Mont Blanc, in all its intimidating splendor, rose in our face. To the left the Brouillard face, to the right the Fréney face, the two separated by the Innominata ridge.

The Fréney face at first appeared pacific; then the sun pulled itself above the morning haze and within minutes rockslides began wiggling down between the four main rock pillars. John studied the glacier, tracking an invisible line that scooped around the debris zone and hooked back to the Central Pillar, our objective. He was pointing out a "reasonably safe" approach when the top of Mont Blanc seemed suddenly to be hit with a mortar. Stones came rumbling down the face—one the size of a vw van bouncing like a rubber ball—and swept right over where John was pointing.

When the roar diminished, John didn't even look at me. "Guess that clinches that."

As the hut keeper had predicted, fusillades of rockfall made climbing the Fréney face out of the question. We haplessly began glassing the Innominata ridge directly above us, our eyes immediately drawn to a red granite pillar split by a gorgeous dihedral. En route to Mont Blanc we'd stopped in at the Office de la Haute Montagne in Chamonix, a constantly updated library of climbs on Mont Blanc, to review new routes. Unbelievably, even the Innominata Direct avoided this obvious feature.

"It's never been climbed," I enthused.

"Might be because of that ten-foot icicle dangling from the first overhang," replied John.

Two hours later we were at the base of the virgin open book.

"I wouldn't waste time when you're directly below the icicle," said John, his way of telling me that if it cut loose at the wrong time, I might be cleaved in half.

The first sixty feet was five-star liebacking; then I was below the icicle, then I was fist-jamming in the overhang right beside it, then the back of my shoulder accidentally touched it and the whole thing let loose.

Miraculously, all the head-crushing junks missed John.

"Good work!" he bellowed up.

That first overhang was wet and wonderful, the second dry and quick, and in less than two hours we were standing atop of the two-hundred-foot pillar talking big again about our newly found route.

It was late, 4:30 PM. There were only two easy chevals and two shorter pillars above us and the route would be completed, but ominously heavy clouds had rolled in. Buffeting wind had come with. The foretold snowstorm was arriving right on schedule. Still, we had four more hours of daylight and headlamps.

"We leave most of our gear up here, storm blows through, then we come back up and knock this baby out," offered John.

I agreed. Made perfect sense at the time, so we bailed. All the way back down to the Eccles hut.

We shouldn't have. We had just snatched defeat from the jaws of victory.

| | |

"The world's climate is getting warmer," states Professor Andreas Kääb, a glaciologist at the University of Zurich, "that is a fact. Why, and how fast, are the questions."

The University of Zurich operates the World Glacier Monitoring Center, and Kääb's office walls are covered with satellite images of glaciers from around the planet.

"There has been a one- to two-degree centigrade increase in the past century, and much of this occurred in the past fifty years."

So what? What's a couple degrees? Turns out the glaciers in Europe and the Himalaya and most in North and South America are "temperate" — the ice stays right around freezing, 32°F or 0°C — and therefore extremely sensitive to changes in temperature. Bump the air temp up just a degree or two and it's like moving an ice cube from the freezer into the frig: it'll melt, slowly but surely. In terms of global warming, the world's alpine glaciers are our canaries in a coal mine.

"Particularly in the past five years, glaciers in the Alps are receding at unprecedented rates. We have also documented dramatic down-wasting [a thinning of the thickness rather than a shortening of the length] of the large glaciers," explains Kääb. "At the present rate of global warming, it is probable that all the small glaciers in the Alps will disappear entirely in the next one hundred years."

Higher temps have also caused the permafrost line to rise, which, according to Kääb, is the salient reason for so many rockslides.

"Formerly, the ice in the joints held these immense slabs of rock in place. Now that the ice is melting, rockslides are inevitable."

Kääb classifies the impact of global warming on the alpine environment into three categories: water, tourism, and hazards. His predictions:

Meltwater will increase, swelling rivers and temporarily generating abundant hydropower. But glaciers, sans cold snowy winters to replace summer losses, are like a savings account without interest. Once you've used it up, it's gone for good.

In tourism, the few remaining summer ski areas will likely close or rely exclusively on snowmaking machines, as will most low-elevation winter ski areas. Only the upper reaches of the larger winter ski areas will have dependable snow, and those structures built on present-day permafrost will begin to collapse. Climbing routes and their approaches throughout the Alps will continue to change, rendering guidebooks at best inadequate. Some routes could become safer, but in general, owing to the increase in rockslides, most will become considerably more dangerous.

Finally, natural hazards will dramatically increase (at least during this multidecade transition phase). Ice avalanches, landslides, and most importantly, glacial lake outbursts, are the greatest threats. Outbursts occur when a glacier melts back, creating a sizable lake, which, held in place only by a loose terminal moraine, eventually bursts this weak natural dam and floods the valley below. Dozens of towns and cities in the Alps lie in the line of water.

"The Alps as we know them," concludes Kääb, "are disintegrating before our eyes."

|||

That night the storm clamped down on Mont Blanc. By morning the incessant thunder of rockslides had vanished. A small drop in temperature, a fresh coat of snow, and the mountain suddenly went silent. Cracking the troll-size door, brilliant white light and snowflakes sprayed into the hut. Back to bed.

The next morning, ditto.

The next morning, ditto. So much snow had now fallen that going up or down was tricky. But we were safe in our tiny cliff dwelling, and happy (John) or claustrophobic (me), as the case may be.

John began reading out loud the best bon mots from Barzun's *From Dawn to Decadence*.

"Dessert without cheese is like a pretty girl with only one eye."

"We cannot be wrong, because we have studied the past and we are famous for discovering the future when it has taken place." Disraeli, 1851.

While the snowstorm railed, Barzun revealed to us through numerous examples how persistently and valiantly mankind has been grappling with the issues of equality, poverty, liberty, and justice—and, discouragingly, how slow humans are to implement effective solutions.

The storm broke late on the fourth day. Whether it was the result of normal weather cycles or another indication of global climate change, we'll never know. Regardless, John and I plowed up through one to two feet of fresh, wet, surprisingly stable snow to Punta Eccles to determine the possibilities of completing our new route—now dubbed the Super Directissima.

"Doesn't look that bad," I said.

"No, it really doesn't," replied John.

Somehow, patently ignoring the obvious, we still believed things had not changed enough for us to change our plans.

|||

If the Alps are transmogrifying so radically, what about the other mountain ranges of the world?

Ditto.

In an August 2001 United Nations report on Bhutan, "a rapid retreat of nearly all glaciers" in the Himalaya and the Karakorum from 1860 to 1980 was recorded. A UN team dispatched to the Everest region found that, compared to fifty years ago when the peak was first climbed, the area is now "unrecognizable as ice has retreated up the mountain." The glacier that was once at the foot of nearby Island Peak is now a lake 100 meters deep, 500 meters wide, and 2 kilometers long and is threatening villages downstream. This is just one of twenty new glacial lakes in Nepal identified as being "in danger of bursting its banks."

Ohio State professor Lonnie Thompson has found that 33 percent of the ice on Kilimanjaro has disappeared since 1980, 82 percent since 1912. On Mount Kenya, the famous Chouinard/Covington Diamond Couloir ice route put up in 1977 is today nothing but an ugly rock gully.

This July in the Peruvian Andes, eight climbers were killed when a block of ice near the summit of Alpamayo broke loose. Thirty-five climbers have died in the Andes in the last five years; locals attribute the increase to warming ice.

And in the United States, the beloved pika, a cousin of the rabbit and a unique species deftly adapted to the alpine environment, appears to be vanishing. In a recent report in the *Journal of Mammology*, Erik Beever of the U.S. Geographical Survey found a 30 percent reduction in numbers between 1994 and 1999, attributing the decline to climate change.

Every month there is new evidence from mountain regions around the world. As for the $64,000 question, the *cause* of global warming, even the recalcitrant Bush administration, a nonsignatory of the fundamental Kyoto Protocol and the last we-need-more-research holdout, has finally acknowledged the truth.

"Greenhouse gases are accumulating in the Earth's atmosphere as a result of human activities, causing global mean surface air temperatures and subsurface ocean temperatures to rise," bluntly states the Environmental Protection Agency's 2002 U.S. climate report. The report even acknowledges that in specific, oil refining, electrical power generation, and automobile use are the primary offenders.

Hard as it is to swallow, the United States, while only 44 percent of the world's population, contributes a devastating 25 percent of the planet's greenhouse pollution.

|||

John and I were up before our alarm went off and off before we were completely awake. The steps we'd postholed the night before gave us confidence until we began scratching our way up the arête proper. The rock was thickly glazed with multiple layers of ice and snow. The new route we had begun five days ago in the heat wave of summer was now a winter climb. We were forced to use crampons and ice axes to reascend what we had originally climbed in rock shoes and bare hands.

We reached our stash of gear, buried beneath two feet of snow, at dawn, but the sky was black with new storm clouds. Prospects looked grim. The consequences of continuing up would likely be severe: a cold bivouac, frozen toes, perhaps worse. We had been defying and denying the conditions on Mont Blanc from the start, but such impertinence was no longer tenable.

Sometimes you have all the evidence you need; you just have to accept it, then change.

"We've got to go down," yelled John through the swirling snow.

So we did.

The First Ascent of Mount Robson | Conrad Kain

On reaching the Robson Glacier after the ascent of Mount Resplendent, I went down to the timber at 6,700 feet. Here I met my *Herren* for Mount Robson. Both were busy about the fire, Mr. Foster (Deputy Minister of Public Works for British Columbia) with cooking, Mr. MacCarthy with gathering wood. After a good supper, we went up, laden with firewood, to the foot of the Extinguisher. The rock bears this name on account of its form (candle extinguisher). On the moraine we made our shelter beside a wall of stones, over which we stretched a piece of canvas and crept under it like marmots into their hole.

I awoke early next morning and felt pain in my eyes, and for a long time I could not open them. It felt as if my eyes were filled with sand. My snow glasses were no good. I saw a starry sky, which was more than we had expected. I applied cold poultices for half an hour and the pain in my eyes began to abate. I lit the fire and wakened my *Herren*. Both were delighted at the sight of a cloudless sky.

At 4:30 AM, after an early but good breakfast, we left our bivouac. We followed the route of the previous day (ascent of Mount Resplendent), over the glacier. Before we came to the Pass, we swerved to the right. From this point began the real climb of Mount Robson. We climbed up an avalanche trough, then under some dangerous ice bridges to the right. The snow was in bad condition. We proceeded without any difficulties toward the steep snow slope that descends from the Dome (10,000 feet) and reached it at 7 AM. We took a rest and deliberated over the route ahead.

Two years ago I spent hours studying this route, and did not take the bergschrund very seriously. From the Dome, one had a nearer survey of the bergschrund. We approached it over the glacier, which is here not very steep. A rib of rock comes down almost to the "schrund." Over this rock I planned to ascend, but after every possible attempt we were forced to give it up, for at this place the glacier breaks off sheer. For about two hundred feet we followed along the bergschrund to the right. Here was the only possibility at hand of overcoming it. After long chopping at the ice, I stood on its 65-degree slope. Across the schrund I made more steps. Then I let both *Herren* follow.

A thin layer of snow lay on the ice, and, owing to the melting of the snow, the ice was in very bad condition for step-cutting. I made the steps in a zigzag. Mr. Foster counted 105 steps to a ledge of rock. The rock, when seen from below, promised good climbing and a rapid advance. But it turned out otherwise. We climbed up an icy wall, and then to our disappointment had an ice slope before us, fifty or sixty meters high. I kept as well as I could to the rocks that protruded here and there, which saved me a few steps. At the top of the slope we had another wall of rock, and above that an almost hopeless ice slope. One could see the tracks of falling stones and avalanches. On this slope I made 110 steps. It was a relief to climb on rocks again, though they were glazed with ice. But unfortunately the satisfaction was short, and for several hundred meters we had to climb again upon a slope of ice and snow. The snow here was in danger of avalanching. For safety, I lengthened the rope on the dangerous slope.

At last we reached the shoulder at noon. I do not know whether my *Herren* contemplated with a keen alpine eye the dangers to which we were exposed from the bergschrund. In the year 1909 this route was attempted by Mr. Mumm and Mr. Amery with the guide Inderbinen from Zermatt. The party were in danger of their lives from an avalanche. I spoke with Inderbinen: he said, "I never before saw death so near."

On the shoulder we took a midday rest. There came a snowy wind that wet us to the bone. We pulled out all the clothing stowed away in our rucksacks. We found the shoulder less broad than we expected. It was a snow ridge, on the northeast side of which were overhanging cornices fringed with long icicles glittering in the sun, a glorious picture.

For a few hundred meters we had to keep to the southeast side. The snow on this side was in good condition, so that we made rapid progress. There was on each side a splendid view into the depths below (*Tiefblick*). The more beautiful view was that of the Robson Glacier, Smoky Valley and Mount Resplendent and the Lynx Range opposite.

From the shoulder to the peak, the route was no longer so dangerous, but complicated by the loose, powdery snow. It was as if we were on an entirely different climb on the southeast side. The complications arose from walls of snow. Never before on all my climbs have I seen such snow formations. The snow walls were terraced. The ledges between the walls were of different widths, and all were covered with loose snow. I often sank in to my hips. There were forms on the walls like ostrich feathers, a truly strange and beautiful winter scene. Unfortunately we had no camera with us. Some of the walls were fifteen to twenty meters high. It was difficult to find a way up from one terrace to another. At one place I worked for over half an hour without effect. We had to go back. A very narrow and steep couloir offered the only possibility. I warned my *Herren* that the piece would take considerable time to negotiate. Both had a good stand and kept moving as much as possible in order to keep warm. The wind was so bad here that I often had to stop. The steepness alone, apart from the wind, made step-cutting very hard work. For a number of steps I had first to make a handhold in the ice, and swing the axe with one hand. I do not think I need to describe this method any more fully, for everyone who has ever been on the ice, knows that cutting steps with one hand is a frightfully slow process. I know that in such places it is not pleasant either for those behind. As soon as I was convinced that I could make it, I called to my *Herren:* "Just be patient, the bad place will soon be conquered, and the peak is ours." Mr. MacCarthy answered: "We are all right here, we are only sorry for you. I don't understand how you can still keep on cutting steps."

When we had the difficult place behind us, the reward was a fairly steep snow slope, with the snow in good condition so that we could all three go abreast. At the top of the snow slope, was another wall, which, however, could be outflanked without difficulty.

The last stretch to the summit was a snow-ridge. I turned to my *Herren* with the words: "Gentlemen, that's as far as I can take you."

In a few seconds both stood beside me on the peak. We shook hands with one another. I added my usual Alpine greeting in German, "Bergheil." Of course, I had to explain the word *Bergheil,* because both knew no German. There is no word in the English language which has the same meaning as *Bergheil.*

On the crest of the king of the Rockies, there was not much room to stand. We descended a few meters and stamped down a good space. It was half-past five o'clock. Our barometer showed exactly 13,000 feet.

The view was glorious in all directions. One could compare the sea of glaciers and mountains with a stormy ocean; Mount Robson is about 2,000 feet higher than all the other mountains in the neighborhood. Indescribably beautiful was the vertical view towards Berg Lake and the camp below. Unfortunately only fifteen minutes were allowed us on the summit, ten of pure pleasure and five of teeth chattering. The rope and our damp clothes were frozen as hard as bone. And so we had to think of the long descent.

As far as the steep couloir, all went well. The descent over this piece was difficult. All the steps were covered with snow. Except for this, we had no difficulties till the shoulder. As it was late, I proposed to descend by the glacier on the south side, for greater safety. Besides the question of time, it seemed to me too dangerous to make our descent over the route of ascent. As a guide with two *Herren,* one has to take such dangers more into account than do amateurs, for upon one's shoulders rests the responsibility for men's lives. Also as a guide one must consider his calling and the sharp tongues that set going on all sides like clockwork when a guide with his party gets into a dangerous situation. It was clear to me that we must spend a night on the mountain. The descent was not quite clear to me. I was convinced that on this side we could get farther down than by the way we came up. My bivouac motto is: "A night out is hardly ever agreeable, and above 3,000 meters always a lottery."

After the shoulder, we had a steep snow slope to the glacier. I made about 120 steps. Once on the glacier, we went down rapidly for a few hundred meters until a sheer precipice barred the way. So far and no farther. Vain was my search for a way down. We had to go back uphill, which was naturally no pleasure. Between rocks and glacier was a very steep icy trench which offered us the only descent. I examined the icy trench for a few minutes, and the ice cliffs overhanging us. I saw the opportunity and, of course, the dangers too. Mr. Foster asked me what my opinion was, whether we could go on or not. I answered, quite truly: "We can; it is practicable but dangerous." Captain MacCarthy said: "Conrad, if it is not too dangerous for you, cutting steps, then don't worry about us. We'll trust to you and fortune."

That made matters easier for me, as I could see that both *Herren* had no fear. I lengthened the rope and left the *Herren* in a sheltered spot. I made the steps just as carefully and quickly as I could. When I had reached a good place I let both *Herren* follow. Mr. MacCarthy went last, and I was astonished at his surefootedness. This dangerous trench took a whole hour to negotiate. The rock was frozen, but the consciousness that we had such terrible danger behind us, helped us over the rocks. In greater safety we rested beneath the rocks.

Below us was the glacier which, seen from above, promised a good descent almost to timberline. I remembered that the glacier had still another break-off and knew that we must camp out. However, I said nothing of this to my *Herren,* but the opposite. I pointed with my axe to the woods with the words: "It will be a fine night down there in the woods beside a big fire." Both chimed in, for the word "fire" makes a very different impression when one is standing in soaking clothes upon ice and snow; from the word "fire" when one is aroused by it from a sound sleep.

We did not find the glacier as good as we expected. We searched our way through ice debris in an avalanche bed. Here on the glacier the sun bade us good night. The sunset was beautiful. I would have been even more beautiful to us if the sun had been delayed one hour. It was a melancholy moment when the last glow of evening faded in the west. We rested and spoke on this theme. Mr. MacCarthy said: "It is as well that the law of nature cannot be changed by men. What a panic it would raise if we succeeded in delaying the sun for an hour! It is possible that somewhere some alpinists will tomorrow morning be in the same situation as we are, and will be waiting eagerly for the friendly sun."

Despite the approach of darkness we went on. About ten o'clock in the evening we reached the rocks. It was out of the question to go any further. Our feet felt the effects of the last seventeen hours on ice and rock, and so we were easily satisfied with a resting place. A ledge of rock two meters wide offered us a good place to bivouac. We made it as comfortable as we could. We built a little sheltering wall about us. Our provision bag still had plenty of sandwiches, and Mr. MacCarthy, to our surprise, brought a large packet of chocolate from his rucksack. We took our boots off. I gave Mr. Foster my pair of extra mitts for socks, so we all had dry feet, which is the important thing in camping out. The *Herren* had only one rucksack between them, into which they put their feet. Both *Herren* were roped up to a rock.

I gave a few hints on bivouacking, for there are some tricks in sleeping out on cold rocks that one can only learn by experience. Fortunately the night was a warm one, threatening rain. Clouds were hanging in the sky, which, however, the west wind swept away to the east. In the valley we saw flickering the campfire of the Alpine Club and of the construction camp of the Canadian Northern and Grand Trunk Railways. I was very tired and went to sleep without any trouble. A thundering avalanche woke me from a sound sleep. I heard Mr. Foster's teeth chatter as he lay beside me. I uttered no word of sympathy, but went to sleep again.

Later I was awakened by a dream. I dreamed that we were quite close to a forest. I saw wood close at hand, and dry branches ready for kindling. In the dream I reproached myself what the *Herren* would think of me, sleeping here in the forest with firewood, but without a fire and almost freezing. With these reproaches I awoke and sat up to convince myself whether the forest and firewood were really so near. But I saw only a few stars and in the east a few gray clouds lit up with the dawn. I could not get to sleep again, but lay quietly and listened to the thunder of the avalanches which broke the almost ghostly silence of Nature. At daybreak it became considerably warmer, so my *Herren,* who had spent a cold and sleepless night, now fell sound asleep.

At six o'clock the friendly beams of the sun reached us. I wakened my *Herren.* Both sat up and described the pain in their eyes, which they could not open. The eyes of both were greatly swollen. It was not a pleasant sight. I thought both were snow-blind. Snow-blind, at a height of 9,000 feet, and in such a situation—that might have an unpleasant ending. After some cold poultices, the pain abated and both were able to keep their eyes open.

I told my dream. Both *Herren* had dreams of a similar nature, which had reference to the cold night. Mr. Foster dreamed that a number of his friends came with blankets and commiserated the barren camping ground, and no one covered him. Mr. MacCarthy, in his dream, implored his wife for more blankets, and his wife stopped him with the curt reply: "O no, dear, you can't have any blankets. Sleeping without any is good training if we want to go to the North Pole."

I searched for a descent over the rocks. After a quarter of an hour I came back.

"Yes, we can make it without further difficulty."

At 6:45 AM we left the bivouac, which will certainly remain in our memory. We did not get down so easily after all. We had to get around sheer walls. The climbing was difficult, and at some places the rock was very rotten. This was very unpleasant for my *Herren.* They could only see a few steps through their glasses and swollen eyes.

As last we had the most difficult part behind us, but not the most dangerous. We had to traverse a hanging glacier. For ten minutes we were exposed to the greatest danger. I certainly breathed freely when we lay down to rest under some overhanging rock. Our barometer showed 8,200 feet, time 10:15 AM. That eight hundred feet had taken three hours to negotiate. I said to my *Herren:* "I am happy to be able to inform you that we have all dangers behind us. We shall reach the green grass in the valley safe and sound even to our swollen eyes."

We crossed loose stone to the southwest ridge. This ridge should be the easiest way up to the peak. From here we had a beautiful view of Lake Kinney below. Without further difficulty we descended through a wild, romantic gorge to the lake. In the gorge we had a slide over old snow. At eleven o'clock we took a long rest and devoured everything eatable we could find left in our provision bag. Then we followed the newly-built trail to camp.

About five o'clock in the afternoon we came, hungry and tired, into camp, where we were hospitably received by our fellow campers with food and drink and congratulations.

From what Donald Phillips himself said, our ascent was really the first ascent of Mount Robson. Phillips's words are as follows: "We reached, on our ascent (in mist and storm), an ice-dome fifty or sixty feet high, which we took for the peak. The danger was too great to ascend the dome."

Phillips and Kinney made the ascent over the west ridge. The west side is, as far as I could see, the most dangerous side that one can choose. Kinney undertook the journey from Edmonton alone with five horses. On the way he met Donald Phillips who was on a prospecting tour. Mr. Kinney persuaded Phillips to accompany him. Phillips had never before made this kind of a mountain trip and says himself that he had no suspicion of its dangers. They had between them one ice axe and a bit of ordinary rope. They deserve more credit than we, even though they did not reach the highest point, for in 1909 they had many more obstacles to overcome than we; for at that time the railway, which brought us almost to the foot of the mountain, was then no less than two hundred miles from their goal, and their way had to be made over rocks and brush, and we must not forget the dangerous river crossings.

Mount Robson is one of the most beautiful mountains in the Rockies and certainly the most difficult one. In all my mountaineering in various countries, I have climbed only a few mountains that were hemmed in with more difficulties. Mount Robson is one of the most dangerous expeditions I have made. The dangers consist in snow and ice, stone avalanches, and treacherous weather.

Ever since I came to Canada and the Rockies, it was my constant wish to climb the highest peak. My wish was fulfilled. For this ascent I could have wished for no better companions. Both *Herren* were good climbers and Nature lovers, and made me no difficulties on the way. Each had a friendly word of thanks for my guiding. In this country people are much more democratic than with us in Europe, and have less regard for titles and high officials; but still it was a great satisfaction to me to have the pleasure of climbing with a Canadian statesman.

Prose Poems | Gary Snyder

THE MOUNTAIN

From the doab of the Willamette and the Columbia, slightly higher ground, three snowpeaks can be seen when it's clear—Mt. Hood, Mt. Adams, and Mt. St. Helens. A fourth, Mt. Rainier, farther away, is only visible from certain spots. In a gentle landscape like the western slope, snowpeaks hold much power, with their late afternoon or early morning glow, light play all day, and always snow. The Columbia is a massive river with a steady flow. Those peaks and the great river, and the many little rivers, set the basic form of this green wooded Northwest landscape. Whether suburban, rural, or urban the rivers go through it and the mountains rise above.

Mt. St. Helens, "Loowit" (said to be the "Indian name")—a perfect snowcapped volcanic cone, rising from almost sea level to (back then) 9,677 feet. I always wanted to go there. Hidden on the north side in a perched basin is a large deep lake.

SPIRIT LAKE

When I first saw Spirit Lake I was thirteen. It was clear and still, faint wisps of fog on the smooth silvery surface, encircled by steep hills of old fir. The paved road ended at the outlet, right by the Spirit Lake Lodge. A ways down the dirt road was a little shingle Forest Service Ranger Station. Farther down was a camp.

Looking out on the lake and across, only forested hills. Cool silence. South of the ranger station a dirt road climbed steadily up to a lighter drier zone. It was three miles to timberline. The mountain above the lake: they reflected each other. Maybe the mountain in the lake survives.

The camp had tent platforms under the big trees in a web of soft fir-floor trails. They were all near the water. It was so dark on the forest floor that there was almost no undergrowth, just a few skinny huckleberries. The camp had a big solid wood and stone kitchen building, and a simple half-open dining hall. There was one two-story lodge in the rustic stone and log construction that flourished (making work for skilled carpenters) during the Depression.

From the camp by the lake we went out on several-day hikes. Loading Trapper Nelson packboards, rolling our kapok sleeping bags tight, and dividing the loads of groceries and blackened #10 can cook pots with wire bail handles. The trails took us around the lake and up to the ridges: Coldwater Mt. Lookout and on to Mt. Margaret and beyond, into a basin of lakes and snowfields nestled below. From the ridges we could look back to Spirit Lake and the mountain with its symmetry and snowfields. We walked through alpine flowers, kicked steps traversing snowfields, glissaded down and settled in by rocky lakes to boisterous campsites and smoky crusty tincan meals all cooked by boys.

THE CLIMB

Walking the nearby ridges and perching on the cliffs of Coldwater Mountain, I memorized the upper volcano. The big and little Lizards (lava ridges with their heads uphill), the Dogshead, with a broad bulge of brown rock and white snowpatches making it look faintly like a St. Bernard. The higher-up icefields with the schrund and wide crevasses, and the approach slopes from timberline. Who wouldn't take the chance to climb a snowpeak and get the long view?

Two years later the chance came. Our guide was a old-time Mazama from Tigard in Oregon. His climbing life went back to World War One. Then he got a big orchard. He wore a tall black felt hunting hat, high corked loggers-boots, stagged-off pants, and carried the old style alpenstock. We put white zinc oxide paste on our noses and foreheads, each got our own alpenstock, and we wore metal-rimmed dark goggles like Sherpas in the thirties. We set out climbing the slidey pumice lower slopes well before dawn.

Step by step, breath by breath—no rush, no pain. Onto the snow on Forsyth Glacier, over the rocks of the Dogshead, getting a lesson in alpenstock self-arrest, a talk on safety and patience, and then on to the next phase: ice. Threading around crevasses, climbing slow, we made our way to the summit just like Issa's

> *"Inch by inch*
> *little snail*
> *creep up Mt. Fuji"*

West Coast snowpeaks are too much! They are too far above the surrounding lands. There is a break between. They are in a different world. If you want to get a view of the world you live in, climb a little rocky mountain with a neat small peak. But the big snowpeaks pierce the realm of clouds and cranes, rest in the zone of five-colored banners and writhing crackling dragons in veils of ragged mist and frost-crystals into a pure transparency of blue.

St. Helens' summit is smooth and broad, a place to nod, to sit and write, to watch what's higher in the sky and do a little dance. Whatever the numbers say, snowpeaks are always far higher than the highest airplanes ever get. I made my petition to the shapely mountain, "Please help this life." When I tried to look over and down to the world below—*there was nothing there.*

And then we grouped up to descend. The afternoon snow was perfect for glissade and leaning on our stocks we slid and skidded between cracks and thumps into soft snow, dodged lava slabs, got into the open snowfield slopes and almost flew to the soft pumice ridges below. Coming down is so fast! Still high we walked the three-mile dirt road back to the lake.

ATOMIC DAWN

The day I first climbed Mt. St. Helens was August 13, 1945.

Spirit Lake was far from the cities of the valley and news came slow. Though the first atomic bomb was dropped on Hiroshima August 6 and the second dropped on Nagasaki August 9, photographs didn't appear in the *Portland Oregonian* until August 12. Those papers must have been driven in to Spirit Lake on the 13th. Early the morning of the 14th I walked over to the lodge to check the bulletin board. There were whole pages of the paper pinned up: photos of a blasted city from the air, the estimate of 150,000 dead in Hiroshima alone, the American scientist quoted saying "nothing will grow there again for seventy years." The morning sun on my shoulders, the fir forest smell and the big tree shadows; feet in thin moccasins feeling the ground, and my heart still one with the snowpeak mountain at my back. Horrified, blaming scientists and politicians and the governments of the world, I swore a vow to myself, something like, "By the purity and beauty and permanence of Mt. St. Helens, I will fight against this cruel destructive power and those who would seek to use it, for all my life."

The Whole Natural Art of Protection | Doug Robinson

In 1967 Royal Robbins returned from climbing in Britain with a new tool and a new game. The tool was nuts, the game clean climbing. Five years later my article "The Whole Natural Art of Protection" appeared in the first real catalog of the Chouinard Equipment Company. That article is often credited with carrying off the clean climbing revolution. There is no doubt that it slam-dunked the endgame, but many interesting events bridged Royal's trip to Britain to that Catalog, and the highlights are worth retelling before we get to that piece.

Returning from England, Royal and his wife Liz quickly climbed Nut-cracker, which was the first time a route had been led clean on its first ascent in Yosemite—probably in the whole country—and he wrote a short piece about it in *Summit*. I was hooked. I filed the threads out of a size-range of brass machine nuts and took them up to the Palisades, where I had begun guiding the summer before. High Sierra rock fractures into a perfect medium for nuts and runners, so by 1969 I had converted the rest of the guides and we were doing first ascents, first clean ascents, and most of our guided climbs without carrying hammers.

Off-season we went to Yosemite and took along our new clean tools, which by then included a few British nuts like the highly prized brass hex from Clog—the first nut any of us had seen that was so small it had to be slung on a loop of swaged aircraft cable—and a sandcast MOAC that is still on my rack. Yosemite's smooth and often flaring cracks made climbing clean a more daunting proposition, and we prudently carried hammers on most of our climbs a while longer. But confidence built until in 1971, Jay Jensen and I climbed hammerless up the East Buttress of Middle Cathedral Rock, the Valley's first clean grade IV. The next summer we pushed it further, up to a grade V on the Steck-Salathe on Sentinel Rock. The clean crux was running it out from small wires on the friction headwall. Still, no one else paid much attention, except in the Palisades and Ventura.

Ventura is a long ways from Yosemite and the High Sierra, but it was already becoming a stop on the fledgling California climbing circuit. It seems that Yvon Chouinard's true favorite sport was, and still is, surfing. So in the late sixties and early seventies the Chouinard Equipment Company, which was nearly in sight of several of California's finest surf breaks, dragged a major focus of the developing front of climbing style right out of the mountains and plopped it down among the unlikely surroundings of oil derricks and palm trees. Chouinard's surfer had brought a focal point of the evolution of climbing down to the beach. So naturally along came climbing's latest development, the clean revolution. Chouinard Equipment was prospering, beginning to outgrow its original tin shed, and it was pretty common to see Jim Bridwell or Dennis Hennek crawl out of an old van in the courtyard on a foggy morning, and fuel up with breakfast at the Vagabond before firing up the forge to make pitons.

On Friday afternoons the company van would unload its last batch of heat treating and we would pile in climbing gear, clip a hammock diagonally inside the back, and party and talk climbing for the long moonlight ride across the Mojave and up to the Eastern Sierra. Depending on the season we might do a new ice route in Lee Vining Canyon, rock on Cardinal Pinnacle, or head on up to the crest to test ice screws. Tom Frost and I tried each successive generation of our evolving design for Stopper nuts in the Buttermilk. I was pleased with our design, but almost more excited to bag the prize of naming them too. There was more intense competition to name products than first ascents in a company that was rolling out such labels as the "climaxe." Meanwhile, Yvon was pushing the hexcentric nut shape. Later I turned an old idea of my dad's—he had done his thesis for a degree in aeronautical engineering on the strength of monocoque construction (tube shapes) for the fuse-lages of airplanes—into the design for Tube Chocks to protect the off-width cracks that were then at the cutting edge of free climbing. Those tools were my first foray into equipment design, but far from my last.

Tom Frost was a real design partner for me in those years, even more than Chouinard. "Ho Douglas, what you got?" Tom would sing out from behind his drawing board, and then we would spend the afternoon crawling around on the pattern paper working, for instance, on turning Don Jensen's cleverly compartmented soft pack design into the Ultima Thule. Tom was known as the silent partner of the big wall Golden Age in Yosemite, the one who produced all the hauntingly classic black-and-white photos from the first ascents of the Salathe and North American Walls. Fewer knew he had been an Olympic five-meter yacht racer and had an engineering degree from Stanford.

Chouinard was more of an intuitive designer, and it was he who had the business vision to start a company and make, for instance, the hard steel pitons that John Salathé had pioneered but wasn't about to produce. But Frost did more for the partnership than to buttress intuition with solid engineering, for his aesthetic sense was as strong in chrome-moly steel as behind the lens of his Leica. Tom Frost is still the most cheerful non-Sherpa I've ever met.

"The Whole Natural Art of Protection" was written especially for the first real catalog put out by the Chouinard Equipment Company (since sold and renamed Black Diamond) in 1972, to spread the word about clean-climbing technique, and to explore its stylistic implications.

"Vedy clean, vedy clean"
—PABLO CASALS

There is a word for it, and the word is clean. Climbing with only nuts and runners for protection is clean climbing. Clean because the rock is left unaltered by the passing climber. Clean because nothing is hammered into the rock and then hammered back out, leaving the rock scarred and the next climber's experience less natural. Clean because the climber's protection leaves little trace of his ascension. Clean is climbing the rock without changing it, a step closer to organic climbing for the natural man.

In Britain, after thousands of ascents of popular routes, footholds are actually becoming polished, but the cracks that protect them are un-scarred and clean. The Nutcracker in Yosemite, which was deliberately and with great satisfaction climbed clean on the first ascent, doesn't have polished holds yet, but has obviously been climbed often and irrever-ently; some sections of crack are corrugated into continuous piton scar for several feet. It can still be done with nuts—they even fit into some of the pin scars—but no one will ever again be able to see this beautiful piece of rock the way the first ascent party did. It didn't have to happen that way. It could still be so clean that only a runner-smooth ring at the base of trees and a few bleached patches where lichen had been worn off would be the only signs that hundreds had passed by. Yet the same hun-dreds who have been there and hammered their marks could still have safely climbed it because nut placements were—and are—frequent, logical, and sound.

In Yosemite, pins have traditionally been removed in an effort to keep the climbs pure and as close as possible to their natural condition. The long-term effects of this ethic are unfortunately destructive to cracks and delicate flake systems. This problem is not unique to Yosemite; it is being felt in all heavily used areas across the country. In the Shawan-gunks a popular route can be traced not by connecting the logical weak-nesses, but by the line of pitons and piton holes up the cliff.

As climbers it is our responsibility to protect the vertical wilderness from human erosion. Clean climbing is one approach to this serious problem.

Right from the start, clean climbing demands increased awareness of the rock environment . . .

The use of nuts begins with solving the environmental problems, but it ends in the realm of aesthetics and style. If technical rockclimbing in places like Yosemite were still confined to the handful of residents and few hundred occasional climbers who bought and used the first Chouinard pitons, then the switch to clean climbing would be purely a matter of individual preference for the aesthetic opportunities it offered, for silent climbing, lightness, simplicity, the joys of being unobtrusive. But the increased popularity of climbing is clearly being felt in the vertical wilderness, and if we are to leave any of it in climbable form for those who follow, many changes will be necessary. Cleanliness is a good place to start.

Then there is the matter of style. When going where cleanliness has been established, the climber may leave his pitons at home and gain a dividend of lightness and freedom; but if on new ground or the not yet clean, he can treat his pins and hammer as the big wall climber does bolts and leave them at the bottom of his rucksack, considering the implications before he brings them into use.

The most important corollary of clean climbing is boldness. When cracks that will accept nuts peter out, long unprotected run-outs can result, and the leader of commitment must be prepared to accept the consequences that are only too clearly defined. Personal qualities— judgment, concentration, boldness, the ordeal by fire—take precedence, as they should, over mere hardware.

Using pitons on climbs like the Nutcracker is degrading to the climb, its originator, and the climber. Robbins may have been thinking of that climb when he wrote, "Better that we raise our skill than lower the climb." Pitons have been a great equalizer in American climbing. By liberally using them it was possible to get in over one's head, and by even more liberally using them, to get out again. But every climb is not for every climber; the ultimate climbs are not democratic. Fortunate climbs protect themselves by being unprotectable, and remain a challenge that can be solved only by boldness and commitment backed solidly by technique. Where boldness has forced a line to come clean, we should tred with respect. There, as well as with unclimbed rock, patience is the key. The clean climber stands humbly before untouched stone. Otherwise one could become guilty of destroying a line for the capable climbers of the future to satisfy his impatient ego in the present. By waiting he might become one of those future capables. Every climb has its time, which need not be today.

Besides leaving alone what one cannot climb in good style, there are some practical corollaries of boldness in free climbing. Learning to climb down is valuable for retreating from a clean and bold place that gets too airy. And having the humility to back off rather than continue in bad style—a thing well begun is not lost. The experience cannot be taken away. By such a system there can never again be "last great problems" but only "next great problems."

Carried out, these practices lead from quantitative to qualitative standard of climbing, affirming that the climbing experience cannot be measured in pitches per hour, a climb cannot be reduced to maps and decimals. Rather, the value turns inward. The motion of climbing, the sharpness of the environment, the climber's reactions are still only themselves, and their dividends of joy personal and private.

Climbing Into a Life | John Daniel

After dropping out of Reed College and kicking around back East, I settled in San Francisco for a year, then drifted back to Portland in 1969
and fell in with a loose confederacy of rock climbers and mountaineers
at Reed. Some were students, some dropouts like me. I liked their learn-
edly outlaw spirit. I tagged along on rock climbs in the Columbia Gorge,
cleaning pitches behind the leaders, learning at the safe end of the rope
a feel for vertical movement and for the unreliable character of Oregon's
volcanic rock. A favorite playground was Horsethief Buttes, east of the
gorge on the Washington side. There we would boulder and do short
top-roped climbs in the afternoon heat, wandering the buttes wherever
our hands and feet led us. In the evening we rested, cooked a pot of
stew on a campfire, passed joints and gallon wine bottles between us,
and drifted off to boulder again by moonlight and sit for a while on the
butte tops, watching lit tugs and barges passing below on the broad and
shining Columbia.

Mount Hood was my first peak. Two friends and I slept a couple of
hours in the car and set out from Timberline Lodge at three or so in the
morning, our boots and ice axes crunching in the crusted snow. Our
slow and steady rhythm mesmerized me, made me feel part of some
ancient quest. This was not the Blue Ridge of northern Virginia. Fat stars
and planets were glowing as I had never seen them in a gulf of space
that expanded as we trekked higher, the dark countryside spreading
wide below with its specks and clusters of human light. At some point
I shouted for pure joy, scaring hell out of my friend Jackson, who was

leading. Above Illumination Rock we stopped to drink water and eat a bite. I noticed a tiny dark motion on the snow. Leaning down, shaking from the cold, I saw a spider—of all creatures!—trucking steadily up the icy grade.

"What are you doing here?" I asked.

"What am *I* doing here?" I answered, and broke up in shivery laughter. One small spider and three small humans all wildly out of place on a frozen mountain, out of our minds, maybe—and doing exactly, it seemed to me, what we'd been born to do. The sovereign radiance of dawn was lighting an expansive, ungraspable wholeness within me and without, a cosmos lit with possibility. The spider never stopped climbing, and after a while the rest of us followed.

Climbing is an instinctive desire. Pretoddlers pull themselves upright before they walk, and soon they climb stairs, furniture, parents, and eventually trees, fitting hands to limbs much as our long-gone ancestors did many millions of years ago in the forests of Africa. To climb rocks and mountains is to be that child, with larger ambitions. But for me it was also, I see now, an escape—from the mess of my parents' marriage, from questions of direction and purpose I couldn't answer, from fears and confusions about personal relationships that I scarcely understood. On cliffs and steep snowfields, usually alone, I knew exactly what I feared. I welcomed the simplifying lens of danger, the way it forced me to focus everything I had on each slight nub or depression in a rock face, to feel the stone's crystalline texture with my fingertips, to stare, momentarily spellbound between moves, at a nest of tiny yellow flowers in a crack six inches in front of my face.

Those flowers were more beautiful than flowers in a garden, and the same was true of birds and clouds and sunsets. The things of the wild flared full of being when they revealed themselves in the course of a climb, most vivid when I was most scared or exhausted. It was like taking a drug, but this way earning the payoff, body and mind and spirit working hard in concert to achieve it. If climbing was an escape, it was also a seeking. For several years I pursued it with hunger—far more hunger than skill—as if peaks and clouds and glacial brilliance were symbols of some secret meaning I was forever on the verge of understanding. Mountains, to me, were monuments of nature's joy. I wanted to feel for myself, *in* myself, that elemental joy. In the wild hills, if anywhere, I sensed, I might discover the sure and undivided self I longed to be.

There were moments when I found it. The most satisfying climb I made was Mount Olympus, the highest peak in Washington's Olympic Range. I hiked the twenty-mile Hoh River trail, from its start in a mossy rainforest of colossal Sitka spruces up through thinning forests shot through with quick little streams. Now and then I glimpsed a craggy skyline, a bright snowfield of the alpine interior. I took two days, not pushing it, as if the approach to Olympus was a purgatory necessary to make myself worthy of the mountain. And then I broke out of the trees into the mountain's presence, almost too bright to behold. I crossed Blue Glacier with its odd whining noises, kicked steps up and over the Snow Dome, and at last dropped my ice axe and climbed the bare summit pinnacle, where I took off my boots and lay cradled in warm stone as windy vapors gathered and dispersed, obscuring and revealing the maze of knifey, white-flanked ridges around me. I had found the center of the world. I lay still as stone, wanting nothing that was not there.

| | |

A young man is a dangerous thing, says a friend of mine who once was one. Being a young man of good breeding and some manners, I directed against myself most of the danger I generated. I rode a motorcycle, a BSA Lightning, despite ditching it in a Portlander's begonia bed the first time I mounted it and ditching it several times thereafter. I liked the power, the rush of air, just as I liked the powerful rush of methamphetamine when it hit my system. No longer was I taking drugs for anything as nuanced as personal insight or spiritual vision. I wanted euphoria. I wanted to feel *right*. I was out in the world, but the world was not confirming me. I lived with friends in San Francisco, worked at various jobs, dabbled in Zen meditation, protested the draft and the Vietnam War, joined encounter groups, and took sporadic college courses and more drugs. Nothing I did seemed to lead anywhere or to fit with anything else—a ramshackle life, and it was not at all clear who was living it.

The recurrent thread, the authentic trail I kept losing and finding again, was climbing. I bought a rack of pitons and rode my motorcycle to Yosemite, where I hung around Camp Four, the climbers' camp, long enough to work up my courage and ask a veteran if he needed a partner that morning. It happened that he did, and so he and eventually others led me onto the bright granite faces. I reveled in the rock's speckled polish, its tiny fingerholds and clean jam cracks, its rich flinty smell in sun warmth, its arched and pinnacled music always rising. I learned technique, pushed myself, began to lead some pitches and scrape up against my limits as a rock climber. I watched others making moves I couldn't do and envied them, but more than their climbing prowess I envied how they were with themselves, how some of them, only a few years older than me, had an ease about them, a fluid and deliberate way, a habit of being in no hurry and sure in every move.

I met a guy of about my own ability, a chemistry grad student at Cal, and we put ourselves to work on weekends practicing for a big wall. We chose the Chouinard-Herbert route on Sentinel Rock, a 1,700-foot line that climbers now scamper up in a few hours. In our primitive era, it was usually done in two days. Early one July morning in 1972, Ted and I scrambled up the brushy scree slope and easy fourth-class pitches, then hit the first roped pitch on the wall itself just as the sun hit us. We weren't bad, we discovered, but we were slow. Wall climbing, as then practiced, was cumbersome. One man led, climbing free where he could, standing in slings where he couldn't; pounding pitons into cracks up the hot vertical granite to a ledge or maybe just a place to hang. He secured himself, drank a quart of water wishing it were a gallon, and went to work raising the haul bag—the climber's equivalent of a steamer trunk—as his partner followed the pitch on a fixed rope, recovering the hardware. Then the partner leapfrogged ahead, at the same plodding pace, up the next pitch. It was an exercise in vertical freight hauling, a laborious raising of bodily mass and the mass of stuff that bodies must have to sustain themselves through two scorching days of hauling mass.

All day we'd been hearing snatches of speech and laughter floating down from a climbing party somewhere on the upper wall. Then came a shout. Something dark was dropping fast out of the brilliance of stone and sky, ripping the air with the sound of an erratic helicopter prop as I crammed myself against the face. The thing had hit the slope five hundred feet down and burst into pieces before I registered what it had been—a pack or a haul bag, crammed full.

"I thought it was a body," said Ted when he reached my belay ledge.

"I did too," I said.

Climbing is a spell, strenuously cast. Rope and hardware, hands and feet, simple will. If the spell breaks, there's only gravity.

It was dusk when we finished the last pitch to the bivouac ledge, which was big enough for two to semi-stretch out and smelled of human shit. Not that we cared. We spent the evening each drinking water and watching the other drink water. Watching like hawks.

"Better save the rest for tomorrow," Ted observed, finishing a long glug.

"Right," I agreed. "We'll need it." I reached for one of the last few quarts and drank half of it. Ted drank the rest of his bottle. We might as well have been discussing foreign policy.

We ate everything in the haul bag that contained a drop of moisture—oranges, a can of corn, a memorable warm cucumber that we snatched from each other's grasp and devoured in big chomps. A thousand feet below, a few lights of sanity moved on the valley floor.

We awoke to pale dawn, the smell of sewage, and the need to move on. Our last swig of water was gone by midmorning. The climbing wasn't especially tough, but the afternoon was a cauldron. We knew it was dumb time, mistake time. We reminded each other to concentrate, to tie the knots right, to place plenty of protection. The last hard pitch was a bulging overhang of semidetached slabs dubbed the Afro-Cuban Flakes by Chouinard and Herbert, far better climbers than we, who had evidently had the time and good humor—and the water—to pause during their first ascent to draw music from the slabs with their hammers. The pitch seemed to take us hours and probably did. As Ted made the lead I watched inner-tubers float the Merced River in the green valley a quarter of a mile beneath me. When he reached the belay point I followed on the fixed rope, swinging wildly over the void as I carelessly unclipped the rope from one after another of the expansion bolts the first ascenders had pounded in to surmount the overhang.

Ted was belaying from a huge ledge. Above, it looked like easy scrambling to the top. The sun was down. We decided to rest briefly, then climb up and over the top and down the easy gully behind Sentinel until we came to water. It would be dark, but we had a flashlight.

An hour later we were still sitting. Moving had turned out to be unlikely. We ate what we could get down without water and fell asleep where we were. My tongue felt huge, my mouth dry as the granite I lay on. Slow, fluent colors, vivid reds and purples, moved through me all night, not dreams exactly, but a kind of hallucinatory tide. I felt empty, weightless. Ted's voice called me to daylight. We packed quickly and clambered up the easy ledges. At the top of Sentinel stood a solitary ponderosa pine, its bark a vibrant orange with black furrows, tigerish, its crown of boughs shot with sun. The tree glowed, seethed in my vision, as if it could not contain its own bright being. As Ted went ahead, I stumbled to the pine and pressed my forehead to its trunk, breathing its hot vanillic aura. I took a flake of bark shaped like a puzzle piece.

We slid and scrambled down the dry gully, telling each other to slow down and be careful as we both slid faster, slipping and scraping ourselves, breathing mouthfuls of dust. Where the gully opened onto the scree slope, a little stream flowed through grass and shrubs and horsetails so green they hurt my eyes. We dumped our packs and knelt in the stream and lifted spilling handfuls to our mouths. The water burned like cold fire inside me. My heart skittered, beat double a few times, settled to a steady boom. We wet our hair, rubbed the grime from our hands and faces, laughed, chattered like children. The stream flowed from its high hidden springs, lively, clear, unmeasured, and free.

|||

As I've written in an essay called "The Impoverishment of Sightseeing," I returned to Yosemite Valley in the 1980s with my wife and mother and was surprised how inert and ordinary the valley walls looked through the frame of a tour bus window. Half Done, Sentinel, El Capitan, all seemed mere visual objects, scenes. My experience of one of the great natural spectacles of the world felt rote and passionless, and I thought I saw the same disconnection in the other tourists that day. Their pleasure in the beauty around them seemed muted, as if, though drawn to nature, they remained somehow insensible to it. As I and the rest of us clicked our photos and showed the valley to our video cameras, it felt as though we were trying to verify that what we saw was actually there and that we were actually seeing it.

In our contemporary world we have split off visual beauty from the greater experience of nature, and in doing so we have forfeited a beauty far more lively and robust. To know that greater beauty requires the exercise of more than the eyes, and it can't be done at a distance. It takes time, sweat, and sometimes pain, a willingness to enter the land and engage it. Backpackers, birders, hunters, fishers, climbers, surfers, river runners, tree sitters, homesteaders, field scientists, small farmers, small ranchers, and backwoods lunatics are more likely to know this beauty than are those who only stop their cars at the scenic vistas. They won't automatically know it—there are climbers who care only about bagging peaks, birders keener on lists than on birds, ranchers to whom grass is little more than poundage of beef—but the fullness of natural beauty is potentially available to them. They have the opportunity to become part, for a time, of places that onlookers can only observe.

As I was climbing and hiking and drifting in the early seventies, I was reading conservation magazines, developing a rudimentary awareness of western environmental issues, the principles of ecology. I was beginning to understand nature conceptually as a living system that places limits on us even as it sustains us. But such understanding is wan and forceless unless we learn it through the body and senses as well as the intellect. The first axiom of ecological awareness, it seems to me, is that the universe does not exist for human convenience and does not especially care if human life, individual or collective, continues or comes to an end. This can't be well understood as a purely abstract proposition. Standing in a Blue Ridge boulder field buzzing with rattlesnakes first brought it home to me, and further experiences have ratified the lesson—hitchhiking in humbling cold one night near Mount Shasta, the heat and the hurtling haul bag on the face of Sentinel Rock, a black bear I watched once in the High Sierra ripping through the contents of my backpack as if she owned it, which she did.

Almost every outing has advanced my ecological education by expanding my sensory imagination. Those thirsty hours in Yosemite's cauldron taught me something my mind only thought it knew—that moisture makes life possible, that its absence sets hard boundaries on where and how and how long life can thrive. Having clambered over fallen old-growth trees in the maritime Northwest and smelled the good dark smells of moss and soil and rotting wood, I better appreciate that a healthy community needs to carefully conserve and recycle its common wealth to sustain itself through time. The word *home* meant something more to me, something I might have learned no other way, when I saw Chinook salmon three feet long shadowing the small streams of their birth in the Idaho Sawtooths, eight hundred river miles and eight tall dams from their lives in the North Pacific. Feeling a twenty-five pounder thrust doggedly against my line in a coastal Oregon river informed me, too, just as eating his flesh would later inform my body. Even the memory of a night spent in the smell of human excrement recurs to me with vivid, if depressing, connections. I think of it when I'm stuck in traffic and the odor of mingled exhaust fumes seeps into my car, and when I drink city tap water that tastes as though it's been drawn from a swimming pool.

But most of what I've learned from my outings, like the language I've absorbed, remains unconscious. It contributes to my being in ways I can't analyze or explain, ways I can only feel grateful for. Somehow, after Sentinel and other climbs and backcountry treks, my steps took on a trace more substance. I belonged a little better to my life. For some of us, the way in must first lead out. Because we don't know who we are we must escape ourselves, forget ourselves, bewilder ourselves in a bigger beauty in order to realize, years later, watching breakers pound a headland or a red-tail adrift in the summer sky, that life is not something still ahead or hoped for, but what we are living, and that smiling inside us, though we don't always know it or act in ways worthy of it, is that undivided self we had desired, but hadn't known how to seek or even to ask for.

Into Africa | Cameron M. Burns

> You may be familiar with the Alps and the Caucasus, the Himalayas and
> the Rockies, but if you have not explored Rwenzori, you still have something
> wonderful to see.
> —DOUGLAS W. FRESHFIELD, 1906

The small, round-faced Bakonjo ranger laced his boots, stood up, smiled, and said, "Hello, I am Josiah. I will go with you." He then slung an old Russian machine gun over his shoulder and we started walking up the road through the village.

Benny Bach, Charlie French, and I—along with a dozen required guides and porters, and the well-armed Josiah Makwano—were about to enter Rwenzori National Park. It was February 2005, and the Rwenzoris were open again and tourist trade was on the rise. The park had reopened in 2001, four years after being closed as a result of fighting along Uganda's unstable border with the Democratic Republic of Congo. The area was still relatively edgy in terms of travel, though, and on a map of Uganda I bought before the trip, Benny, Charlie, and I noted that large swaths of the southwestern portion of the country had bold red text stating things like "Caution: roads in this area may be mined" and "Travel warning in this region due to civil unrest in Rwanda and Congo."

We were in the Rwenzoris partly because we'd always wanted to go, and partly because I had agreed with a publisher to update a 1997 book I'd done on Kilimanjaro and Mount Kenya, the agreement being that I'd add the three tallest peaks of the Rwenzoris, Mounts Stanley, Speke, and Baker, to the book.

Prior to the trip, we had pored through books on the Rwenzoris and examined the remote valleys on the southern edge of the range. One peak, Keki ("Cake-ee"), grabbed our attention quicker than the rest because, as Henry Osmaston and David Pasteur had written in their excellent guide to the Rwenzoris: "13,500 feet . . . this appears to be steep-sided and may be difficult to climb. No ascent has been recorded." Later, in a book from the 1930s, we found a watercolor painting of Keki, and it looked a lot like Hallett Peak in our own Rocky Mountain National Park: steep walled and likely fun climbing. Andrew Wielochowski's map of the Rwenzoris had Keki marked too, but the way to get to the mountain seemed anything but straightforward. Also, the more maps we looked at, the more we realized that this portion of the range was something of an unknown, a black hole in mountain geography. Trails varied from map to map, and it was pretty unclear how we'd even get to Keki; we soon labeled our lack of information the "Keki Hole." We got a hold of Osmaston, and, thirty-two years after the publication of his book, he told us via e-mail that indeed, the plumcake-shaped hunk of land was, as far as he knew, still unclimbed.

Our plan became pretty simple: wander up the big three (Mounts Stanley, Speke, and Baker), then do a little "wildcatting," as Benny likes to call it—exploring new ground.

Thus, armed figuratively with considerable research and literally with Josiah Makwano, who was there in case the wars weren't really quite over, we wandered through the village of Nyakalengija and into the woods.

Global Weirding and Malaria

Our first week was spent trudging up the standard trekking routes on the main summits. Sadly, though, before even our first peak, Mount Speke, one of our guides, Eric Baluku, suffered a debilitating bout of malaria and had to be sent home. Many westerners—acutely aware of the well-publicized effect of AIDS on Africans—seem to forget about malaria, but malaria is still one of the biggest killers in all Africa. According to the

World Health Organization, "there are at least 300 million acute cases of malaria each year globally, resulting in more than a million deaths. Around 90 percent of these deaths occur in Africa, mostly in young children." All the local people in East Africa I've met have had relatives die from it, and according to several knowledgeable Bakonjos, most of the Rwenzori guides and porters suffer from it. Eric was "replaced" a few days later by a small, smiling chap named Fred Bosco.

We wandered over Mount Speke from east to west—a trip our requisite guide, a Catholic minister named Peter Babughagle, had done in the 1970s—to learn that the huge glacier that had once existed on Speke's east side three decades ago was now completely gone. Peter was in total disbelief, as if someone had stolen his pants while he was eating supper. Two days later we wandered up Mount Stanley, to the highest point in the range, Margherita (5,109 meters), as the glaciers underfoot flowed with melting ice faster than a swimming pool being drained.

As in mountains around the globe, especially those on the equator, the Rwenzori ice sheets are melting as a result of global warming. Before the regional turmoil of the 1990s, scientists had repeatedly ventured into the Rwenzoris to examine glacial retreat, and come away with shocking discoveries about equatorial ice fields. In 1990, a group of Austrian researchers found the Rwenzori glaciers had been retreating at about twelve meters per year for the previous two decades. In June 2003, after the region had become relatively safe to travel in again, British geographer Richard Taylor led a team that surveyed the ice on Mounts Stanley and Speke, and learned that the Elena Glacier had retreated about 140 meters, give or take, since 1990, while the Speke Glacier had retreated 311 meters in the same period. Glaciologists have for a long time painted rocks at the glaciers' snouts, to measure the retreat. Moreover, as Taylor's team noted in a report, "the data appear to indicate further that the retreat rate has been exponential, rather than linear." Worse, the report concludes, "snow will disappear from the Rwenzori mountains in the next two to three decades and possibly by the year 2023."

This glacial retreat doesn't just hurt tourism. As reporter Ian Sample noted in the London *Guardian* in 2003, "Were they [the icefields] to vanish completely, it could have a big impact on those living alongside the rivers and streams the glacial melt waters feed."

It's tough to stand in a spectacular place like on the Elena Glacier, watching environmental deterioration race along and know that, just like you, I am the cause. My strongest memory of that moment is the distraught look on Charlie's face as we stood on the pockmarked, dirty, and beat-up ice sheet, which was covered with a half inch of water, all of it draining quickly downhill. It was like watching a whopper rain roll off a tilted parking lot. The havoc being wreaked by our modern fossil-fueled ways was more than disturbing—it was, on the warm ice, chilling.

We wandered up Mount Baker a couple of days later and then, finally, had a chance to give back. Charlie had spent half our sole rest day staring at a pretty slab, opposite the Kitandara Hut in the middle of the range, and suggested it needed climbing—not just by us, but by the whole crew: some twelve porters and the guides themselves. We set up a top-rope.

Reaching summits is a fine reward in the mountaineering world, whatever the route, whatever the difficulty, and regardless of the suffering, but teaching folks in an exotic region of the world—one that will surely see more and more visitors and where rock-climbing skills are virtually unknown—was the highlight of our journey.

Into the Darkness

The next day we set off into the unknown, the Keki Hole. It was time to disappear down one of the Rwenzoris' unfrequented valleys and play Stanley and Livingstone.

By this point, about ten days into our jaunt, the local guides and porters had become trusted friends. We were sharing meals and gear, and they had even sent one porter out to their village, Nyakalengija, to get us gumboots (Wellingtons) for walking. The mud and moss, and the wild steepness of the Rwenzori valleys, all combine to make foot travel a serious undertaking. Indeed, after leaving Kitandara Hut, hiking the nonexistent trail, well marked on the maps, of course, required a full day for us to cover a couple of kilometers.

The gumboots, though, stuck to rock as well as any climbing shoes, and we soon had the entire crew of Ugandans out bouldering in the forest. It was surreal.

After cresting Bamwanjara Pass, we entered the upper Kamusongi River valley, and, at last, found Keki. It turned out to be a miserable little hump of foliage. There was nothing we could do except scramble up the dirty hummock where, on top, we found a thirty-year-old cairn. Our new peak was a bust. We were crap at playing African explorer; Stanley and Livingstone were chuckling in their graves. There was nothing to do but continue down the valley, as we'd arranged a final pickup at the southeastern edge of the mountains, at a small mining town called Kilembe. We stumbled on through the mud, lamenting shoddy research—the only kind we were good at.

Monarchs in the Mist

A few kilometers later, as the descent steepened, the topography began to change. The valleys became steeper, and the rock walls skirting them got taller and taller. By nightfall, at a rock shelter called Mutinda, we found ourselves sitting under a cluster of towers and walls that were a cross between Venezuelan *tepuis* and Costa Rican highlands. The next day, we clawed our way up grass humps and sideways trees and bagged an elegant-looking spire, the low-fifth-class rock climbing made harder by huge sheets of moss that peeled off when we mantled onto ledges. We gave the route M2, from the moss-climbing rating system. It was February 11, my first daughter's birthday, so we dubbed the peak Zoe's Needle, and descended. Halfway down, I decided to try another, nearby summit. After all, I have two little girls, and when birthdays come along, they both get something, no matter how silly.

While Benny and Peter Babughagle headed back to camp, Charlie and I headed up to attempt a similar summit. We ditched the rock gear, expecting lower-fifth-class rock at the most, and were soon soloing up a dirty chimney that had much harder climbing than expected. Charlie backed off, but our second "guide," Fred, soloed the chimney behind me—eyes as wide as platters. We built a cairn on the summit, down-climbed the chimney, and descended to camp. Mollie's Tower was in the bag.

Naming the summits of these mountains after monarchs was a trend first kicked out by the Duke of Abruzzi in 1906, when he named Margherita, Alexandria, Elizabeth, and a dozen other summits for European monarchs, explorers, and colonial rulers. I figured we were continuing the tradition; Princesses Zoe and Mollie, when I called them via satellite phone, were most excited, though a bit uncertain of what Africa was (and probably who I was). We continued out to Kilembe. In all, it was a modest excursion, but it opened our eyes to the possibilities tucked away on the edge of the great Congo basin.

Back in the village of Nyakalengija, we held something of a going-away party, in which we handed out tips and thanked our crew of locals. It was a sad farewell. Over the course of fifteen days, three *abbajungus* from the West had grown tight with eighteen Bakonjos they'd never met before—and they seemed to think we were okay too, cash or no cash.

Back to Civilization

Africa takes your breath away. Not only is it a stunningly diverse and beautiful continent, but I'd argue it has the worst troubles of any place on earth. After you've met dozens of youngsters with no parents, after you've listened to stories from Western doctors about the incidence of AIDS, after you've read about rhino poaching, and wars, and poverty, crime, injustice, starvation, and corruption, you're left with the impression that the challenges of Africa are just too vast—that little can be done for the so-called Dark Continent. Not entirely true—you just need to tackle them piece by piece, inch by inch.

Although I've always thought climbing, a subset of tourism, a pretty selfish activity, in places like Uganda, mountain enthusiasts represent the front line of economic development and, hopefully, stability. Between July and December of 2001, there were 118 foreign visitors to the Rwenzoris, according to park statistics. In the dry season of the northern winter (January, February, etc.) of 2005, there were hundreds and hundreds of foreign visitors—mostly trekkers, but a few climbers as well. And the Ugandan government is planning to foster the tourism.

According to park officials, the best aspect of our visit was that we had prompted the reestablishment of a route through the southern section of the mountains, something they had longed to do for years so that they could offer visitors more than the standard Bujuku-Mubuku Circuit trek, and to inject some cash into a village (Kilembe) subject to the fits and starts of a mining economy. Sure, we'd made an impact on the planet—who doesn't?—but it felt good knowing we brought much-needed cash to a people living on the edge of the world and in the shadow of multiple historical hiccups.

As for the more global issue of climate change, we all have to work on it. I've long believed energy policy is not just a federal or international issue. It's a state, regional, and local issue too. And a community, neighborhood, and even family issue. Many individuals don't think they alone can have an impact, but our fossil fuel system is not impenetrable to Joe Sixpack.

Before our 2005 Rwenzori excursion I'd tried to offset my portion of plane travel greenhouse gas emissions by cycling to work. After returning home, it took me only four hours worth of web-clicking to switch my family's electricity supply to "full" wind (we had been at two 100-kilowatt-hour "blocks"), installed compact fluorescent light bulbs in sockets that didn't already have them, applied to my homeowners' association to put up solar panels, and signed my family up as the first family entity to join the Chicago Climate Exchange, so we could "offset" greenhouse gas emissions (my wife is adjusting the family menu to address my methane contribution).

Visiting the Rwenzoris made me realize climbing trips aren't entirely selfish adventures. Climbers have long led the fights to save crags, mountain regions, and entire ecosystems. And, when it comes to global weirding, climbers, like all consumers, can do their part, by pressuring manufacturers, government officials, carmakers, and others whose decisions have huge impacts on climate change, to make better products and policies.

I'm exceptionally lazy, but cutting my greenhouse gas emissions nearly in half was easier than any boulder problem I've ever tried. And, if as consumers we can help preserve the mountain places we love—places like the Rwenzoris—just a little bit longer, then we might, in fact, help tackle both Africa's and our own issues.

Solo in Queen Maud Land | Mike Libecki

I have had the opportunity to explore many of the remote places of the world for first ascents, unique culture, and mystery, but what unites them all is their immensely fragile environments. They are raw, beautiful, and often times frightening, especially in Arctic regions. The most powerful realization is how vulnerable the wildlife, plant life, and minerals are. From what I have witnessed, there is a valid need to make sure these pristine patches of the earth do not succumb to devastation by ignorant humanity. It doesn't matter if it is someone like myself, an avid climber on a solo expedition, or the power-hungry mining and energy industry. Thousands of climbers are traveling to the farthest ends of the earth every year as much or more than scientists and explorers. It is necessary that the climbing community also become teachers to exemplify proper etiquette to best preserve our pristine playgrounds. In the last unspoiled areas of the planet, one person can make the difference between pure and blemished environment. One grain of rice can tip the scales.

My first major expedition was to Baffin Island, one of the Canadian Arctic islands, which possesses the earth's largest concentration of the steepest, most remote big walls. It would also be my first major challenge to be environmentally conscious. My partners and I followed protocol we had learned in Yosemite: leave nothing behind, including feces, even while living on a granite wall for a month. We contained every bit of solid waste, from both male and female partners, brought enough fuel to burn our waste into ashes, then carried the ashes out. Compared to this task, the climbing and subzero suffering was the easiest part of the journey. Imagine three people's feces contained and brought down from a month of living on a wall—the smell, the weight, the filthy chore.

To what extent will climbers and adventurers commit to treat the planet with positive etiquette for just the principle? Would it have really affected the plant, mineral, and wildlife if we had left our feces to decompose on the rock? I think not. But what if thousands of climbers left their feces year after year in these remote areas? Compare the impact of the small numbers of climbers and mountaineers to the hungry energy industry going to remote places for research and toil. It is simple: if each human, regardless of their reason to be in the wilderness, can make a commitment to treat the environment like we would treat our own families, a positive outcome may be our planet's future. Climbers have an opportunity — a responsibility — to become leaders not only while on the rock, but off the rock as well.

In the present day, when environmental issues are brought up, I think of politics and the media: global warming, oil drilling in the Arctic, and life-giving water polluted around the world, just to name a few. Of course to me, the media is attempting to brainwash us about our social leaders and their promises to keep our planet healthy. I don't care if it is an issue for or against the earth's well-being, I have learned not to believe what I hear. What I do believe, though, are my own experiences in these remote environments. Like many climbers, I have seen that these places are changing drastically and in grave danger.

For example, in a meager span of six years from 1998 to 2003, I witnessed a global warming trend. What I encountered on ten expeditions, five in Baffin Island and five in Greenland, proved that the warming trend is reality. Exactly why is another question. In Baffin Island, in the course of these six years, I saw the same frozen fjord's ocean melt earlier each year. The results were similar in Greenland: glaciers had shrunk and once-white ice-capped mountains had turned brown. It is fact that the Arctic is getting warmer and the icecaps are melting. Whether it is a result of long-term human desecration or a natural cycle of our planet and universe, I am not sure. What I am sure of is playing my part to see that Mother Earth is treated like the holy temple She is.

Environmental issues that bring out the rebel side of me and really piss me off are the desecrations of the earth factually caused by human stupidity and laziness. I witnessed this on my first expedition to Queen Maud Land, Antarctica. My partner and I are skiing along on the shiny electric-blue icecap of Antarctica, perfect fresh frozen air numbing our lungs and nostrils, each breath a cleansing of the soul. With each motion of our skis a moment of fantastic, pristine bliss. These moments are the reason for my obsession with expeditions. Twenty-four-hour sunlight, perfect dark blue azure skies, snow crystals swirling around us like tiny diamonds, huge towering granite swords rising thousands of feet into the sky surrounding us as we gaze upon them in awe, knowing we would soon climb them. I was sure at any moment a wizard riding his pet dragon would fly out of the skyline to greet us. Beautiful, fantastic, a dream come true, right? Wrong. An hour later, we could see blurring heat waves rising off the icecap, creating a sea-of-green mirage. The music of skis gliding in rhythm stopped. This was no mirage. Protruding just inches above the icecap was an almost perfect square field of 150 hundred-gallon green fuel barrels marked BP Jet Fuel. Over the last several years the large fuel barrels had sunk into the ice and been encased by spindrift. In another year they would be hidden beneath the surface like fossils. Pollution fossils. Lazy-human fossils. Dozens of snow petrels lay dead on and around the barrels. The worst thing was not that our dreamland moment of fantasy was suddenly shattered, but that the barrels were all labeled with the name of a government organization that I would rather not mention. This is one of the government organizations one must obtain permission from to come here. What excuse could there be? If we can take it in, can we not take it out? These holy lands graciously welcome us with open arms, and we leave them violated?

Queen Maud Land is the most fragile, pristine environment I have had the honor to embrace. Despite the unbelievable fuel-barrel junkyard I found on my first trip to Antarctica, it is one of the most unexplored areas of the planet as well as possibly the most remote big wall climbing area. Antarctica is the last continent that humans have the opportunity to keep serene and unpolluted. Fortunately, the world feels the same way:

one must follow many strict guidelines, enforced by the Antarctic Treaty, just to step foot in Antarctica. I have never had to cut through so many layers of environmental red tape to travel anywhere before, and it's about damn time. Just as climbers can model behavior, the incredible continent of Antarctica can model results. Maybe someday the entire planet will require environmental access laws, and these laws will be enforced. From the example of the fuel barrels scarring the once clean environment, you can see not only why there is a need for strict guidelines, but how climbing expeditions have shaped my environmental beliefs.

|||

In 2005, I went to Queen Maud Land solo. As the gales of November whipped and thrashed my fragile nylon tether, I felt like a lone sailor out at sea. But the sea I had come to explore consisted of clear-blue solid ice. I did not have a sail rigged to a mast, but rather a kite connected to my harness, skis, and sled. I came to reconnoiter and climb remote granite islands that are both threatening and magnificent. They are like giant granite bouquets blooming out of vases of ice—by far the most uniquely shaped formations I have ever seen. How did I get here?

For the last fifteen years, I have looked through my eye-windows into the world with the feeling of being seventeen years old, a teenage boy. I am thirty-two now, and I can see and feel myself changing. For the first time in my life, when I look into a mirror I can see my dad looking back. Good-bye teenage boy, hello adult man.

The new feeling of adulthood was first like a rebirth, with renewed optimism and the courage to take life to greater heights. I felt something like a professional kid, with newfound strength to continue my lifestyle of climbing in the remotest areas of the planet, and to do so while being a father, having a comfortable home for my family, and giving back to the community. Now I even listen to the news channel in my truck instead of rocking out to bootleg Grateful Dead jams circa 1977. What happened to me? As surely as a compass needle points north, I am becoming an adult.

Random events during my Antarctic trip in 2005 confirmed this metamorphosis. For the first time, I indulged in what I had always considered the classic adult vices: coffee and tobacco. My entire life, I had made fun of my parents for indulging in this combo. How could a cancer stick followed by jitter juice be a delight? Just before leaving Cape Town on my way to Antarctica, as I bought a few backup salamis at a market, a pouch of tobacco caught my eye. I left with the pouch of Old Toby and fifty rolling papers.

According to my map, a few hundred square miles in Queen Maud Land are home to countless spires, towers, and ships' prows of granite. I had the opportunity of a lifetime to spend almost three hours flying over the area for a stunning aerial reconnaissance. It seemed impossible that so many unclimbed formations in the world-class category could exist in such a relatively small area. At one point, perhaps in the time of Gondwanaland and Laurasia, these geographic works of art must have been home to dragons and wizards and are part of the reason fairytales exist. I felt like an ancient warrior right out of a book, coming to save a sweet, beautiful maiden imprisoned at the top of the unclimbed spear-tip summits, guarded by subzero temperatures, fierce numbing winds, and rotten stone, like ferocious, frost-breathing dragons.

I pointed to a group of granite swords. The toylike, bi-wing airplane landed on the glassy ice and slid back and forth like a fish swiveling around a boat deck. The Russian pilots laughed and gunned the single-propeller engine like kids in a go-cart. The pilots seemed perplexed that I would attempt to climb one of these strange towers of stone by myself. When I stepped out into the numbing breeze, I felt the same way.

To go alone to Queen Maud Land has been on my list of dreams for many years. All the solo expeditions I had done had been part of a stair-case of training to prepare for this journey. The sound of the propeller faded to silence, and I stood alone on the clear icecap; perfect sculptures of shiny ice flames surrounded me. It was 0°F when the last light of the sun winked away. The tall, ominous granite and I regarded each other with suspicion. I shuttled loads to set up my camp. When the rustling of gear and skis gliding on ice subsided, there was only the breeze, my heartbeat, and my breath. Utter solitude. Living alone in temperatures as cold as my home freezer for the next five weeks would prove some of my father's advice: "Be careful what you wish for, because you might just get it."

There were two real concerns: the katabatic winds and the rotten granite. I had learned to fear both during the Antarctic summer of 2003–4 when I climbed a big wall about forty miles away. The lurking wind turned balmy, sunny, 20°F days into dangerous negatives in minutes. I also would never forget my previous experience on the worst rock of my life. Since leaving Salt Lake City on this journey, I had been possessed with worry about the rock quality. But I wore a halo of hope that I would find solid stone on the steep-sharp granite formations that disguised their danger in gorgeous grandeur. The towers here are so fantastic that one's fear is replaced with a feeling akin to the erotic.

My first objective was to attempt a stunning shield of rock that reminded me of the Ship's Prow off the coast of Baffin Island where I climbed solo in temperatures that never rose above 25°F. I was now back in a similar situation on the opposite side of the planet, and, though the temperatures here would be colder, at least I would not have to worry about polar bears raiding my camp. Before long I had three pitches fixed, with the high winds and freezing temperatures forming the crux. Unfortunately, the unpredictable quality of rotten rock became drastically evident on the fourth pitch. As I traversed a small ledge under a hollow spiderweb of cracks, two haul-bag-sized flakes stood in my way. They were balanced so perfectly it seemed that a gust of wind could set them loose. They had to go.

On a good stance, with bomber gear, I gently touched one of the flakes, and they both went crashing toward the ground. I was expecting the simple thrill of a wall trundle, but then a chain reaction started, and all around me pool-table-shaped flakes exploded and roared with fury. Before my adrenaline had a chance to kick in, a truckload of granite let loose, continuing the thunder and destruction. I tucked into fetal position. The earth shook and screamed like King Kong. It sounded like the entire wall was crumbling: doomsday. All of the stone that would have been my route erupted in the most intense movement of earth I have experienced. I smelled fire, heat, raw organic energy.

After the end-of-the-world explosions bellowed across the icecap and boomed off the nearby walls, I heard only ringing and a deep hum in my head, then the crackling of stones bouncing down the wall toward me. I hid behind my eyelids, curled into a ball, and took the stoning like a witch tied to a post. Then there was silence, a chilly wind, bright blue sky, and a happy sun gleaming. It was as if I was in a straitjacket. I suddenly gasped for breath as if I had just been under water for three minutes. I was hot and wet despite the freezing wind—then I realized I had peed my pants.

I rappelled the route, shivering. Fortunately, my route had been veering right, and my ropes below were unscathed. As my tears slowly seeped, I thought of my daughter. I thought of my adult duties, and not only how much my daughter needed me but just how much I needed to be with my daughter. Tears froze on my face. I crawled into my bag, drank the rest of the warm liquid in my thermos, bit off a few chunks of hard salami, and tried to sleep. My iPod fed me therapy in the form of Johnny Cash songs: "One," "Nobody," "Solitary Man," and "I See a Darkness." In my mind I could still hear the crashing roar of the earth. I could still smell it.

When I awoke I felt a new energy. I took the day to digest the experience and consider my options. It was the first time I had backed off a solo route, and it humbled me to the bone; I had to come to terms with the fact that this experience had been near ultimate danger, and I had had no choice but to go down. But my psych-addiction-obsession for solo climbing is energy I cannot control; it guides me like iron to a magnet. I had put every bit of my heart and soul on the line to get here. I thought of another adult saying that my mom repeated: "Be true to yourself and be thankful for what you've got." I still had plenty of time to find another objective.

I put on my skis to go take a look at a beautiful, tall, skinny spire nearby, a route I had scoped earlier that led to a café-table-sized summit. Despite being terrified on the first route I attempted, I still yearned to stand on the top of this spire.

I found some solid stone but also, of course, pitches of kitty litter. There were times I would try to place a No. 1 Camalot, and after finally whittling down the pebbles I'd end up placing a No. 3; a knifeblade placement would turn into a three-quarter-inch angle hole. The wind-chill controlled my schedule, and I often had to rappel back to camp because of dangerously numb feet and toes. I tiptoed with each move and wore free climbing shoes the entire time for precision, despite the frozen toes I obviously would have to endure. I fixed ropes and needed only one wall camp. I could barely sleep while thinking of the next day's work in the steeps, shadowed by fear from that first monumental rockfall experience.

I made the summit after sixteen days of work. Standing on top was glorious, but most of my enjoyment while getting there had been consumed by my fear of the rotten rock. Nonetheless, I found myself screaming in joy as I put on my Year of the Rooster mask atop the needlelike Windmill Spire.

Safely back at camp, I was hypnotized by a magnificent horizontal sunset of Barbie pink and orange sherbet rolling across the horizon. I could see the first ship's prow I had attempted. It mocked me in glorious sunlight. I had yearned to stand on top of its amazing summit. Three days before the Russians would return for me, I skied to the back of the formation, and after several hours on a beautiful dragon-back ridgeline I found myself on top. I thought of my daughter again, but this time I was laughing instead of crying.

| | |

Back home, I had to take pain pills for the aftereffects of frozen toes. Before long I was pulling off dead flesh that looked like strings of dried squid from where my toenails used to be. I felt deeply honored to have witnessed such raw power on this journey. I am back to my usual green tea and coffee a couple times a week. The tobacco didn't make it home, and I mock myself for the brief nicotine fix.

Transformation into adulthood is an interesting journey. The single most important thing I have realized, as I evolve from boy to adult and father, is that I need to teach my daughter that she must believe in her dreams, regardless of what they may be, and to go after them. Old age and then death are inevitable. The time is now. Dream big and live those dreams.

I have plans to go back to Queen Maud Land, Antarctica, many more times. My goals are not only to climb more of the world-class vertical granite mountains, but to live in what I call the "now," embracing moments of pure reality. Also, I want to bring out the sinister barrels left there to rot, or most likely to be forever frozen in the icecap. In my mind, being in Antarctica is about as close as you can get to the moon without leaving the earth's orbit. I wonder if there is a junkyard left on the moon by lazy humans. To me, environmental etiquette is about not only the mathematical consequences, but the principle. If I, or anyone else is going to be able to enjoy this part of the earth, our actions must result in the area being undefiled. My experiences in Antarctica have been life-changing, enlightening, and humbling. I only hope others can find the same emotion and growth I have in such virgin terrain. Stumbling on a junkyard in an area thought to be untouched kills the entire reason for going on these trips. Without these fantasylands kept pristine, the experience will never be the same.

It's important to share my experiences in these lands-of-the-lost, because the wild experiences in these faraway places have heightened my environmental sensibility. I am not only a climber on a mission for mystery, adventure, and summits, but a representative of the climbing community as environmental leaders.

3: connection

Connection. This is the third way to experience the alpine world. When the ice speaks to your axe, when the light and the wind coax you out of one couloir and into the next, when you skip the loose block without thinking . . . you are connected. Connection is a way of perceiving that recognizes and acts on the overlap between the human and the world.

Ron Kauk says "make friends with the rock," and in that open interaction between person and place we've come a long way from conquering peaks for queen and country. For me, connection is practical knowledge of nature, and it suggests that climbers are fundamentally intertwined with the world of rock and snow and cloud. Of course, climbing isn't the only way to integrate yourself with your world, but the rowdy pack of writing from the mountains shows it's one powerful way. Look at the Scottish climber W. H. Murray, who wrote of a moonlit winter climb, "in the architecture of hill and sky, as in great art and music, there is an everlasting harmony with which our own being had this night been made one." There are dozens of such expressions in climbing literature, and it's become a commonplace because it's rooted in something significant. The harmony here is a consonance between person and place generated by climbing.

There's more: this connection is the lived expression of a longtime philosophical goal for environmentalists—surmounting the subject/object divide. Here is the challenge from way back. In the seventeenth century a Frenchman who was not a climber insisted human knowledge begins with "I think, therefore I am." René Descartes thus expressed the modern confidence that your mind is as separate from the world's matter as any boat from the ocean that floats it. So, the important business is thinking, and the physical body and the rough, rough earth are secondary objects for your mind to manipulate. We are all heirs to Descartes, and we all inherited a natural world conceived as an inert mechanical object to be acted upon by the thinking human subject.

A few centuries down the boulevard, environmental thinkers say this hierarchy of mind above body, thought above world, leads Western people to treat nature as an object for profit and convenience, instead of a part of ourselves. Apparently our philosophical heritage and our profit-driven culture have generated a wall separating us from the nature we inhabit, and this separation allows us to strip-mine, clear-cut, and pollute the land we live in.

But is there some way beyond the separateness Descartes identified? This is where climbing comes in. Its intense physical attention to the ice or rock pushes people to experience nature as an extension of themselves and, thereby, to know it as more than the passive resource our culture of consumption and extraction tells us it must be.

The American philosopher David Abram captures some of this connecting in his concept of "participatory perception": "perception always involves . . . the experience of an active interplay, or coupling, between the perceiving body and that which it perceives." Abram describes an intermingling, or "coupling," between the human self and the physical world that is not separate, but is the realization of harmony between the perceiver and the perceived. Climbing is one activity that clarifies and demonstrates this anti-Cartesian participation. Look, for instance, at the first piece in the section below where Henry David Thoreau climbs Mount Katahdin: "I stand in awe of my body, this matter to which I am bound becomes so strange to me. . . . What is this Titan that has possession of me? . . . *Contact! Contact! Who* are we? *where* are *we*?" His climbing experience destabilizes the separation between human self and wild other.

Prominent American environmental writers have conjured this connection from their experience. Mary Austin writes of a "transaction" between her "spirit and the spirit of the land." Thoreau asks us in *Walden:* "Am I not partly leaves and vegetable mould myself?" And in these contemplations of connection we get a sense that the physical world is not simply an object for humans to instrumentalize, but is instead a living part of each one of us. John Muir's politics could certainly place him in the "Caretaking" chapters, but he knows something about connection too: "Climb the mountains and get their good tidings. Nature's peace will flow into you as sunshine flows into trees." Here Muir illuminates climbing as a vehicle for recognizing and embracing the overlap between the human self and the physical world that is also our flesh and our future. So connection is a way of knowing just beneath the surface of habitual perception. The climbing narratives that follow show what happens when the intense demands of alpinism, aid climbing, or rock craft push the human actor directly onto the stage of this world.

If we start with Thoreau, it's a surprisingly short leap to Yvon Chouinard in Yosemite. The long days on the aptly named Muir Wall leave Chouinard's group physically exhausted, but suddenly open to a sustaining, natural force: "with the more receptive senses we now appreciated everything around us. Each individual crystal in the granite stood out in bold relief. . . . This unity with our joyous surroundings, this ultra-penetrating perception gave us a feeling of contentment that we had not had for years." Chouinard's experience illustrates the climber's unique perspective on a unity forged with nature between hot hot sun and hard hard stone. This unity between self and environment is readily apparent in Lynn Hill's triumphal story of free climbing the Nose. Here Hill reports the desperate challenge of thin moves and the inspiring vigor she draws from "an open mind and spirit" in that place. She describes "a sense of liberation and strength" pouring from the Yosemite granite into her.

These stories, from golden Yosemite to wind-ravaged Patagonia to Terry Gifford's imagined future, turn on the gentle hub of connection and make us look long and clear at the relation between climbers and the world that sustains us all.

Ktaadn | Henry David Thoreau

By six o'clock, having mounted our packs and a good blanket full of trout, ready dressed, and swung up such baggage and provision as we wished to leave behind upon the tops of saplings, to be out of the reach of bears, we started for the summit of the mountain, distant, as Uncle George said the boatmen called it, about four miles, but as I judged, and as it proved, nearer fourteen. He had never been any nearer the mountain than this, and there was not the slightest trace of man to guide us further in this direction. At first, pushing a few rods up the Aboljacknagesic, or "open-land stream," we fastened our batteau to a tree, and traveled up the north side, through burnt lands, now partially overgrown with young aspens and other shrubbery; but soon, recrossing this stream, where it was about fifty or sixty feet wide, upon a dam of logs and rocks, and you could cross it by this means almost anywhere, we struck at once for the highest peak, over a mile or more comparatively open land still, very gradually ascending the while. Here it fell to my lot, as the oldest mountain-climber, to take the lead: so scanning the woody side of the mountain, which lay still at an indefinite distance, stretched out some seven or eight miles in length before us, we determined to steer directly for the base of the highest peak, leaving a large slide, by which, as I have since learned, some of our predecessors ascended, on our left. This course would lead us parallel to a dark seam in the forest, which marked the bed of a torrent, and over a slight spur, which extended southward from the main mountain from whose bare summit we could get an outlook over the country, and climb directly up the peak, which would then be close at hand. Seen from this point, a bare ridge at the extremity of the open land, Ktaadn presented a different aspect from any mountain I have seen, there being a greater proportion of naked rock, rising abruptly from the forest; and we looked up at this blue barrier as if it were some fragment of a wall which anciently bounded the earth in that direction. Setting the compass for a north-east course, which was the bearing of the southern base of the highest peak, we were soon buried in the woods.

We soon began to meet with traces of bears and moose, and those of rabbits were everywhere visible. The tracks of moose, more or less recent, to speak literally covered every square rod on the sides of the mountain; and these animals are probably more numerous there now than ever before, being driven into this wilderness from all sides by the settlements. The track of a full-grown moose is like that of a cow, or larger, and of the young, like that of a calf. Sometimes we found ourselves traveling in faint paths, which they had made, like cow-paths in the woods, only far more indistinct, being rather openings, affording imperfect vistas through the dense underwood, than trodden paths; and everywhere the twigs had been browsed by them, clipt as smoothly as if by a knife. The bark of trees was stript up by them to the height of eight or nine feet, in long, narrow strips, an inch wide, still showing the distinct marks of their teeth. We expected nothing less than to meet a herd of them every moment, and our Nimrod held his shooting-iron in readiness; but we did not go out of our way to look for them, and, though numerous, they are so wary, that the unskillful hunter might range the forest a long time before he could get sight of one. They are sometimes dangerous to encounter, and will not turn out for the hunter, but furiously rush upon him and trample him to death, unless he is lucky enough to avoid them by dodging around a tree. . . .

We had proceeded on thus seven or eight miles, till about noon, with frequent pauses to refresh the weary ones, crossing a considerable mountain stream, which we conjectured to be Murch Brook, at whose mouth we had camped, all the time in woods, without having once seen the summit, and rising very gradually, when the boatmen, beginning to despair a little, and fearing that we were leaving the mountain on one side of us, for they had not entire faith in the compass, McCauslin climbed a tree, from the top of which he could see the peak, when it appeared that we had not swerved from a right line, the compass down below still ranging with his arm, which pointed to the summit. By the side of a cool mountain rill, amid the woods, where the water began to partake of the purity and transparency of the air, we stopped to cook some of our fishes, which we had brought thus far in order to save our hard bread and pork, in the use of which we had put ourselves on short allowance. We soon had a fire blazing, and stood around it, under the damp and sombre forest of firs and birches, each with a sharpened stick, three or four feet in length, upon which he had spitted his trout, or roach, previously well gashed and salted, our sticks radiating like the spokes of a wheel from one centre, and each crowding his particular fish into the most desirable exposure, not with the truest regard always to his neighbor's rights. Thus we regaled ourselves, drinking meanwhile at the spring till one man's pack, at least, was considerably lightened, when we again took up our line of march.

At length we reached an elevation sufficiently bare to afford a view of the summit, still distant and blue, almost as if retreating from us. A torrent, which proved to be the same we had crossed, was seen tumbling down in front, literally from out of the clouds. But this glimpse at our whereabouts was soon lost, and we were buried in the woods again. The wood was chiefly yellow birch, spruce, fir, mountain-ash, or round-wood, as the Maine people call it, and moose-wood. It was the worst kind of traveling; sometimes like the densest scrub-oak patches with us. The cornel, or bunch-berries, were very abundant, as well as Solomon's seal and moose-berries. Blue-berries were distributed along our whole route; and in one place the bushes were drooping with the weight of the fruit, still as fresh as ever. It was the seventh of September. Such patches afforded a grateful repast, and served to bait the tired party forward. When any lagged behind, the cry of "blue-berries" was most effectual to bring them up. Even at this elevation we passed through a moose-yard, formed by a large flat rock, four or five rods square, where they tread down the snow in winter. At length, fearing that if we held the direct course to the summit, we should not find any water near our camping-ground, we gradually swerved to the west, till, at four o'clock, we struck again the torrent which I have mentioned, and here, in view of the summit, the weary party decided to camp that night.

While my companions were seeking a suitable spot for this purpose, I improved the little daylight that was left in climbing the mountain alone. We were in a deep and narrow ravine, sloping up to the clouds, at an angle of nearly forty-five degrees, and hemmed in by walls of rock, which were at first covered with low trees, then with impenetrable thickets of scraggy birches and spruce-trees, and with moss, but at last bare of all vegetation but lichens, and almost continually draped in clouds. Following up the course of the torrent which occupied this—and I mean to lay some emphasis on this word *up*—pulling myself up by the side of perpendicular falls of twenty or thirty feet, by the roots of firs and birches, and then, perhaps, walking a level rod or two in the thin stream, for it took up the whole road, ascending by huge steps, as it were, a giant's stairway, down which a river flowed, I had soon cleared the trees, and paused on the successive shelves, to look back over the country. The torrent was from fifteen to thirty feet wide, without a tributary, and seemingly not diminishing in breadth as I advanced; but still it came rushing and roaring down, with a copious tide, over and amidst masses of bare rock, from the very clouds, as though a water-spout had just burst over the mountain. Leaving this at last, I began to work my way, scarcely less arduous than Satan's anciently through Chaos, up the nearest, though not the highest peak. At first scrambling on all fours over the tops of ancient black spruce trees (*Abies nigra*), old as the flood, from two to ten or twelve feet in height, their tops flat and spreading and their foliage blue, and nipt with cold, as if for centuries they had ceased growing upward against the bleak sky, the solid cold. I walked some good rods erect upon the tops of these trees, which were overgrown with moss and mountain-cranberries. It seemed that in the course of time they had filled up the intervals between the huge rocks, and the cold wind had uniformly levelled all over. Here the principle of vegetation was hard put to it. There was apparently a belt of this kind running quite round the mountain, though, perhaps, nowhere so remarkable as here. Once, slumping through, I looked down ten feet, into a dark and cavernous region, and saw the stem of a spruce, on whose top I stood, as on a mass of coarse basket-work, fully nine inches in diameter at the ground. These holes were bears' dens, and the bears were even then at home. This was the sort of garden I made my way *over*, for an eighth of a mile, at the risk, it is true, of treading on some of the plants, not seeing any path *through* it—certainly the most treacherous and porous country I ever traveled. . . . But nothing could exceed the toughness of the twigs—not one snapped under my weight, for they had slowly grown. Having slumped, scrambled, rolled, bounced, and walked, by turns, over this scraggy country, I arrived upon a side-hill, or rather side-mountain, where rocks, gray, silent rocks, were the flocks and herds that pastured, chewing a rocky cud at sunset. They looked at me with hard gray eyes, without a bleat or a low. This brought me to the skirt of a cloud, and bounded my walk that night. But I had already seen that Maine country when I turned about, waving, flowing, rippling, down below.

When I returned to my companions, they had selected a camping-ground on the torrent's edge, and were resting on the ground; one was on the sick list, rolled in a blanket, on a damp shelf of rock. It was a savage and dreary scenery enough; so wildly rough, that they looked long to find a level and open space for the tent. We could not well camp higher, for want of fuel; and the trees here seemed so evergreen and sappy, that we almost doubted if they would acknowledge the influence of fire; but fire prevailed at last, and blazed here, too, like a good citizen of the world. Even at this height we met with frequent traces of moose, as well as of bears. As here was no cedar, we made our bed of coarser feathered spruce; but at any rate the feathers were plucked from the live tree. It was, perhaps, even a more grand and desolate place for a night's lodging than the summit would have been, being in the neighborhood of those wild trees, and of the torrent. Some more aerial and finer-spirited winds rushed and roared through the ravine all night, from time to time arousing our fire, and dispersing the embers about. It was as if we lay in the very nest of a young whirlwind. At midnight, one of my bedfellows, being startled in his dreams by the sudden blazing up to its top of a fir-tree, whose green boughs were dried by the heat, sprang up, with a cry, from his bed, thinking the world on fire, and drew the whole camp after him.

In the morning, after whetting our appetite on some raw pork, a wafer of hard bread, and a dipper of condensed cloud or water-spout, we all together began to make our way up the falls, which I have described; this time choosing the right hand, or highest peak, which was not the one I had approached before. But soon my companions were lost to my sight behind the mountain ridge in my rear, which still seemed ever retreating before me, and I climbed alone over huge rocks, loosely poised, a mile or more, still edging toward the clouds—for though the day was clear elsewhere, the summit was concealed by mist. The mountain seemed a vast aggregation of loose rocks, as if sometime it had rained rocks, and they lay as they fell on the mountain sides, nowhere fairly at rest, but leaning on each other, all rocking-stones, with cavities between, but scarcely any soil or smoother shelf. They were the raw materials of a planet dropped from an unseen quarry, which the vast chemistry of nature would anon work up, or work down, into the smiling and verdant plains and valleys of earth. This was an undone extremity of the globe; as in lignite we see coal in the process of formation.

At length I entered within the skirts of the cloud which seemed forever drifting over the summit, and yet would never be gone, but was generated out of that pure air as fast as it flowed away; and when, a quarter of a mile further, I reached the summit of the ridge, which those who have seen in clearer weather say is about five miles long, and contains a thousand acres of table-land, I was deep within the hostile ranks of clouds, and all objects were obscured by them. Now the wind would blow me out a yard of clear sunlight, wherein I stood; then a gray, dawning light was all it could accomplish, the cloud-line ever rising and falling with the wind's intensity. Sometimes it seemed as if the summit would be cleared in a few moments and smile in sunshine: but what was gained on one side was lost on another. It was like sitting in a chimney and waiting for the smoke to blow away. It was, in fact, a cloud-factory,—these were the cloud-works, and the wind turned them off done from the cool, bare rocks. Occasionally, when the windy columns broke into me, I caught sight of a dark, damp crag to the right or left; the mist driving ceaselessly between it and me. It reminded me of the creations of the old epic and dramatic poets, of Atlas, Vulcan, the Cyclops, and Prometheus. Such was Caucasus and the rock where Prometheus was bound. Æschylus had no doubt visited such scenery as this. It was vast, Titanic, and such as man never inhabits. Some part of the beholder, even some vital part, seems to escape through the loose grating of his ribs as he ascends. He is more lone than you can imagine. There is less of substantial thought and fair understanding in him than in the plains where men inhabit. His reason is dispersed and shadowy, more thin and subtile like the air. Vast, Titanic, inhuman Nature has got him at disadvantage, caught him alone, and pilfers him of some of his divine faculty. She does not smile on him as in the plains. She seems to say sternly, why came ye here before your time? This ground is not prepared for you. Is it not enough that I smile in the valleys? I have never made this soil for thy feet, this air for thy breathing, these rocks for thy neighbors. I cannot pity nor fondle thee here, but forever relentlessly drive thee hence to where I *am* kind. Why seek me where I have not called thee, and then complain because you find me but a stepmother? Shouldst thou freeze or starve, or shudder thy life away, here is no shrine, nor altar, nor any access to my ear. . . .

The tops of mountains are among the unfinished parts of the globe, whither it is a slight insult to the gods to climb and pry into their secrets, and try their effect on our humanity. Only daring and insolent men, perchance, go there. Simple races, as savages, do not climb mountains—their tops are sacred and mysterious tracts never visited by them. Pomola is always angry with those who climb to the summit of Ktaadn. . . .

| | |

Perhaps I most fully realized that this was primeval, untamed, and forever untamable *Nature*, or whatever else men call it, while coming down this part of the mountain. We were passing over "Burnt Lands," burnt by lightning, perchance, though they showed no recent marks of fire, hardly so much as a charred stump, but looked rather like a natural pasture for the moose and deer, exceedingly wild and desolate, with occasional strips of timber crossing them and low poplars springing up, and patches of blueberries here and there. I found myself traversing them familiarly, like some pasture run to waste, or partially reclaimed by man; but when I reflected what man, what brother or sister or kinsman of our race made it and claimed it, I expected the proprietor to rise up and dispute my passage. It is difficult to conceive of a region uninhabited by man. We habitually presume his presence and influence everywhere. And yet we have not seen pure Nature, unless we have seen her thus vast, and drear, and inhuman, though in the midst of cities. Nature was here something savage and awful, though beautiful. I looked with awe at the ground I trod on, to see what the Powers had made there, the form and fashion and material of their work. This was that Earth of which we have heard, made out of Chaos and Old Night. Here was no man's garden, but the unhandselled globe. It was not lawn, nor pasture, nor mead, nor woodland, nor lea, nor arable, nor waste-land. It was the fresh and natural surface of the planet Earth, as it was made forever and ever,—to be the dwelling of man, we say,—so Nature made it, and man may use it if he can. Man was not to be associated with it. It was Matter, vast terrific,—not his Mother Earth that we have heard of, not for him to tread on, or be buried in,—no, it were being too familiar even to let his bones lie there—the home this of Necessity and Fate. There was there felt the presence of a force not bound to be kind to man. It was a place for heathenism and superstitious rites,—to be inhabited by men nearer of kin to the rocks and to wild animals than we. We walked over it with a certain awe, stopping from time to time to pick the blueberries which grew there, and had a smart and spicy taste. Perchance where *our* wild pines stand, and leaves lie on their forest floor, in Concord, there were once reapers, and husbandmen planted grain; but here not even the surface had been scarred by man, but it was a specimen of what God saw fit to make this world. What is it to be admitted to a museum, to see a myriad of particular things, compared with being shown some star's surface, some hard matter in its home! I stand in awe of my body, this matter to which I am bound has become so strange to me. I fear not spirits, ghosts, of which I am one,—*that* my body might,—but I fear bodies, I tremble to meet them. What is this Titan that has possession of me? Talk of mysteries!—Think of our life in nature,—daily to be shown matter, to come in contact with it,—rocks, trees, wind on our cheeks! the *solid* earth! the *actual* world! the *common sense! Contact! Contact! Who* are we? *where* are we?

The Muir Wall | Yvon Chouinard

Just beyond this glorious flood the El Capitan Rock, regarded by many as the most sublime feature of the valley, is seen through the pine groves, standing forward beyond the general line of the wall in most imposing grandeur, a type of permanence. It is 3,300 feet high, a plain, severely simple, glacier-sculptured face of granite, the end of one of the most compact and enduring of the mountain ridges, unrivaled in height and breadth and flawless strength.
— JOHN MUIR, *The Yosemite*

More than any other mountain or formation, El Capitan has been responsible for the changing philosophy and the rising standards of American climbing. I speak not only of rock climbing but of ice as well, for new standards of ice climbing are being established by Yosemite-trained "rock specialists."

The new philosophy is characterized by small expeditions going into remote areas and trying new and extremely difficult routes with a minimum of equipment, no support parties or fixed ropes to the ground; living for days and weeks at a time on the climb and leaving no signs of their presence behind. This purer form of climbing takes more of a complete effort, more personal adjustment, and involves more risk, but being more idealistic, the rewards are greater.

Probably the basis for this type of climbing was established by the naturalist John Muir. He used to roam the Sierras for weeks, eating only bread and whatever he could pick off the land, sleeping under boulders in only his old army overcoat, and rejoicing with the summer storms. He chose to accept nature as it was without trying to force himself onto the mountains but rather to live *with* them, to adjust *himself* to the rigors of this sort of life.

It was a vigorous life indeed, but his writings tell us of his communion with nature and his profound mystical experiences. Scientists will explain that when the body is weakened by fasting the senses become more acute and receptive. This partly explains Muir's mysticism but does not explain how, even though he was essentially fasting, he still managed to keep his prodigious strength. The answer to this is simple; he was fully adjusted to his environment and to eating less food.

This same attitude was later accepted by John Salathé and "Axe" Nelson, who trained their bodies to do with very little water in anticipation of their 1947 Lost Arrow climb. Their five-day ascent with only one pint of water per man per day is still the most remarkable achievement in American climbing.

The nine-day first ascent of the North American Wall in 1964 not only was the first one-push first ascent of an El Capitan climb, but a major breakthrough in other ways. We learned that our minds and bodies never stopped adjusting to the situation. We were able to live and work and sleep in comparative comfort in a vertical environment. When the food and water ran low, we found that we could obtain an enormous amount of energy from eating just ten raisins. We reached the summit feeling as if we could go on for another ten days. No longer would we ever be afraid of spending so many days on a climb. Whether it was a Yosemite wall or a long Alaskan ridge.

After this climb we asked ourselves the inevitable question, "What's next?" The answer was obvious . . . another first ascent on El Cap in one push with two men instead of four. This would not only double the workload and responsibility, but would also considerably decrease the safety factor.

It is the unknown that frightens brave men, and there are unknown factors in trying a new route on this great wall. In the spring of 1965, after studying our proposed route for two years, calculating our equipment down to the last piton and cup of water, and weighing the consequences of failure high up on the face, T. M. Herbert and I felt at last ready for the big push.

Our proposed line started to the left of the Salathé Wall route, ascended some inside corners and arches, crossed the Mammoth Terraces, and continued more or less up, keeping to the left of the south face or Nose route.

JUNE 14: In the cool early morning we walked to where we had left our duffel bags and equipment the day before. The climb begins at the Moby Dick slab, a popular two-pitch climb of F9 severity. From the ledge at the top we dropped down *en rappel* for twenty feet to the left and began nailing up. The pitons held well, but they were awkward to place in the inside corner that leaned left. There was gardening of dirt and grass before a piton could be placed and, as usual, belays in slings. We had to place two bolts in order to reach a sixty-foot-long horizontal flake, and from these we hung our hammocks and had a secure, restful sleep.

JUNE 15: I completed the traverse, placing the pitons very carefully so that the flake would not expand. Them T. M. continued on, alternating pitons and bolts in a dangerous-looking loose arch. After reaching a troughlike groove, the climbing became easier and we rapidly gained height. Toward sundown T. M. pendulumed to a large ledge where we were to spend the night. Somehow our hauling system got fouled and a terse word was exchanged and much-needed water spent in perspiration before we were able to lift our two fifty-pound bags onto the ledge. The strain of the climbing, the terrible California sun, and that ever-present fear and uncertainty were all working away, and were reflected in us.

We had a fine ledge where we could lie out at full length and use our hauling bags for extra warmth. Besides, in the morning there were no problems having to repack the bags hanging from the pitons. The single fact that we had a ledge put us back into an elated mood, and we joked and talked until we fell asleep.

JUNE 16: As we had expected, the third day turned out to be mostly moderate free climbing up the right side of the Heart. In the late afternoon we reached another fine ledge a pitch above the enormous Mammoth Terraces. The last lead was done in the rain as the weather had quickly turned from oppressive heat to a fine drizzle. When it began to pour in earnest we crouched in our cagoules and waited. In a brief break T. M. started nailing the next day's lead, while I belayed and collected water that was running down the rock. But the water had a bright green color and tasted so foul that we decided to keep it only as a reserve for the last day.

JUNE 17: For the first half of the fourth day we followed a single crack and then switched to another that we followed until we were forced to quit climbing early when the intermittent rain settled into a downpour. Since we were obviously in for a nasty bivouac, we prepared for it as best we could. We even tried to hang our hammocks above us as a shield against the torrents of rain. It never stopped all night and the cold was intense, as in a high mountain storm. Soaked through, we huddled together to keep warm. T. M. had a particularly bad night, shivering so violently that he could hardly speak. When he did, he sounded almost delirious. We were despondent and for the moment had lost the vision and our courage. Yet we kept any thoughts of retreat to ourselves.

JUNE 18: The returning light restored our courage. A perfect crack in an overhanging corner allowed us to gain height rapidly while the overhanging wall shielded us from the rain. At the top of the corner T. M. began placing bolts across the blank area, doing a fantastic job of stretching out the distance between them. This traverse we hoped would lead us to the Gray Bands from where we would reach the beginning of the upper part of our route. After resting from the exhausting work of placing eleven bolts, all horizontally, he dropped down, went around a corner, and began to layback up vertical flakes. Losing voice contact with me, he painstakingly backed down until he could belay from the top of a very shaky flake. It was a tremendous effort and certainly saved the day. I just had time to finish the next pitch and to reach the Gray Bands before dark. We rappelled down to a good ledge and fumbled around in the dark to set up our bivouac. My down jacket was hopelessly soaked from the constant rain and so T. M. gave me his sweater, which had to do for the rest of the climb.

JUNE 19: The cold gray dawn revealed an appalling sight. Barring us from the summit was one thousand feet of wild, overhanging wall capped by a thirty-foot ceiling. A quick inventory showed two days' worth of food and water and only nine expansion bolts. There was no going down from here. The only practical retreat would be to traverse Gray Bands for four hundred feet to the Nose route, up which we knew we could make it to the top in two or two-and-a-half days. Aside from the uncertainty of the way ahead and our short supplies, we were physically and mentally exhausted from the strain of the climbing and the cold, wet bivouacs. Should we retreat or go on? Here was that line that had to be crossed of which Herzog speaks so eloquently in *Annapurna*. The cost of a failure can be dear, but the values to be gained from a success can be so marvelous as to change a person's whole life.

After all, why were we here but to gain these personal values? Down below there were only ten people who even knew we were up here. Even if we were successful, there would be no crowds of hero worshippers, no newspaper reports. Thank goodness American climbing has not yet progressed to that sorry state.

Our decision made, T. M. led upward. At this point the route becomes vague in my mind. The artificial climbing blends into the free. The corners, dihedrals, jam cracks, bulges, are all indistinguishable parts of the great, overhanging wall. The pitches never end, and one day merges into another. I recall only bits and pieces. A horrible flaring chimney sticks out in my mind, and the most difficult pendulum in my life. Always the overhangs and bulges keep us from knowing exactly where to go. And I remember a wonderful peregrine falcon aerie deep back in a chimney; soft white pieces of down stuck on to the crystals of the gray granite.

JUNE 20: The view below our hammocks was terrific—2,500 feet between us and the ground. But that was another life and we began to discover our own world. We now felt at home. Bivouacking in hammocks was completely natural. Nothing felt strange about our vertical world. With the more receptive senses we now appreciated everything around us. Each individual crystal in the granite stood out in bold relief. The varied shapes of the clouds never ceased to attract our attention. For the first time we noticed tiny bugs that were all over the walls, so tiny they were barely noticeable. While belaying, I stared at one for fifteen minutes, watching him move and admiring his brilliant red color.

How could one ever be bored with so many good things to see and feel! This unity with our joyous surroundings, this ultra-penetrating perception gave us a feeling of contentment that we had not had for years. It reminded T. M. of his childhood days when the family all came together on the porch of his home to sit and watch the setting sun.

The climbing continued to be extreme, and in our now weakened state strenuous pitches took us hours to lead. T. M. is normally a fairly conservative climber, but now he was climbing brilliantly. He attacked the most difficult pitch of the climb, an overhanging series of loose flakes, with absolute confidence; he placed pitons behind the gigantic loose blocks that could break off at any moment, never hesitating and never doubting his ability.

JUNE 21: Awakening on the eighth day, we promptly devoured the last few bites of food and the last of our water. Four bolts were left; four hundred feet to go, and always that summit overhang weighing on our minds. It was going to be close. When the cracks were good they were all one size; we had constantly to drop down and clean our pitches in order to use the same pitons higher up. Often cracks were bottoming, which meant having to put pitons back to back and tying them off with only the tips holding. The slow progress was extremely frustrating. The rain continued to fall in a silvery curtain that stayed a good twenty-five feet away from us. Hanging from pitons under an overhang we placed our last bolt, hung by a "cliff hanger" on a tiny flake, and barely reached a good crack to our left.

Our friends on top urged us on with promises of champagne, roast chicken, beer, and fresh fruit. But the summit overhang still barred us, and we almost insanely tried one blind crack after another. Finally with the help of a light from above, we placed the last piton. We took a few halting steps on the horizontal and abandoned ourselves to a gastronomic orgy.

Looking back up at our route late one afternoon when a bluish haze covered the west side of El Capitan, it seemed to have lost a bit of its frightfulness but appeared even more aloof and mysterious than before. It is far too deep-rooted to be affected by the mere presence of man. But we had changed. We had absorbed some of its strength and serenity.

Freeing the Nose | Lynn Hill

Returning to El Cap felt like coming home, I realized as I headed up the wall on my first attempt to free the Nose, in 1993. Some twenty years had passed since my first view of this grand monolith, when I had come on a camping trip to Yosemite with my family. Later it had been a rite of passage when I struggled my way up the Nose with Mari and Dean in 1979, climbing the route using aid during our three-day ascent. Then, thirteen years later, I had made a speed ascent with Hans Florine in just over eight hours. Now, at age thirty-three, my mission was to free climb every inch of this legendary three-thousand-foot rock formation.

My partner was a British climber named Simon Nadin, a tall man with a soft voice and a sunny-faced complexion, whom I had met at a World Cup competition in 1989. That year, Simon had entered his first competition; by year's end he was the first World Cup champion in the history of the sport. I felt at ease around Simon and respected his under-stated personality. As a climber, he had bundles of natural talent. In addition to being a good sport climber, Simon was used to doing bold, naturally protected routes in England. Simon, like me, had served an apprenticeship in traditional climbing style as opposed to sport climbing alone. When Simon and I had had a chance encounter at Cave Rock, on the shore of Lake Tahoe, we discovered our mutual desire to try to free climb the Nose. Though Simon had never climbed a big wall, I trusted him to be my partner on this towering cliff where swallows and per-egrines swooped. Within an hour of our meeting, Simon had postponed his return flight to Britain. Five days later, we were already two-thirds of the way up the wall, sleeping on a ledge beneath the Great Roof.

We woke up on our bivy ledge two thousand feet above the ground with the first rays of light spilling into the valley. As we looked down from our perch, the giant pine trees on the valley floor appeared like small heads of broccoli. Despite our airy position and bright sunshine illuminating the day, I didn't feel a sense of lightness. Getting to this point had taken us two days, and now, on our third day on the route, the force of gravity was weighing on us heavily. We were twenty-one pitches up the wall, and we had climbed eighteen hours without pause the previous day, finally quitting at midnight. The fatigue from all that free climbing, and the backbreaking work of dragging up two ropes, a heavy rack of gear, and a cumbersome haulbag, made us wake feeling tired and fuzzy-headed. As I looked at the Great Roof looming above my head, I felt my swollen hands throb with each beat of my heart.

The Great Roof pitch begins with a corner shaped like an open book with a crack at its center. The rock to either side is smooth, and the width of the crack at times pinches down to a quarter of an inch. The corner rises straight up for about 100 feet, but then it begins to tilt to the right, leaning over until it becomes a large roof shaped like a breaking wave of granite. To free climb it, a climber must surf sideways on smooth, featureless rock with his or her fingers jammed into the crack above. We knew this was one of the longest pitches of the entire route and its impressive architecture appeared unrelenting in its continuity. To make matters worse, the intensity of the midsummer heat radiated from the rock, making our skin ooze with perspiration.

"It looks like you get the first shot at leading the Great Roof," I said, handing the gear over to Simon. We had been swinging leads all the way up the wall.

"I guess I'll give it a try," he said softly in his adorable English accent.

Simon looked graceful as he cruised up the first three-quarters of the pitch, lay backing and jamming his way up the crack that split the center of the right-facing corner. But just before arriving under the Great Roof, his progress came to a distinct halt.

Simon slumped his weight onto the rope and shouted down to me, "The crack is too thin. I can't even find a way to hang on up here."

Watching such a talented climber become increasingly frustrated with each unsuccessful effort, I couldn't help but share his sense of frustration.

"You might have a better chance at this pitch than me," he shouted before lowering back down to the belay and turning the lead over.

This was the section that John had in mind when he pointed to my small fingers and said they would be my secret weapon. Ironically, my height of five-foot-two is often a shortcoming on the most difficult face climbs, where there are inevitably moves with long reaches between holds, but on the Great Roof it appeared the tables were turned and perhaps my small size would be an advantage.

When I arrived at the first difficult section below the roof, I immediately understood why Simon was having such a hard time hanging on. Though I was able to wedge my fingertips into a few small openings in the crack, the face on either side was utterly devoid of features to stand on. At one point, the only edge of rock I could use to stand on was located at shoulder height and I needed to make a powerful kick just to get my foot up onto this hold. Underneath the roof itself, I had to duck my head down inside the curl of this granite wave, while wedging two fingertips of each hand straight up into the crack above my head. In order to keep my feet from skating off the smooth surface of the rock, I needed to maintain a perpendicular angle with my feet pressed flat against the vertical rock below. Moving from this rock-surfing position involved strenuous yet delicate tai-chi-like dance steps to coordinate finger moves and foot shuffles. After trying countless combinations of hand and foot sequences, my strength and concentration were nearly spent. I knew it would be possible to free climb this pitch, but I wasn't sure I would have enough strength to do it that day. I didn't have the luxury of coming back another day, nor did I have the energy to refine the sequence any further. My only hope of free climbing this pitch on my next try was to perform each move with as much grace and finesse as possible. I lowered down to the belay to rest before giving it my best effort.

After a twenty-minute rest, I started up again feeling surprisingly strong and fluid. But as soon as I began the most difficult series of moves, my timing was off and my body position faltered. I thrust my fingertips into a small opening in the crack just as my right foot popped off the face. In the next instant, I was airborne, then the rope caught my fall and I swung sideways into the corner. I hung on the rope, panting, with two thousand feet of air below my feet, and then I lowered back to Simon.

"One more try. I'll do better next time," I said, voicing my mantra of hopeful determination.

While I rested, a team of Croatian climbers passed us. They moved quickly, climbing in traditional aid style. Down on the meadows I noticed that the pines were casting long shadows. We had limited energy and daylight left. Either I would make the first free ascent of this pitch on my next try, or we would have to abandon our all free attempt and finish climbing to the top.

While resting at the belay, I looked across the valley at the face of Middle Cathedral. On its mottled wall I noticed a play of shadows form the shape of a heart. I have always noticed the symbols around me, and this heart on stone reminded me of the values that have always been most important in my life and in climbing. My own development as a climber has been an extension of the experiences, passion, and vision of others. For me, free climbing the Great Roof was an opportunity to demonstrate the power of having an open mind and spirit. Though I realized that I could easily fall in my exhausted state, I felt a sense of liberation and strength knowing that this was an effort worth trying with all my heart. I had a strong feeling that this ascent was a part of my destiny and that somehow I could tap into that mysterious source of energy to literally rise to the occasion. I said nothing to Simon of my private thoughts, and when I returned to the roof, I realized that this was the moment of truth.

This time, as I began the most difficult sequence of moves, I could feel my strength waning, but willpower alone seemed to fuel me past the move where I had fallen on my previous attempt. Inches before the end of the traverse, my foot slipped off the face again and I began tipping backward. Because I had crunched my body into a tight and awkward position under the roof, my head butted into the ceiling above me, unexpectedly steadying me. I propelled myself onward, extended my right arm as far as I could, and shoved my fingers into a small slot. I composed my breathing for a moment, then focused on making a few final moves onto the belay ledge where one of the Croatian climbers stood staring at me wide-eyed. He had just witnessed the first free ascent of the Great Roof and he was as surprised as me at what had just taken place. Simon shouted up some words of congratulations, then came up the pitch using aid.

Simon didn't need to say anything for me to understand the disappointment he felt in having failed to free climb the Great Roof himself. Years later, I read an interview in which Simon spoke about his feelings watching me free climb the Great Roof that day:

"One more attempt was all the dwindling light would allow. I tried hard to stay cheery and not upset Lynn's concentration. Dejected that I had failed at the first obstacle, the consolation of just doing the Nose wasn't enough. Lynn's free ascent of this pitch was inspirational. She had been on the edge, feet popping off several times but somehow summoning up enough reserves to complete it."

The hard climbing was not over yet, though. There was one more pitch above Camp Six called the Changing Corners that had never been free climbed, and it had a reputation among the few who had tried it for being "reachy," meaning that the key holds were far apart. I knew that there was a good chance I would not be able to find an alternative way to make it past this blank section of rock.

Sensing that Simon needed a bit of cheering up, I said, "I think you'll have a much better chance of free climbing the pitch above Camp Six. Brooke Sandahl told me that this section involved a long reach with virtually nothing in the way of intermediate holds. There's a good chance that you'll be able to free climb it and I won't. If that's the case, we may be successful in making the first free ascent of the Nose as a team."

In retrospect, I don't know if my comments inspired or intimidated him. Simon merely nodded with a look of mixed emotions as he prepared to climb the next pitch. We climbed a little higher that evening, finally bivouacking on the ledge at Camp Five.

The next morning we organized our gear and shared our last food: one-half of an energy bar and one date each. We started ahead of the Croatian climbers, and it was Simon's turn to lead up a difficult pitch called the Glowering Spot. It turned out to be a horrendous way to start the day. This pitch follows an incipient crack to the left of a grass-filled corner that throws the climber into a frenzy of technical stemming and shallow finger jams. Rated 5.12d, and protected by small wired stoppers that are tedious to wiggle into the crack, Simon was grunting with fatigue by its end. As I climbed up behind him, struggling to stay on the rock without slipping, one of the Croatians appeared behind me, aid climbing upward, right at my heels.

Having climbed twenty-eight pitches, we arrived at Camp Six at eleven-thirty AM, tired but hopeful of being able to continue our free ascent. Brooke had already tried to free climb the pitch above us a year earlier by deviating to the left of the original line, up a steep face, then back right across a blank section of rock. I went up first to check out the crux moves and was quickly discouraged. Getting across the crux section involved reaching out to a tiny hold a full arm-stretch away, with nothing on the sheer face below to stand on. Taller climbers could stand on a small crystal of rock on the face, but this hold was located so low down on the face that I wasn't able to reach the crucial hold with my arms spread apart in a nearly iron-cross position. After a few tries, it was obvious that the mechanics necessary to make this move were not going to work for me. Simon went up next. Though he was able to make it past the first reachy move, he was stopped by the next section, which involved an acrobatic jump to the right. After a few tries, he too determined that the moves were too difficult in his tired condition.

As a last resort, I tried climbing up the original line that nearly all climbers had followed for the previous thirty-five years. This way climbed a shallow, flaring corner to our right. The walls to either side of this feature were smooth, and little in the way of a crack split the corner itself. The climbing was desperately hard and our spirits had been withered away by hunger and fatigue. We had only a few hours of daylight left to make it to the top, so we reluctantly decided that we had no other choice but to abandon the all free effort. We had made a valiant effort to free climb this route, but a mere ten-foot stretch of blank rock had foiled us.

| | |

Over the next few days, which I spent at a family reunion in Idaho, I thought of the moves that had stopped us. Getting up those few feet had seemed so improbable, but after considering the possibilities from a fresh perspective, I was convinced that it was worth giving it another try.

The following week I returned to Yosemite with my friend Brooke, a talented and passionate climber with an understated manner who turned out to be an ideal partner on this landmark ascent. Brooke revealed to me that when he was a young boy learning to climb with his father, he had looked at pictures of the Nose route and thought, *One day I'm going to free climb that route.* Brooke was eager to try it again himself. We hiked nine miles to the top of El Capitan, rappelled down to the pitch above Camp Six, and set to work on this enigmatic section of climbing. Brooke focused on trying his own face climbing variation; I focused on climbing the original line. Climbing up this corner demanded the ingenuity of movement that I had rarely ever encountered. We spent three days working on this pitch, and by the end I had pieced together a sequence of moves that went together like a crazy dance. I had invented a wild tango of smears with my feet, tenuous stems, back steps and cross steps, lay backs and arm bars, and pinches and palming maneuvers. Ironically, instead of being stopped by the reachy variation, I discovered that the original route turned out to be much better suited for a person of my body dimensions.

September heat dogged us, but I was able to climb this pitch with only one fall. Brooke was not successful on his variant, but seeing how close I was to success, he was keen to join me in our effort to make a free ascent of the entire route from bottom to top. When we returned to the Nose a few days later, we were well stocked with food and water, and we both felt a sense of harmony in this magical place. When we arrived at the Great Roof, I went up once to familiarize myself with the moves, then made a successful free ascent on my first try. Next Brooke gave it a try for the first time since his ascent in 1991 when the crack was soaking wet. Though he felt it was possible for him to free climb this pitch, he knew it would be too hard to do that day, so we continued climbing up to our bivy ledge at Camp Five. At the end of the same day, I led the Glowering Spot pitch while I was still limber from the day's climbing.

The morning of our final day, I woke up on the ledge at Camp Five and opened my eyes to look straight up the giant dihedral at the last several hundred feet of the climb. There, above, was the Changing Corners pitch that would make or break our free attempt. I had just dreamed that I had free climbed this pitch, and I felt a strong sense of excitement about what was soon to unfold. The weather was cool and I felt relaxed.

Brooke put me on belay and I started up knowing I would have to link the complex set of moves together exactly the way I had imagined them over the past several days. To get up the Changing Corners section, I had worked out a maneuver involving a bizarre contortion that seemed like a disappearing act. Using a carefully coordinated sequence of opposite pressures between my feet, hands, elbows, and hips against the shallow walls of the corner, I turned my body 180 degrees around.

"That looks like a contortion only Houdini would make up," Brooke yelled up as I spun around from my double-arm-bar contortion. When I reached the belay, I felt a tingle of disbelief run through me. Though we had several pitches to go, none were as hard as this one. Rating the difficulty of such a pitch is almost impossible. Even after having done it, I would say the most accurate grade would be to call it "once, or maybe twice, in a lifetime." I rated it 5.13b/c, but it could have just as easily been rated 5.14b. Scott Burke, who spent 261 days over a three-year period in an effort to free climb the route in 1998, was quoted as follows in *Climbing:* " 'There are no holds,' he said, claiming difficulties of 5.14b. If his grade holds, the Nose sports one of the hardest free pitches in Yosemite and in America and ranks as the hardest free climb of its size in the world."

Brooke shouted up a stream of congratulations, then he turned serious. "Looks like a storm, we better punch it all the way to the top today."

A dark wall of clouds was rolling in overhead leaving a few raindrops in its wake. Nothing is more miserable than being caught in a rainstorm on El Cap. It takes only minutes for the cliff to become a sheet of water and for hypothermia to set in.

The last pitch before the summit was one of the most exciting pitches I've ever done. With nearly three thousand feet of exposure to the ground on an overhanging wall with 5.12c face climbing at the lip of a bulge, this was a spectacular way to conclude such a monumental climb.

Brooke and I bivouacked on the summit, curled around a campfire next to Mr. Captain: a venerable old juniper tree that was gnarled from centuries of lightning strikes and winter blizzards. The storm passed by and the evening sky was bright with stars and a fulsome moon. We huddled around the fire, relishing its warmth, laughing and reliving the most powerful moments of our climb. I felt a rush of emotion knowing that the combination of both or our dreams and efforts had led us to this historic moment. Though Brooke had climbed all but two sections free, he admitted that he was glad not to have completed the entire route free. He felt that free climbing every pitch would have taken away some of the mystery of this great climb and might have left him with a sense of emptiness about what to do next. But that night as we fell asleep under the bright stars, we both felt a sense of completion—as though everything we had ever done had led us to this summit.

The Sorcerer | Barry Blanchard

Glazed lumps of ice bulged from the log like blown glass; I stabbed my ski poles into the flow of the North Ghost River and fought for balance. Stepping sideways on the lumps proved to be the preferred technique, and I was very much into technique. Falling here would be poor style; it would end a day of ice climbing before it began.

I made the far bank and turned to watch my partner, Carlos. He teetered across, dawn dancing his reflection on the serrated chrome of the river's surface. The North Ghost rushed on. It would run out through the copper foothills of Alberta and merge into the Bow; two damns down the way it would flow through my birthplace, the city of Calgary. I remembered fishing the Bow River as a boy, spinning lures cast from an abandoned bridge abutment, suckers and snags and rarely a rainbow or Rocky Mountain whitefish, with big 1960s sedans rumbling commuters along Memorial Trail on the opposite bank.

Carlos and I edged up the riverbank and walked by fire circles and the stumps of a camp. We tacked up a cut line, not talking much but sweating a lot. At Johnson Lakes we left the cut line and slid onto the ice. Bottom plants were visible through feet of ice clear as glass. I glanced ahead to the forest and, above, to the dominant and defiant walls of limestone one thousand feet high sweeping away and defining my left horizon—the front range of the Rockies. This ice would melt and merge into the North Ghost and Bow, eventually flow through my childhood; I thought about how my life had largely been a migration upriver, away from the city, into this land.

|||

At the edge of the second lake we entered the forest.

|||

The tart smell of pine, shade that made the overcast day darker, rigid dead branches that clawed at my suit like bone fragments and sounded like a wire brush dragging over a grocery bag. The drumming of our climbing boots on frozen moss and horseshit. There are wild horses here. Humans are animals—we walk the easiest line just like other animals. I followed the horseshit.

After an hour we passed the Sorcerer, a six-hundred-foot waterfall that I'd climbed several times because it is beautiful. An hour later we entered the south fork of Johnson Creek, and a valley that I was to later describe in a radio interview as the place that I would choose to sit and read my favorite book: *The Old Man and the Sea*.

The valley is an integration of forest, limestone, and water that I haven't words to describe . . . I'd use grace if I was pushed. Undisturbed land, beauty and perfection beyond my ability to understand but not beyond my ability to feel: my heart rate stepped up, colors intensified, sounds became crisper, the wind tickled my flesh, and I could smell a storm in the air. A way of being, so long neglected, that I don't know its name. I'll call it losing the subject/object split, becoming part of the land, letting the land, Alberta and the West, define me . . . possibly more than I'll ever know.

|||

Four rope lengths of polished silver ice clung to the sheer limestone at the head of the valley, Hydrophobia, the waterfall that Carlos and I had come to climb. Our "reason" for being there. I wondered if I would ever evolve beyond my need for a "reason."

Diffuse light enhanced the ice with a silver glow. Holding my weight on my ice axes, I kicked hard at an ice pillar. The crampon bounced, then skated crazily across the vertical ice—the binding had broken. I swore and thrashed myself into a position to place an ice screw. Hanging from the screw, I jury-rigged the crampon with a compression strap, enough to finish the lead. Carlos would have to lead the rest of the climb.

The squall came fast. A turbine of snow and screaming wind that fell over the front range in an explosive wave. Shards of snow drove head-long into my eyes, forcing tears, blinding me. Ice welded my eyelashes shut and glazed my exposed brow, froze the front of my brain until my temples throbbed. A strong gust slapped us tight to the anchor. I screamed to Carlos for retreat. He shouted that he wanted to "do" the last pitch. We cowered, I shivered, the squall let up a bit. I clenched my eyes hard to melt the ice. Carlos started up. I paid out rope and fought for warmth, squeezed my body into a fist, tried to be as strong as the storm. I suffered.

| | |

The storm passed and warmth returned as I seconded. Carlos looked like an alpinist, snow clinging to every fold, ice growing in clumps from his whiskers. We congratulated ourselves, rappelled back to the south fork of Johnson Creek, and started walking.

Standing waves of snow encased the bottoms of large limestone boulders; farther down the gray skeletons of trees reached through the frozen river of snow. Thousand-foot limestone walls opened to the living forest. Silently, I thanked the valley, then crossed the threshold back into the forest; fresh snow clung to all of the trees. Four hours later, by headlamp, we were back at the car.

A Near View of the High Sierra | John Muir

Mount Ritter is king of the mountains of the middle portion of the High Sierra, as Shasta of the north and Whitney of the south sections. Moreover, as far as I know, it had never been climbed. I had explored the adjacent wilderness summer after summer, but my studies thus far had never drawn me to the top of it. Its height above sea-level is about 13,300 feet, and it is fenced round by steeply inclined glaciers, and cañons of tremendous depth and ruggedness, which render it almost inaccessible. But difficulties of this kind only exhilarate the mountaineer.

|||

My general plan was simply this: to scale the cañon wall, cross over to the eastern flank of the range, and then make my way southward to the northern spurs of Mount Ritter in compliance with the intervening topography; for to push on directly southward from camp through the innumerable peaks and pinnacles that adorn this portion of the axis of the range, however interesting, would take too much time, besides being extremely difficult and dangerous at this time of year.

All my first day was pure pleasure; simply mountaineering indulgence, crossing the dry pathways of ancient glaciers, tracing happy streams, and learning the habits of the birds and marmots in the groves and rocks. Before I had gone a mile from camp, I came to the foot of a white cascade that beats its way down a rugged gorge in the cañon wall, from a height of about nine hundred feet, and pours its throbbing waters into the Tuolumne. I was acquainted with its fountains, which, fortunately, lay in my course. What a fine traveling companion it proved to be, what songs it sang, and how passionately it told the mountain's own joy! Gladly I climbed along its dashing border, absorbing its divine music, and bathing from time to time in waftings of irised spray. Climbing higher, higher, new beauty came streaming on the sight: painted meadows, late-blooming gardens, peaks of rare architecture, lakes here and there, shining like silver, and glimpses of the forested middle region and the yellow lowlands far in the west. Beyond the range I saw the so-called Mono Desert, lying dreamily silent in thick purple light—a desert of heavy sun-glare beheld from a desert of ice-burnished granite. Here the waters divide, shouting in glorious enthusiasm, and falling eastward to vanish in the volcanic sands and dry sky of the Great Basin, or westward to the Great Valley of California, and thence through the Bay of San Francisco and the Golden Gate to the sea.

Passing a little way down over the summit until I had reached an elevation of about ten thousand feet, I pushed on southward toward a group of savage peaks that stand guard about Ritter on the north and west, groping my way, and dealing instinctively with every obstacle as it presented itself. Here a huge gorge would be found cutting across my path, along the dizzy edge of which I scrambled until some less precipitous point was discovered where I might safely venture to the bottom and then, selecting some feasible portion of the opposite wall, reascend with the same slow caution. Massive, flat-topped spurs alternate with the gorges, plunging abruptly from the shoulders of the snowy peaks, and planting their feet in the warm desert. These were everywhere marked and adorned with characteristic sculptures of the ancient glaciers that swept over this entire region like one vast ice wind, and the polished surfaces produced by the ponderous flood are still so perfectly preserved that in many places the sunlight reflected from them is about as trying to the eyes as sheets of snow.

|||

Now came the solemn, silent evening. Long, blue, spiky shadows crept out across the snowfields, while a rosy glow, at first scarce discernible, gradually deepened and suffused every mountain-top, flushing the glaciers and the harsh crags above them. This was the alpenglow, to me one of the most impressive of all the terrestrial manifestations of God. At the touch of this divine light, the mountains seemed to kindle to a rapt, religious consciousness, and stood hushed and waiting like devout worshippers. Just before the alpenglow began to fade, two crimson clouds came streaming across the summit like wings of flame, rendering the sublime scene yet more impressive; then came darkness and the stars.

Icy Ritter was still miles away, but I could proceed no farther that night. I found a good camp-ground on the rim of a glacier basin about eleven thousand feet above the sea. A small lake nestles in the bottom of it, from which I got water for my tea, and a storm-beaten thicket near by furnished abundance of resiny firewood. Somber peaks, hacked and shattered, circled halfway around the horizon, wearing a savage aspect in the gloaming, and a waterfall chanted solemnly across the lake on its way down from the foot of the glacier. The fall and the lake and the glacier were almost equally bare; while the scraggy pines anchored in the rock-fissures were so dwarfed and shorn by the storm-winds that you might walk over their tops. In tone and aspect the scene was one of the most desolate place I ever beheld. But the darkest scriptures of the mountains are illumined with bright passages of love that never fail to make themselves felt when one is alone.

I made my bed in a nook of the pine thicket, where the branches were pressed and crinkled overhead like a roof, and bent down around the sides. These are the best bedchambers the high mountains afford—snug as squirrel nests, well-ventilated, full of spicy odors, and with plenty of wind-played needles to sing one asleep. I little expected company, but, creeping in through a low side door, I found five or six birds nestling among the tassels. The night wind began to blow soon after dark; at first only a gentle breathing, but increasing toward midnight to a rough gale that fell upon my leafy roof in ragged surges like a cascade, bearing wild sounds from crags overhead. The waterfall sang in chorus filling the old ice fountain with its solemn roar, and seeming to increase in power as the night advanced--fit voice for such a landscape. I had to creep out many times to the fire during the night, for it was biting cold and I had no blankets. Gladly I welcomed the morning star.

The dawn in the dry, wavering air of the desert was glorious. Everything encouraged my undertaking and betokened success. There was no cloud in the sky, no storm tone in the wind. Breakfast of bread and tea was soon made. I fastened a hard, durable crust to my belt by way of provision, in case I should be compelled to pass a night on the mountaintop; then, securing the remainder of my little stock against wolves and wood rats, I set forth free and hopeful.

III

All along my course thus far, excepting when down in the cañons, the landscapes were mostly open to me, and expansive, at least on one side. On the left were the purple plains of Mono, reposing dreamily and warm; on the right, the near peaks springing keenly into the thin sky with more and more impressive sublimity. But these larger views were at length lost. Rugged spurs, and moraines, and huge, projecting buttresses began to shut me in. Every feature became more rigidly alpine, without, however producing any chilling effect; for going to the mountains is like going home. We always find that the strangest objects in these fountain wilds are in some degree familiar, and we look upon them with a vague sense of having seen them before.

On the southern shore of a frozen lake, I encountered an extensive field of hard, granular snow, up which I scampered in fine tone, intending to follow it to its head, and cross the rocky spur against which it leans, hoping thus to come direct upon the base of the main Ritter peak. The surface was pitted with oval hollows, made by stones and drifted pine needles that had melted themselves into the mass by the radiation of absorbed sun-heat. These afforded good footholds, but the surface curved more and more steeply at the head, and the pits became shallower and less abundant, until I found myself in danger of being shed off like avalanching snow. I persisted, however, creeping on all fours, and shuffling up the smoothest places on my back, as I had often done on burnished granite, until, after slipping several times, I was compelled to retrace my course to the bottom, and made my way around the west end of the lake, and thence up to the summit of the divide between the head waters of Rush Creek and the northwest tributaries of the San Joaquin.

Arriving on the summit of this dividing crest, one of the most exciting pieces of pure wilderness was disclosed that I ever discovered in all my mountaineering. There, immediately in front, loomed the majestic mass of Mount Ritter, with a glacier swooping down its face nearly to my feet, then curving westward and pouring its frozen flood into a dark blue lake, whose shores were bound with precipices of crystalline snow; while a deep chasm drawn between the divide and the glacier separated the massive picture from everything else. I could see only the one sublime mountain, the one glacier, the one lake; the whole veiled with one blue shadow — rock, ice, and water close together, without a single leaf or sign of life. After gazing spellbound, I began instinctively to scrutinize every notch and gorge and weathered buttress of the mountain, with reference to making the ascent. The entire front above the glacier appeared as one tremendous precipice, slightly receding at the top, and bristling with spires and pinnacles set above one another in formidable array. Massive lichen-stained battlements stood forward here and there, hacked at the top with angular notches, and separated by frosty gullies and recesses that have been veiled in shadow ever since their creation; while to right and left, as far as I could see, were huge, crumbling buttresses, offering no hope to the climber. The head of the glacier sends up few finger-like branches through narrow *couloirs;* but these seemed too steep and short to be available, especially as I had no axe with which to cut steps, and the numerous narrow-throated gullies down which stones and snow are avalanched seemed hopelessly steep, besides being interrupted by vertical cliffs; while the whole front was rendered still more terribly forbidding by the chill shadow and the gloomy blackness of the rocks.

Descending the divide in a hesitating mood, I picked my way across the yawning chasm at the foot, and climbed out upon the glacier. There were no meadows now to cheer with their brace colors, nor could I hear the dun-headed sparrows, whose cheery notes so often relieve the silence of our highest mountains. The only sounds were the gurgling of small rills down in the veins and crevasses of the glacier, and now and then the rattling report of falling stones, with the echoes they shot out into the crisp air.

I could not distinctly hope to reach the summit from the side, yet I moved across the glacier as if driven by fate. Contending with myself, the season is too far spent, I said, and even should I be successful, I might be stormbound on the mountain; and in the cloud darkness, with the cliffs and crevasses covered with snow, how could I escape? No; I must wait till next summer. I would only approach the mountain now, and inspect it, creep about its flanks, learn what I could of its history, holding myself to flee on the approach of the first storm cloud. But we little know until tried how much of the uncontrollable there is in us, urging over glaciers and torrents, and up perilous heights, let the judgment forbid as it may.

I succeeded in gaining the foot of the cliff on the eastern extremity of the glacier, and there discovered the mouth of a narrow avalanche gully, through which I began to climb, intending to follow it as far as possible, and at least obtain some fine wild views for my pains. Its general course is oblique to the plane of the mountain-face, and the metamorphic slates of which the mountain is built are cut by cleavage planes in such a way that they weather off in angular blocks, giving rise to irregular steps that greatly facilitate climbing on the sheer places. I thus made my way into a wilderness of crumbling spires and battlements, built together in bewildering combinations, and glazed in many places with a thin coating of ice, which I had to hammer off with stones. The situation was becoming gradually more perilous; but, having passed several dangerous spots, I dared not think of descending; for, so steep was the entire ascent, one would inevitably fall to the glacier in case a single misstep were made. Knowing, therefore, the tried danger beneath, I became all the more anxious concerning the developments to be made above, and began to be conscious of a vague foreboding of what actually befell; not that I was given to fear, but rather because my instincts, usually so positive and true, seemed vitiated in some way, and were leading me astray. At length, after attaining an elevation of about 12,800 feet, I found myself at the foot of a sheer drop in the bed of the avalanche channel I was tracing, which seemed absolutely to bar further progress. It was only about forty-five or fifty feet high, and somewhat roughened by fissures and projections; but these seemed so slight and insecure, as footholds, that I tried hard to avoid the precipice altogether, by scaling the wall of the channel on either side. But, though less steep, the walls were smoother than the obstructing rock, and repeated efforts only showed that I must either go right ahead or turn back. The tried dangers beneath seemed even greater than that of the cliff in front; therefore, after scanning its face again and again, I began to scale it, picking my holds with intense caution. After gaining a point about halfway to the top, I was suddenly brought to a dead stop, with arms outspread, clinging close to the face of the rock, unable to move hand or foot either up or down. My doom appeared fixed. I *must* fall. There would be a moment of bewilderment, and then a lifeless rumble down the one general precipice to the glacier below.

When this final danger flashed upon me, I became nerve-shaken for the first time since setting foot on the mountains, and my mind seemed to fill with stifling smoke. But this terrible eclipse lasted only a moment, when life blazed forth again with preternatural clearness. I seemed suddenly to become possessed of a new sense. The other self, bygone experiences, Instinct, or Guardian Angel—call it what you will,—came forward and assumed control. Then my trembling muscles became firm again, every rift and flaw in the rock was seen as through a microscope, and my limbs moved with a positiveness and precision with which I seemed to have nothing at all to do. Had I been borne aloft upon wings, my deliverance could not have been more complete.

Above this memorable spot, the face of the mountain is still more savagely hacked and torn. It is a maze of yawning chasms and gullies, in the angles of which rise beetling crags and piles of detached boulders that seem to have been gotten ready to be launched below. But the strange influx of strength I had received seemed inexhaustible. I found a way without effort, and soon stood upon the top-most crag in the blessed light.

How truly glorious the landscape circled around this noble summit! —giant mountains, valleys innumerable, glaciers and meadows, rivers and lakes, with the wide blue sky bent tenderly over them all. But in my first hour of freedom from that terrible shadow, the sunlight in which I was laving seemed all in all.

III

Could we have been here to observe during the glacial period, we should have overlooked a wrinkled ocean of ice as continuous as that now covering the landscapes of Greenland; filling every valley and cañon with only the tops of the fountain peaks rising darkly above the rock-encumbered ice waves like islets in a stormy sea—those islets the only hints of the glorious landscapes now smiling in the sun. Standing here in the deep, brooding silence all the wilderness seems motionless, as if the work of creation were done. But in the midst of this outer steadfastness we know there is incessant motion and change. Ever and anon, avalanches are falling from yonder peaks. These cliff-bound glaciers, seemingly wedged and immovable, are flowing like water and grinding the rocks beneath them. The lakes are lapping their granite shores and wearing them away, and every one of these rills and young rivers is fretting the air into music, and carrying the mountains to the plains. Here are the roots of all the life of the valleys, and here more simply than elsewhere is the eternal flux of Nature manifested. Ice changing to water, lakes to meadows, and mountains to plains. And while we thus contemplate Nature's methods of landscape creation, and, reading the records she has carved on the rocks, reconstruct, however imperfectly, the landscapes of the past, we also learn that as these we now behold have succeeded those of the pre-glacial age, so they in turn are withering and vanishing to be succeeded by others yet unborn.

But in the midst of these fine lessons and landscapes, I had to remember that the sun was wheeling far to west, while a new way down the mountain had to be discovered to some point on the timber line where I could have a fire; for I had not even burdened myself with a coat. I first scanned the western spurs, hoping some way might appear through which I might reach the northern glacier, and cross its snout, or pass around the lake into which it flows, and thus strike my morning track. This route was soon efficiently unfolded to show that, if it were practicable at all, it would require so much time that reaching camp that night would be out of the question. I therefore scrambled back eastward, and descended the southern slopes obliquely at the same time. Here the crags seemed less formidable, and the head of a glacier that flows northeast came in sight, which I determined to follow as far as possible, hoping thus to make my way to the foot of the peak on the east side, and thence across the intervening cañons and ridges to camp.

The inclination of the glacier is quite moderate at the head, and, as the sun had softened the *névé*, I made safe and rapid progress, running and sliding, and keeping up a sharp outlook for crevasses. About half a mile from the head, there is an ice cascade, where the glacier pours over a sharp declivity and is shattered into massive blocks separated by deep, blue fissures. To thread my way through the slippery mazes of this crevassed portion seemed impossible, and I endeavored to avoid it by climbing off to the shoulder of the mountain. But the slopes steepened and at length fell away in sheer precipices, compelling a return to the ice. Fortunately, the day had been warm enough to loosen the ice crystals so as to admit of hollows being dug in the rotten portions of the blocks, thus enabling me to pick my way with far less difficulty than I had anticipated. Continuing down over the snout, and along the left lateral moraine, was only a confident saunter, showing that the ascent of the mountain by way of this glacier is easy, provided one is armed with an axe to cut steps here and there.

The lower end of the glacier was beautifully waved and barred by the outcropping edges of the bedded ice layers which represent the annual snowfalls, and to some extent the irregularities of structure caused by the weathering of the walls of crevasses, and by separate snowfalls which have been followed by rain, hail, thawing and freezing, etc. Small rills were gliding and swirling over the melting surface with a smooth, oily appearance, in channels of pure ice—their quick, compliant movements contrasting most impressively with the rigid, invisible flow of the glacier itself, on whose back they all were riding.

Night drew near before I reached the eastern base of the mountain, and my camp lay many a rugged mile to the north; but ultimate success was assured. It was now only a matter of endurance and ordinary mountain-craft. The sunset was, if possible, yet more beautiful than the day before. The Mono landscape seemed to be fairly saturated with warm, purple light. The peaks marshaled along the summit were in shadow, but through every notch and pass streamed vivid sunfire, soothing and irradiating their rough, black angles, while companies of small, luminous clouds hovered above them like very angels of light.

Darkness came on, but I found my way by the trends of the cañons and the peaks projected against the sky. All excitement died with the light, and then I was weary. But the joyful sound of the waterfall across the lake was heard at last, and soon the stars were seen reflected in the lake itself. Taking my bearings from these, I discovered the little pine thicket in which my nest was, and then I had a rest such as only a tired mountaineer may enjoy. After lying loose and lost for a while, I made a sunrise fire, went down to the lake, dashed water on my head, and dipped a cupful for tea. The revival brought about by bread and tea was as complete as the exhaustion from excessive enjoyment and toil. Then I crept beneath the pine tassels to bed. The wind was frosty and the fire burned low, but my sleep was none the less sound, and the evening constellations had swept far to the west before I awoke.

House of Wind | Steph Davis

The wind is thundering above. From the shelter of the langa trees I hear it whirling and leaping out on the glacier. There's no hope of good weather tomorrow. We could just as well stay at base camp.

"Stay," say the Italians, "tonight we make pizza!"

"Stay," say the French, "tonight we are making fondue!"

But if I prowl around Campo Bridwell for one more day, I may kill someone. Maybe Dean. Better to forge across the glacier in a headwind and arrive soaked and exhausted at high camp so we can sit in a smaller tent, eat less interesting food, and feel productive as we accomplish nothing.

|||

We slide down almost vertical scree and baked dirt to the moraine. Pack straps and pigtails whip my face as we wind up and around crevasses. It's been almost an hour since we left Bridwell.

The wind races about maniacally as we crest the final rise. I step cramponless onto bare ice, and a two-directional gust hurls me down, then spins away faster than I can refill my lungs.

Shakily, I rise. Dean and I look at each other wide-eyed and dart for the nearest flat spot on the ice, dropping to our knees just as the wind rushes in again. It pummels us thoroughly and then spirals off, allowing us to scuttle a little farther before it wheels back and dives in harder.

Caught, I freeze like a deer in headlights and drive my ski poles down, bracing desperately until I can flatten. Again, the wind twists away. Again, I bolt across uneven ice in its ebb until I hear the whir of approaching jet engines and, gun-shy, fling myself down.

But this time the wind leaps high without touching us, leaving me to stagger up foolishly from under my pack. And then, capriciously and with an impressive backhand, it pivots and slams me flat.

Forward progress has lost its meaning. It is simply a thing I do. There is no end. There is no goal. There is only dogged, fitful motion. The wind consumes all time and speech, breathes them in and out like harmonica chords.

I think of pilgrims prostrating themselves with each step toward Mecca. A truly incomprehensible form of worship, I've always thought . . . and yet, here I am.

America in Spain | Terry Gifford

In God's wilderness lies the hope of the world, the great fresh, unblighted,
unredeemed wilderness.
—JOHN MUIR

It's a bit of a museum piece really, and will become more so when the oil
runs out. It's a climb from the era of Before Climate Change (BCC). But it
also provides a snapshot of the way ACC Spain is trying to educate visitors
to its national parks a hundred years after John Muir gave America the
idea that nerve-torn city folk will forever need a place to reconnect with
nature. As we begin the period of new awareness that will come to be
called After Climate Change (ACC), we can see that the problem was that
whatever was gained in recreation was lost on return to the industrial
exploitation of resources back in the cities. When the rocks and water
and woods of weekend recreation still became the weekday resources for
"growth" over the last hundred years in America and Europe, our species
was locked into the heady intensity of self-destruction that, perhaps too
late, we recognize as climate change. And climbing is part of it, as I realized when we went to find the rock climbed called America in the Sierra
Espuña National Park in the south of Spain's Costa Blanca, west of the
industrial town of Murcia.

It's a museum piece because this climb is the first to be described in
the first guidebook for our oil-fuelled winter flights to the Costa Blanca
from the long dark UK gray of Sheffield at New Year. That guidebook, in
German and English, was simply titled *Sun Rock*. Rock lovers also being

sun lovers, as well as cheap wine lovers and tapas lovers, for a week over New Year we simply became lovers in Spain. Bolts induced a sense of safety, although long trade routes in wonderful positions were available, shorts were worn whenever slightly possible, and helmets were left at home (the death rate remains high over Christmas and New Year). It was an international atmosphere at the crag, and you often met again climbers you'd first met on a remote Scottish crag during the previous Whit weekend at the end of May. Now the influx from the darker corners of Europe is not confined to a two-week period; there are more guides on offer, more cheap apartments, more queues for climbs, plus websites for the latest tips and info, but the ambience and the delights remain much the same. In many ways the America climb exhibits all the signs of being created just before the beginning of that *Sun Rock* era.

Yet it also reveals the signs of Spain's attempts to catch up with the example of John Muir's inspiration in America. A discrete little parking area in the woods has a signpost pointing up a forest track closed to cars. Since the publication of *Sun Rock,* the long walk in is now being enforced, although local farmers who have mountain almond terraces can disturb the silence of the dappled light in the woods. (I decline to make a cheap joke here about America's inability to ban cars from Muir's temple, Yosemite Valley.) When my wife Gill and I went up that track in search of America, all around us were snapped trees and broken branches from the last storm winds to strike the woods. We came to a new interpretive board telling us that in this Barranco de Leyva we could now expect to see the returned golden eagle and the peregrine flying among the choughs we could hear calling from the crag above the trees. The board also mentioned the archaeological treasures hidden in the Barranco—an ice well (*nevera*), a castle, and an ancient donkey trail built by the Moors through the crags high across the shaded south side of the valley, at the head of which is an old climbers' *refugio* recently restored. As we walked up the broad forest track, we noticed, at each side, the recent diggings of wild boar at the roots of their favorite rhubarb plants.

"Let's hang a bag on a tree around here," I suggested, "with juice and food for later. I think the descent must be down that gully that curves down through the crag up there."

"I hope we can remember which one," called Gill, as I scrambled up through the fallen branches to find a suitably hidden small tree.

Farther up the road, at a big boulder on the right, a little cairn marked the start of the ascent up scree that was strewn with wood. Soon we saw the paler scar of the chipped word "America" that betrayed an earlier age of Spanish climbing. Nowadays they tend to paint names at the foot of climbs. We sat and emptied the rucksack.

A cool wind was sweeping down the Barranco toward the sea. Gill noticed something odd about my apparent delay.

"It's not like you *not* to be rushing to get your harness on," she observed.

"I want to see what the weather's going to do before we launch our-selves on a five-pitch route." I sat back in the intermittent sun looking at the sky at the head of the Barranco. "I don't like the look of those big black clouds coming over the back of this mountain."

Reading the weather in this part of Spain is an art based more on experience and intuition than reason. It's one of the ways John Muir knew that humans would have to reconnect with the dynamics of nature by being in the mountains. The poet Keats had a notion of the state that climbers have to attain in order to read mountain weather, as well as the rock itself: "capable of being in uncertainties, mysteries, doubts, without any irritable reaching after fact and reason." In Wales, the previous week-end, in the high cwm holding the slabs of Carnedd y Filiast, I'd looked down from the stances of Left Edge and felt a growing desire to do some-thing for a place like that, charged by its mysterious power. I am still in a state of uncertainty about whether the best thing to do might be not to go there at all, to leave totally undisturbed the orchids and the newly returned spring ring ouzel that seemed to have called up a mate during the day we all shared that magical place together. The previous weekend, climbing in the Lake District up the long valley of Longsleddale, we'd completely failed to reconnect with the natural signs. To my surprise and horror, I pulled up on a platform on the arête of Dandle Buttress to find my eyes level with a jumble of twigs in the center of which were four blue speckled eggs. The pair of ravens flying around us and perching on rocks opposite had been silent, and I'd misread their unusual restraint. When we returned to the stile below the crag we found the written message we'd missed at its foot: "There is a climbing restriction on this crag for Ravens. 1 March—31 May. To be reviewed. National Park Authority and BMC."

Still in a state of uncertainty, I tied on, turned toward the gray slab, and began a reading of the rock of America. Sharp edges for my fingers gave me confidence for the friction moves across the top of the slab, before a steep step in a corner gave way to a ramp of vegetation hiding rock holds. On a grassy ledge I belayed below two linked holes fronted by a vertical bar of rock—a perfectly created thread belay.

"You know," panted Gill as she neared the belay, "when white girls thought brown skin was beautiful? Climbing girls who were tan-seekers would hate climbing through this sharp stuff." Gill was acutely aware in Spain that we were in the new era of ACC.

"I think the next pitch traverses across to that diagonal crackline," I suggested.

Delicately at first and then with more vigorous use of high side pulls, I worked my way crablike up toward the edge of the buttress. Profiled on the skyline, I looked up for a while and then shouted back to Gill.

"There's been a lot of rockfall up there where the old line used to go. Every other block has come away. It looks loose. I'm going across to a bush, and I'll bring you up."

The lack of rain combined with the temperature variations of ACC have altered a lot of traditional climbs here. Many old classics in Spain are now quite dangerous.

To get to the bush I gingerly crossed a bowl of thorny vegetation covered in loose stones fallen, with the odd sun-blanched twig, from above. Even our latest developments in helmet technology could still be dented by a sharp stone falling a long way. At the bush, as I waited for Gill to follow, I noticed a faded line sling lying in the spiky vegetation, telling an old story.

What looked a mere scramble up steps of rock above became a battle with spikes and bushes that hid every crucial hold. The moves were often harder than they looked from below. I found myself experimenting with the thinnest of line threads more than once, when I could not find rock that offered cracks to take nuts. Lying in some prickly stuff, I came across an ancient channel peg, perhaps dropped by the first ascensionists. At the end of a full sixty meters of rope I came to a sloping shelf under a tree. Above it a fistwide corner crack rose with stacked bulging blocks on its left.

Gill came up sweating and annoyed.

"I'm spiked to death!" she shouted. "Never mind the tan-seekers, I could do with a complete covering that had thorn-proofing!"

"This must be the crux," I said to calm her down. "I'll go up and then haul the sack."

Standing on the first block and feeling the crystalline grip of the bottom of the crack, I saw that this was committing.

"It's certainly intimidating," I said openly, as the psychological trainers these days advise. "But," I reminded myself, "it's only a *Sun Rock* grade four."

I reached up left, found a sharp edge and pedaled up, reached with my right hand to jam a big Friend into the crack. Above it my fist bit. One more long reach and I was standing on a block under the next bulge. After the briefest of breathers I reached left again. The hold was less positive this time, but I'd no time to search further. Leaning back on my painful fist jam, I memorized the small foot-ledges, and, with a sense that I ought to break out left at the top, I reached for the poor hold again and heaved myself upward. With one hand over the top I leaned back, trying to get my left foot up to the rounded edge of a block. It rested only on the lower part of it, but I had to keep going. My foot stayed in place. I pulled onto the top of a tower and tied to a big flake that seemed to be firm.

Gill did not find this pitch easy, but after a long pause one move below the top, she moved up, reached right to unclip the rope from the last runner, and arrived beside me. She leaned into me, panting.

"A *Sun Rock* grade four?" she questioned.

I checked our photocopy of the historic document.

"That pitch was a four. But you're right. It really ought to be a five." I pointed upward.

"There's one long easy pitch left. Why don't you top out?"

Gill grabbed the rack and raced off. Just behind the tower were two marks where the holes from the old two-bolt belay had been filled in. Delighting in slabs and cracks, she made her way toward twin cracks that ended, finally, at the top. Suddenly Gill heard the electric cry of the choughs, saw the blue of wild iris in the limestone pavement, and smelled the rosemary she had crushed underfoot. Far beyond there were summits hidden by heavy clouds. So far our reading of the sky had been good enough.

When I arrived, I consulted the *Sun Rock* text again.

"It says here that the descent is to the west."

"But that gully we saw is to the east," said Gill.

"Yes, that's odd. The book's crag diagram shows it to the east, too. But the text definitely says west."

I had just finished coiling the rope when Gill was suddenly shouting at two figures who had also topped out farther along the crag to the east.

"Hola!" she called with a wave.

"Hola!" they called back.

"We don't want to be caught here in an electrical storm," I said, glancing up at the boiling clouds. "We must find this gully to the west."

And I set off, jumping the cracks in the limestone as Gill followed behind.

We were stopped by shouts behind us. The gestures of the other climbers indicated that the descent was to the east, in their direction. So we walked over to the couple who were also ready to find the descent.

The man and woman were both Spanish engineers. Their climb had been a much harder grade than ours, farther right where long clean lines offer transparent quality on this mile-long cliff. The descent gully was, indeed, the obvious one I'd identified from below, and it curved around the base of the cliff toward our stash of sustenance.

We wanted to return to trace the Moorish trails to the castle and find the deep-lined shaft made for turning winter snows into summer ice. But this, we knew, would be dependent on the cheap flights from the UK that were contributing to our ACC problems, not solving them. For all our awareness of ACC, we were still locked into the mindset of BCC nineteenth-century America. The doublethink of Muir's time persists in us. We still cannot take learning from recreation into approaches to resources. Climbing, as much as it briefly reconnects us personally with nature, is still environmental escapism. When, we have to ask ourselves, do we stop coming here to climb sun rock? When, perhaps, ought we get around to asking ourselves, Do we visit only crags we can reach by bicycle from home? In contact with wilderness "lies the hope of the world." Was Muir wrong? Do we have to say that he was actually far too optimistic, as we persist in running away from our own ultimate and necessary environmental redemption?

Untethered in Yosemite | David Stevenson

I do not expect in this lifetime to be bored by Yosemite Valley. Or ever to tire of driving eastward through the Wawona Tunnel. That first glimpse of El Cap from the car window has never failed to lift my spirits, to give me an almost visceral thrill, to humble me. That is why, I suppose, I so admire those who never leave. I don't believe they stay because they have no other options, no sense of the larger world outside the Valley, nothing else to which they are so well suited. Though all these may also be true, I believe they are secondary to the certain knowledge that for them Yosemite is unmatched. "This is the place," they say in effect, as Brigham Young is to have said at the physical end of a spiritual journey.

Perhaps for its indigenous peoples Yosemite was an Eden, but we can't know exactly what they thought—Eden being a Western concept and the record of mid-nineteenth-century Miwok secondhand and sketchy, at best. In the first writing about the Valley, *Discovery of Yosemite, and the Indian War of 1851, Which Led to That Event,* Lafayette Bunnell describes almost simultaneously the holy beauty of the place and the vanquishing of the first peoples who lived there. This historical moment is like Renato Rosaldo's "imperialist nostalgia": "the phenomena of mourning what one has destroyed."

I spent the summer of 1999 on the eastside of the Sierra, in the small mountain town of Lee Vining just down from Tioga Pass, the east entrance to Yosemite National Park. In describing the place to those with no concept of where it might be, I always say, "just east of Yosemite" the way I might have said "Detroit" years ago when asked where I was from, when in truth it was suburbs west of the city. After this summer they will say: "Yosemite, hey! Where that woman got her head chopped off?" Yeah, I admit. It happened about thirty miles away as the crow flies, but I think by the time I heard about it they had caught the guy. I felt bad for the victim, of course, but I also felt that a sacred space, a spiritual refuge, had been violated. I learned in tenth grade biology class that too many rats in the terrarium lead to aberrant behavior, or as the Yosemite National Park literature warns us: the Valley receives four million visitors per year, most concentrated in the two or so square miles of the valley floor, despite that the park itself occupies 1,200 square miles of largely undeveloped landscape.

In *Savage Dreams*, Rebecca Solnit reexamines the etymology of the name "Yosemite," finding that it means probably not "grizzly," as long thought, but "some among them are killers." Ironically, it was the white settlers who named the place with a Miwok word, despite that it was also they, the white men, who were the killers. The Miwok were expelled from their valley homeland of nearly a millennia by the Mariposa Battalion, Bunnell, the aforementioned writer, among them. Chief Tenaya, who saw his son brutally murdered by the whites, prophesied and threatened: "Yes, sir, American, my spirit will make trouble for you and your people, as you have caused trouble for me and my people." And, indeed there are some killers in the Valley today. I've always thought stupidity, gravity, and bad judgment to be the top three, but I suppose we can now add psycho-killer to the list.

|||

Early in June I'm climbing up the southeast slope, the easy route, of Mount Morrison. Morrison is on the eastside of the Sierra, east and south of Yosemite, just off highway 395. I'm alone. It is, after all, the easy route. A few miles in and I can feel a blister forming on my heel, probably a large one.

I sit on a rock looking up into the basin below Mount McAddie, a wild unvisited place just a few miles from the highway. My foot will be wrecked if I continue; I'm still at the beginning of a long day, yet I don't seriously consider turning back.

I just want to be *up there*. That choice to continue seems significant somehow, or maybe significant that it didn't even come to being a choice. And for a while, the rest of the day, I feel *untethered*.

The climb is not quite so easy as I thought it would be, completely covered in snow and steep in parts. But it's also shorter than I had imagined, and soon I'm up there with the whole glorious panorama of the Sierra to myself. I can see north past Mono Lake toward Reno, east across Nevada, south to dozens and dozens of giant Sierran peaks whose individuality is subsumed by a sense of totality: granite, snow, and blue sky forever and ever. I feel giddy; as Emerson had it: "glad to the brink of fear." I take a lot of photographs, knowing as I snap them off they will bore anyone but me. I write mushy sentimental stuff in the summit register, words I would surely disown at sea level. And I return, thinking of those who choose to stay untethered, not for an afternoon, or a weekend or a summer, but past the point of no return. Out there, up there.

|||

In Yosemite Valley at the base of Nutcracker: the line or the *queue* as the Aussie kid would have it. He and his partner Tom are just ahead of us. Ahead of them are two Japanese couples and three guys just starting up — nine in all; if solitude and wilderness are inextricably linked in our minds, this day will offer neither. Nutcracker is a moderate Yosemite classic with historic significance; Royal Robbins put the route up in the sixties without using any pitons — a revolutionary act at the time. The line of climbers is expected. Tom has taken off his shirt and spread out his gear on it, immune apparently to the mosquitoes. In two previous "attempts" on Nutcracker I've given in to heat and fear in varying proportions. This day the weather is perfect, the hour not too late. We will wait.

Then the leader of the three-person team backs off, is lowered down the wall. His friend goes up only to take a thirty-foot fall that miraculously leaves him much bloodied and shaken, but otherwise unhurt. For a while this does not deter them and they plan to re-attack, but soon good judgment prevails and the bleeding man goes for medical help. They ask would we please retrieve their gear, left at their high point. Of course. Four of the others start up a variation, and suddenly it's our turn. It has been agreed, but not in spoken language, that my partner, Jim, will be taking the hard leads. I believe this intuitive mutual knowledge is based on the fact that I now live in the Midwest, that my children are young, my waistline expanding — the usual excuses. This day marks twenty years since the first time Jim and I roped up together.

The climb is as advertised, a classic; the weather a dream. Even the other people, the waiting, are not factors that interfere with our pleasure. The crux moves are hard, as advertised, but soon we are on the summit — having overcome a surprising stretch of unprotected terrain near the top. The summit block, too, is a dream with its spectacular views of the Cathedral group to the west and Half Dome looming above us to the east. Despite the day's share of four million visitors driving through the Valley, soon to be standing in lines for cabin reservations, ice cream cones, and T-shirts exhorting "Go Climb a Rock," and despite the numbers of climbers on the route, we have the summit all to ourselves. You can walk off this one more or less hassle-free, and, all in all, we got what we wanted out of the day, though it's hard always to say exactly what that is.

|||

As a Forest Service employee on the eastside, I have access to the Yosemite National Park public news bulletins that are faxed to us daily. I should add here an important difference between national parks and national forests; parks are operated basically like museums: they are, in effect, *preserved;* forests are operated more like a business with a "multiple use" mandate. Recreation is one of the uses for the forest, but not the one that pays the bills: mining, grazing, and logging rights on national forest lands are sources of millions of dollars of income for the federal government. The budget for operating the Forest Service, however, is doled out by Congress and seems to bear no logical, much less financial, connection to the monies that the Forest Service takes in.

The first Yosemite news bulletin that catches my eye this summer is about the BASEjumper who landed safely after leaping off El Cap, ran from waiting, tipped-off rangers, thumbed his nose at them, and leapt into the raging Merced River. BASE stands for Buildings, Antennae, Spans, and Earth, the fixed objects from which these skydivers leap. Robbie Slater, before he was killed descending from the summit of K2, had done the exact same thing, from the leap off the Big Stone to the escape into the river. This fellow, however, has not been seen since, an outlaw, the stuff of legends.

The second news bulletin out of Yosemite announced the rockslide on the Glacier Point Apron. The Apron is a huge slab of granite that rises from just south of Curry Village, site of one of the largest concentrations of humanity within the park. The U.S. Geological Survey estimated the rockfall at about 525 tons. In a strange twist, a climber died while belaying, but his friends above him survived. Accidents of geology seem closest to the hand of God, do they not? According to the USGS, these rocks "have been exposed to weathering for more than the last one million years." If your number's up, you're number's up, right?

Yosemite Search and Rescue had a spotting scope set up in the Curry Village parking lot. Watching the cracks in the rock expand, watching *geology*. I mention to the spotter that the story as reported in the *Los Angles Times* didn't make "climbing sense" to me.

"Hey," he said, "whatever you can say to make the family feel better. Why say anything else?"

Then in response to the question he was doubtless tired of hearing: "Gravity's the same today as it was yesterday. Rock will fall, but you can't say when."

|||

Late in the afternoon after our little climb of Nutcracker, Jim and I are wandering around the tourist sites stopping regularly to rehydrate, taking in the scene. Jim calls his wife, and there at the phone booth next to him is Ron Kauk. Moments earlier I had contemplated purchasing a poster of Kauk on a climbing route called Peace, rated 5.13c on a scale whose uppermost limit was 5.9 when originally designed. The route is in northern Yosemite in Tuolumne Meadows, almost six thousand vertical feet above the valley floor. Kauk had made the first free ascent of Astroman (the east face of Washington Column) and of Midnight Lightning, the world's most famous bouldering problem in Camp 4. I had seen him climb in the International Sport Climbing Championships at Snowbird when I lived in Salt Lake City.

Most of us were there to see the French phenom of the day, Patrick Edlinger, and I suppose *technically speaking* he was the best. But when Kauk climbed there was an electric hushing of the crowd. It might have been that his presence hadn't been expected, or that he, unlike all the rest, did not wear Lycra tights. It may too have been that he was an American. But I think something else was recognized that day, and it was, again, intangible. It had to do with fluidity and grace; it had to do with the only real kind of style: acquired by aspiring to no style — *aspiring* is not even the right word where a zenlike verb is required. What emanated from Kauk had something to do with climbing and nothing to do with competition. When he popped off near the top of the final overhang, he had somehow nonetheless given us a vision of how it might be done.

And now here he was talking into a pay phone. And then sitting back down at a table of friends.

He looks like an ordinary person, except, I suppose, better looking. In any other American endeavor a person of his stature probably would be sitting in the leather seats of a BMW talking on a cellular phone. There can be no doubt that he pays a high price for his life as he lives it.

That night in Camp 4 we see the Japanese from Nutcracker: filterless cigarettes all around and two one-gallon bottles of Canadian Club on the picnic table. Camp 4 is actually now called Sunnyside Walk-in Campground. The name Camp 4 is a remnant of the 1960s, the golden age of Yosemite climbing. Mostly climbers stay here, and it's packed with folks—three tents to a site, no reservations, fourteen-day limit. It's hard, on this day impossible, to get a campsite in midsummer. We're on our way to site 19 where two guys said we could sleep in their tent while they did the high bivy to get an early start on Snake Dike, the easiest climbing route on Half Dome. At site 19 there are six tents. We don't even know the guys' names—they were behind us on Nutcracker. A person appears and directs us to the tent we're looking for. I would be remiss here if I did not mention that this person was a dwarf.

We then go to site 26 to return the gear left by the guys who fell. Then across the road to the Mountain Room Bar, which is devoid of climbers and filled with people watching the NBA Finals, eyes glued to the two TVs. Here is the difference I think: *these* people are tethered to *this* world. A couple days later I'm back at work on the eastside thinking about going to the Tiger Bar down in June Lake to watch a basketball game myself. Alan, a firefighter who lives a few cabins over, says, "It's the finals?"

"Yep." It's not a comfortable role: being Alan's connection to world news.

"Who's playing?"

I tell him and he looks at me in disbelief. "Shee-oot," he says, "are we still in Kosovo?" We were.

He shakes his head and laughs at himself and/or the larger forgotten world.

|||

The next morning I am up early in Camp 4. A familiar-looking man in running shorts—he looks like a Euro (what is that look anyway?) but is coming from the Search and Rescue tents. The muscles in his legs are those of a world-class athlete. Wind- and sun-burned. Hard.

An hour later he's drinking coffee in the lounge, and I realize suddenly he's Werner Braun. About ten years ago he had climbed Astroman over fifty times. I remember the first time seeing his name and thinking Von Braun, the rocket man. But this man is Braun, and the climb is Astroman.

I can't describe Astroman to you very well. It has a climbing pedigree rarely matched; the first ascent was made by Yosemite climbing pioneers Warren Harding, Glen Denny, and Chuck Pratt. This was an aid climb, accomplished over a long period of time: the east face of Washington Column. All three were significant figures in the climbing world. During the climb, Steve Roper ferried water up fixed ropes to the climbers and took photos, published by Harding's prior arrangement in the *Oakland Tribune*. This was the first money — thirty dollars — Roper made from climbing; later he would write the first climbing guidebook to Yosemite. This was 1959.

The first free ascent of the same route was made by John Bachar, John Long, and Ron Kauk in 1975. A free ascent is a climb made in a *purer* style; no hanging or resting on gear — hands and feet on rock only. They rechristened it Astroman. Six luminous visionaries of two generations.

I was telling the story of seeing Werner Braun to young Sean, a first-time visitor to the Sierra and an accomplished climber; that is, he had done some hard sport routes at Smith Rock up in Oregon. He didn't know of Braun or Astroman.

"Have *you* done it?" he asked me, referring to Astroman.

I laughed. "No."

"Are you going to do it?"

"No," I said. And I remembered the day I knew I wouldn't do Astroman, which would have been any day I had consciously given it any thought. Bob Schneider and I, Bob who had actually done it years earlier in an aid climb, talking in the indoor climbing gym. Some climbs recede from you, others you can keep in sight out there on the horizon. Two guys in their forties, climbing in a gym. No, we would never do Astroman.

But this concept was lost on the youth Sean, to whom everything is still possible.

|||

News bulletin number three: early in June a hiker loses his footing in the river and is shot over Nevada Falls: a 492-foot drop to the valley floor. A multitude of signs in a wide variety of languages warns against this exact thing. How could someone do this stupid thing? Could it be that here the "Danger" that signs warn us of is so literal, so immediate, and that elsewhere it's not? That the other warnings cluttering our lives are crying wolf too loudly, too often? There are warnings and there are *warnings*, right? This occurrence happens nearly every summer.

|||

Jim and I drive up to Tuolumne Meadows. The Italians are behind us on a route called South Crack above Tenaya Lake. Their leader overlaps us at belay stations, a cheerful fellow singing Neil Diamond songs in Italian. He wishes to know if Budweiser is the best American beer. Is there any climbing in Chicago? There's really only one word of English he understands perfectly: *run-out*. The word refers to expanses of rock that the leader cannot protect and risks a long and serious fall should he lose his grip or footing. Tuolumne, and South Crack, are known for run-out routes. The Italian sings out randomly, trilling the *r*: "rrdun-out!"

I tell Jim about the first time I did South Crack. That time, a man appeared behind me, silently. It was a surprise because usually you can hear the clanking and tinkling of climbing hardware. He climbed through—passed me. He was soloing, which is why I didn't hear his gear jangling—he had none. We were about four or five hundred feet off the deck. All I could think to say to him was, "How many times have you done this route?"

"I don't know," he said. "About two hundred."

Untethered.

|||

At the top Jim and I see a man in a red hat. He's yelling "Down!" and waving wildly. A crazy Euro-tourist we figure, "down" his only word of English. Soloed something in his driving moccasins, no doubt, and now doesn't know how to get down.

Down, he yells.

We are above and beyond him by a couple hundred yards, on the long slow road down—cairns and dirt paths.

When we get back to the car there's the guy in the red hat. He was trying to show us the fastest way down, he says. We laugh, having thought it was *he* who was asking *us* how to get down.

"No," he says, he used to guide here. That was the way he took clients down.

It's a small world, and I suddenly realize to whom we're speaking: T. M. Herbert? I venture.

"Yes," he says.

In Yosemite the golden age is recent enough that the gods mingle casually with mortals, as if they were not gods at all. I know my history.

Herbert, whose son Tommy is a world-class rock climber as well, says he stopped soloing South Crack the previous year. Too old, he says—it's sensible to stop soloing 5.8. Hard to disagree with that.

He's sixty-three.

Figures he's done South Crack 250 times, and Great White Book, the route he'd soloed today, about 500.

The Italians in their Speedos are lying out on flat rocks on the edge of Tenaya Lake.

Once at this very spot Kathy Roper sat reading a book at the lakeshore while her husband Steve and I climbed a short route on the rock above. Day hikers paused to watch a bear roam the opposite shore. A tourist remarked to Kathy that he'd "seen trout, bears, and idiots," nodding upward in our direction.

|||

Later in the summer I am at Mirror Lake with my family: wife and two boys, six and eight years old. The hike to Mirror Lake is short; the trail is paved and you can take a bus—for free—halfway there from Curry Village. Hence there are lots of people at Mirror Lake; families abound, frat boys at a bachelor party, folks on rented mountain bikes. This is the farthest east in the Valley I've ever been, and here below Half Dome the approach to the climbing routes on the northwest face looks as unappealing as I've always heard it to be: loose and dirty rock, steep, slabby, long, etc. Suddenly two guys with mega-loaded packs—a battered white FISH haul sack among them—appear. They unweight their loads slowly—as one must shed one hundred plus pounds of stuff—and sit on the sand. They begin to take their shoes off to cross the river—there's a slow-motion aspect to their actions.

I'm wondering why they'd be coming down this way--the standard descent off the top is a walk-off down the trail. So I ask. A traverse, they say, we've done a traverse. Nine days on the wall, twelve nights total. Plus another trip up to retrieve gear. They ask if I climb.

I'm hesitant to say yes, because compared to them I'm really just fooling around. I say yes, but so they don't get the wrong idea, add that I've never slept on a porta-ledge.

They look better than I'd feel if I were them, although their hands look hammered—swollen like sausages is the standard climber's cliché. I mention that, but they didn't seem to notice. Later my wife would say they had a look on their face that she couldn't quite describe. I recognize it though.

Later on the hike down I catch up to them and we talk climbing. At first I feel like I'm intruding on private space, mythic ritual: the end of the hike out, the return to the world. We talk about the ice climbing in Lee Vining, the *American Alpine Journal*, the Bugaboos. My son Macklin is delighted with Jay's advice: if we go to the Bugaboos, be sure to cover the tires and hoses of the car with chicken wire so the porcupines won't eat them, exactly the kind of advice a six-year-old expects will be helpful in this world. Without gushing, I try to express the enormity of my admiration for what they've just done. Only very late in the conversation did they admit it was a first ascent. A superb achievement, but the world that understands it for what it is, the world that appreciates it, is very small. All too soon their climb will become (for everyone but them) a line on a photograph, a few words on a page. I ask if they've named it, but no, they haven't got around to that yet.

Later still, I'll realize that I had met Jay before (I'll also remember that, in another life, I had slept on a porta-ledge; bad memory is one of the necessaries of continuing to climb). I see Jay at the store sitting at a picnic table, a point of stillness among the blur of tourist activity. You might say he was in a daze. But, as I've said, I know the look—I've seen it in the mirror. He's been untethered, and now he's in between. Exhaustion, contentedness, stillness, at peace, spaced, happy to be alive, to be unburdened of the pack, to be sitting down on a bench, happy to be holding a bottle of beer, the beady coolness of the glass against one's hand, too tired to remember to drink of it.

|||

Could it be that that all visitors to the Valley since, and including Lafayette Bunnell, have been seeking the same thing? The climbers, the tourists, the BASEjumpers, the people watching television in the Mountain Room Bar, the Europeans in their Speedos? David Robertson has speculated that "perhaps what we seek most in the wilderness is a return to a new and different Eden." Of course, Yosemite's status as wilderness is much in doubt, since the concept insists that a place be both relatively uninhabited and undeveloped. A small area that receives four million visitors a year cannot really be wilderness. Despite that some of the climbing routes are crowded, in my experience it has always been possible to get away from "it all." I have sat on ledges just a few hundred feet off the valley floor as the sun set and watched its golden light pour through the mouth of the valley, illuminating the granite walls and spires and glinting off the Merced as if it were a river of mercury. Though I know there are thousands of people below me, they are unseen, swallowed up by the canopy of black oak and lodgepole pine that covers even most of the buildings and roads. And, somehow—it seems miraculous—there is silence. Something happens. It may be that I have found, as Robertson says, "a natural regeneration and mental and spiritual well-being." But there's something about those words, that language, that I distrust, as if they were not descriptors of experience but a kind of betrayal of it. I'm not sure that language can ever describe this feeling very well, and maybe that too is why I'll keep returning year after year to Yosemite, still a paradise, as the third millennium begins.

recommended readings

FIFTY CLIMBING CLASSICS

Alvarez, Al. *Feeding the Rat* (1988). A thought-provoking portrait of one British mountaineer and, by extension, the whole climbing community. The author is a journalist, poet, and climber, whose writing is fresh and engaging.

Blum, Arlene. *Annapurna: A Woman's Place* (1978). The story of the 1978 American Annapurna expedition and the success followed by tragedy of its all-woman team. Engagingly told, it is a thoughtful exploration of one ambitious expedition, and one distinct effort against prejudice.

Boardman, Peter. *The Shining Mountain* (1985). Early writing by a gifted climber and sensitive author. Boardman sets the stage for his powerful ascents and soulful partnership with Joe Tasker. This work is packed with hard climbing and good writing.

Bonatti, Walter. *Mountains of My Life* (1994). The story of Bonatti's role in the troubled 1954 Italian K2 expedition, and the story of Bonatti's other incredible accomplishments in a lifetime of alpinism and adventure.

Bonington, Sir Christian. *I Chose to Climb* (1966). The autobiography of the young Chris Bonington, twentieth-century Britain's best-known mountaineer. Here the reader experiences Bonington's early climbs, shares his emotion, and feels his powerful ambition.

———. *Annapurna South Face* (1971). The story of the all-star British and American expedition to one of the biggest and hardest mountain faces in the Himalaya.

Bowman, W. E. *The Ascent of Rum Doodle* (1983). The great mountaineering parody caricatures participants of an imagined expedition and leaves readers laughing themselves breathless.

Buhl, Hermann. *Nanga Parbat Pilgrimage* (1956). Nanga Parbat was the German 8,000 m peak, and Buhl tells its story, as well as the story of his epic first ascent.

Child, Greg. *Postcards from the Ledge* (1998). A collection of mountain journalism sometimes touching and sometimes funny. Child is one of the world's finest all-around climbers, and these stories talk about hard climbing from the inside.

Chouinard, Yvon. *Climbing Ice* (1978). The very best of the how-to books. It models both climbing practice and the attitude that made the author a master.

Craig, David. *Native Stones* (1987). A nature poet and climber asks, Why climb? And his answer touches on environmentalism, ethics, intimacy, and risk.

Davidson, Art. *Minus 148* (1969). You've been cold? Read about the first winter ascent of Denali, with heart-stopping temperatures and a wild cast of climbing characters.

Diemberger, Kurt. *Summits and Secrets* (1991). A collection of the Austrian mountaineer's best writings, with sensitivity to nature, observations about his human experiences, and strong ascents of his youth.

Greig, Andrew. *Men on Ice* (1977). Scintillating poetic drama from a climber poet.

Harrer, Heinrich. *The White Spider* (1959). The riveting history of the Eiger *nordwand* by one of the 1939 first-ascent party.

———. *Seven Years in Tibet* (1954). The story of German climbers taken prisoner during World War II and escaping to Tibet. Hunger and harsh-altitude difficulty is followed by Harrer's fascinating story of the young Dalai Lama and life in the "forbidden city," Lhasa.

Haston, Dougal. *In High Places* (1973). The autobiography of a hard man. Haston tells the story of his own youth and fabled accomplishments in the Alps, the Himalaya, and all over the vertical world.

Herzog, Maurice. *Annapurna* (1952). One of the great tales of mountain suffering. The first 8,000 m peak is climbed by a French party, and the descent is as harrowing as it is inspiring.

Hornbein, Thomas. *Everest: The West Ridge* (1968). The great American accomplishment on Everest recounted by an articulate member of the party.

Houston, Charles, and Robert Bates. *K2: The Savage Mountain* (1954). Two of the "Harvard Five" recount the 1953 American expedition that missed the summit, but found fame for a hard and heroic descent from the world's second-highest mountain.

Hubank, Roger. *Hazard's Way* (2001). A fictional rendering of Edwardian Britain and its climbers, this is the rare climbing novel that works. In it a young man decides between pleasing his family and following his heart to the rocks.

Hunt, John. *The Ascent of Everest* (1954). Everest's first ascent told with precision by the military man who oversaw the operation. A good read in connection with Krakauer's *Into Thin Air* and Tenzig Norgay's *Tiger of the Snows*.

Jones, Chris. *Climbing in North America* (1976). The first thorough history of climbing on this continent, with inspiring photos and route descriptions from a hard-climbing transplanted Brit.

Krakauer, Jon. *Into Thin Air* (1998). You know this one. The Everest debacle told by the gifted climber and writer who was tied into the midst of it all.

Messner, Reinhold. *All Fourteen 8000ers* (1988). Messner, the first person to climb all the 8,000 m peaks, tells the stories both of physical achievement and mental suffering that put him there. The best mountain writing by the world's best mountain climber.

Muir, John. *The Yosemite* (1912). Any of Muir's Sierra writings is an inspiration, and this one brings readers to the heart of American climbing—the Valley. This work is part guidebook, part natural history, part Hetch Hetchy testimonial, and all richly described by the grandfather of American environmentalism.

Murray, W. H. *The Evidence of Things Not Seen* (2002). An unusual and moving collection by a mid-twentieth-century hero of Scottish climbing. He wrote his first book in a German POW camp, and brings a mix of close observation and stoic acceptance to the alpine world he loves.

Newby, Eric. *A Short Walk in the Hindu Kush* (1973). A writer's tale of one small expedition to the big mountains. Newby's work is prized for its very British humor and sly understatement.

Norgay, Tenzing. *Tiger of the Snows* (1955). The other side of the 1953 Everest story. A Sherpa's own perspective on the climbing and the beauty and the challenges of empire.

Patey, Tom. *One Man's Mountains* (1987). Accomplished British climber and humorist puts his own quirky lens to some of the twentieth century's most stirring characters and ascents.

Pritchard, Paul. *Deep Play* (1998). A prize-winning effort from a world-class climber who tells his own story and meditates on the benefits of risk.

Rebuffat, Gaston. *Starlight and Storm* (1968). Inspiring stories from the mid-twentieth-century efforts to scale the great north faces in the Alps. Rebuffat is motivated by love of beauty and the austere natural world that surrounds him and his talented peers.

Robinson, Doug. *A Night on the Ground, A Day in the Open* (1996). Described as "John Muir meets Jack Kerouac," Robinson recounts three decades of mountain pleasure and mountain strain in this tidy collection.

Rowell, Galen. *The Vertical World of Yosemite* (1974). A collection of photos and stories from the Valley, sure to inspire sweaty hands and a trip to that crucible of American climbing.

Salter, James. *Solo Faces* (1980). Arguably the finest fictional rendering of the alpine life. Based loosely on Gary Hemming's tragic life, the climbing day is polished to shine by this master stylist.

Sayre, Woodrow Wilson. *Four Against Everest* (1964). A story of friendship and extreme climbing by this high-altitude filmmaker and athlete.

Shipton, Eric. *Blank on the Map* (1938). An exploration of the central Karakoram, with Shipton and Bill Tilman in fine form on the peaks and on the page.

Simpson, Joe. *Touching the Void* (1989). The classic survival tale by a strong-willed Brit left for dead in the Andes. Alternately hilarious and tear-jerking, this book has touched climbers and nonclimbers alike.

Steck, Allen, and Steve Roper. *Fifty Classic Climbs* (1979). A runaway favorite for climbers to love and hate, this book tells the story and brings the crowds to a selection of North America's best routes.

Stephen, Leslie. *The Playground of Europe* (1871). Eminent Victorian professor, Alpine Club founder, and father to Virginia Woolf looks back on the golden age of the Alps with humor and insight.

Stuck, Hudson. *Ascent of Denali* (1914). The story of the first ascent of North America's highest peak by a remarkable dogsledder and his hardy companions.

Tasker, Joe. *Savage Arena* (1982). Evocative writing, strong personalities, and the hardest climbs on the planet make this a must-read. Tasker describes his own maturation in the mountains, conjures the feel of seventies climbing, and guides readers through the perils and rewards of hard, hard alpinism.

Tilman, H. W. *Snow on the Equator* (1940). The African alpine adventures of this wonderful writer and stiff-upper-lipped Brit.

———. *Mischief in Patagonia* (1956). Another favorite from the phlegmatic Tilman. Here he decides to climb in Patagonia and concludes he'll learn to sail by sailing there from the UK. Incredible adventure at sea and ashore.

Turner, Jack. *Teewinot* (2001). A year of close natural observation in the Tetons. By turns climber, guide, naturalist, and angry commentator, Turner puts one range and a whole world of ideas into sharp focus in this Thoreauvian effort.

Ullman, James Ramsay. *Banner in the Sky* (1954). Young adult fiction that turns the Matterhorn into a testing ground for physical and emotional growth. This book has been a crowd pleaser for fifty years.

Vause, Mikel. *Rock and Roses* (2002). An edited collection of women's mountain writing. This assembles pieces from a powerful cast of climbers who prove the mountains are not just for men.

Venables, Stephen. *Lost Mountains* (1987). A leading alpinist recounts two very bold, very light Himalayan expeditions. This is a book about particular climbs and a dramatization of the joyful small-party ethics of modern super-alpinism.

Waterman, John. *In the Shadow of Denali* (1984). Stories of Alaska high-altitude suffering and success from one of the country's best writers. Waterman knows alpine climbs and climbers and brings them all to life in muscular prose.

Whymper, Edmund. *Scrambles Amongst the Alps* (1871). Stories of Victorian alpinism, told with verve by the young and brooding Matterhorn first ascensionist. A historical classic that is also a good read.

contributors

Barry Blanchard, an Alberta native, is the face of Canadian alpinism. His routes are penciled across the Rockies, and his writing is admired for its honesty and its impact.

Arlene Blum is a central figure in women's mountaineering, famous for leading the first American—and all woman—ascent of Annapurna. She holds a PhD in chemistry, has inspired thousands with her speeches, and is the author of *Annapurna* and *Breaking Trail*.

Cameron M. Burns is an Australian, a Coloradan, and a family man who has made first ascents all over the world and authored multiple books, including guides to Kilimanjaro, California's fourteeners, and the desert Southwest.

Yvon Chouinard, mountaineer, surfer, fly fisherman, and visionary green business prophet, was at the center of Yosemite's golden age, and established hard routes in good style across North America's steepest ranges. His most recent book is *Let My People Go Surfing*. "The Muir Wall" was first published in the *American Alpine Journal* in 1966.

John Daniel is a prize-winning environmental writer. Now he's the subject of environmental scholarship, but Daniel's first publication was in *Climbing Magazine*, and he is the author of many books, including *Winter*

Creek, Wild Song, and *Rogue River Journal.* "Climbing Into a Life" is drawn from *Winter Creek.*

Steph Davis, a Moab resident, is a central figure in the new generation of strong American climbers. She has freed El Cap, put up hard desert routes in Utah, and summited in Patagonia. Her book is titled *High Infatuation* (Mountaineers, 2007).

Terry Gifford is a leading environmental scholar, poet, and mountain writer. This Englishman writes about climbing and its promise for environmental awareness. His many books include *The Joy of Climbing* and *Reconnecting with John Muir.*

Lynn Hill, California rock climber and inspirational storyteller, is known for her achievements on the world's hardest rock routes. She tells her story in the book *Climbing Free,* from which "Freeing the Nose" is drawn.

Steve House, known for his bold ascents and the clear, provocative prose he publishes in the climbing magazines, won the coveted Piolet d'Or in 2006. "The Mind of the Observer" first appeared in *Alpinist,* #8.

Mark Jenkins, adventurer and columnist for *Outside Magazine,* is an accomplished climber and author of *The Hard Way, Off the Map,* and *To Timbuktu.*

Conrad Kain (1883–1934), Austrian-born, was North America's most famous guide, and his exploits as a climber and teacher are legendary across the Canadian Rockies. "The First Ascent of Mount Robson" first appeared in the *Canadian Alpine Journal.*

Rev. George Kinney (1872–1961) was a Canadian clergyman and wilderness adventurer. Kinney made several attempts on Mount Robson, explored wild British Columbia, served in World War I, and lived the rest of his life in service to his faith. "The Capture of Mount Robson" comes from a manuscript archived at the Whyte Museum of the Canadian Rockies.

Mike Libecki is a Utah adventurer and photographer drawn to remote places and renowned for hard, solo aid climbs.

Jeffrey Mathes McCarthy is chair of Environmental Studies and associate professor of English at Westminster College in Utah. He is an active climber with first ascents in Alaska and the Pacific Northwest. His writing is published in both academic and climbing journals.

Chris McNamara is a young California climber best known for his hard aid routes in the west and influential through his guidebook company SuperTopo.com.

Karen McNeil died in 2006 on Alaska's Mount Foraker. She was a cheerful spirit, an acclaimed alpinist, and an outspoken champion for women in climbing.

Peter Metcalf, a wilderness advocate, business leader, and the CEO of Black Diamond Equipment, has a powerful resume of Alaskan climbing.

John Muir (1838–1914), the grandfather of American environmentalism, was an impassioned mountaineer who devoted his later life to sharing and protecting the natural world he loved. "A Near View of the High Sierra" first appeared in Muir's *The Mountains of California* (1894).

Doug Robinson is a California mountaineer and writer known for his Sierra climbing, skiing, and guiding. He is the author of many essays and the book *A Night on the Ground, A Day in the Open* (Mountain N' Air Books, 1996).

Gary Snyder, environmental icon, poet, and mountaineer, has been a lucid voice of reason and beauty in his essays and his poems. His many books include *The Practice of the Wild, Mountains and Rivers Without End*, and *Danger on Peaks*. The prose poems are taken from *Danger on Peaks* (Shoemaker & Hoard, 2004).

David Stevenson, nature writer and literary scholar, has climbed across the American West and Midwest. He is book review editor for the *American Alpine Journal*. A longer version of "Untethered in Yosemite" appeared in *Weber Studies*.

Henry David Thoreau was an American naturalist, writer, and free spirit. If Muir is the grandfather of American environmentalism, then surely Thoreau is its godfather. His Katahdin climb is taken from *The Maine Woods* (1864).

Jonathan Waterman is an environmentalist, writer, and arctic adventurer. He lives in Colorado and is the author of many books, including *Where Mountains Are Nameless* and *In the Shadow of Denali*. "Denali" is drawn from *In the Shadow of Denali* (Lyons Press, 1998).